ROADS TO
FALAISE

ROADS TO FALAISE

'COBRA' & 'GOODWOOD' REASSESSED

KEN TOUT

SUTTON PUBLISHING

First published in the United Kingdom in 2002 by
Sutton Publishing Limited · Phoenix Mill
Thrupp · Stroud · Gloucestershire · GL5 2BU

British Library Cataloguing in Publication Data
A catalogue record for this book is available from the British Library.

ISBN 0-7509-2822-0

Typeset in 11/16pt Photina MT.
Typesetting and origination by
Sutton Publishing Limited.
Printed and bound in England by
J.H. Haynes & Co. Ltd, Sparkford.

Contents

List of Illustrations   vii

Acknowledgements   ix

Intention   xv

1.   Flowers in the Hedgerows   1

2.   The Sadness of Sergeant Sid   19

3.   Halt! Who Goes Where?   32

4.   World's Worst Traffic Jam   49

5.   The Bull Meets the Matadors   71

6.   Grim Guards and Hamstrung Rats   94

7.   Crestfallen at the Crest   110

8.   Cobra under the Carpet   128

9.   Cobra Strikes at Last   147

10.   Cobra Hydraheaded   165

11.   Shambles at Chambois   181

12.   Very Unfriendly Fire   193

Notes and References   205

Bibliography   221

General Index   227

Index of Units Mentioned   235

LIST OF
ILLUSTRATIONS

Maps

Flowers' Hedgerows   xi
Normandy, June–August 1944   xii
Operation Goodwood, Normandy, July 18–21, 1944   xiii
Aerial photo, first day of Goodwood (*as map*)   xiv

Plate Section between pages 110 and 111

1 Bob Levine returns to Mont Castre.
2 Author and *bocage* hedgerow.
3 Jim Flowers with former enemy Fritz Uhlig.
4 Sid Jones in his 80s.
5 Sgt Sid Jones with 1944 fitters.
6 Railway arch between Soliers and Bras.
7 Ruins of Caen.
8 Col Hans von Luck.
9 Gens Montgomery, Dempsey and O'Connor.
10 'London' bridge over the Orne.
11 The air bombardment.
12 Sherman tanks in open country.
13 Maj Gen G.P.B. 'Pip' Roberts.
14 Reconstructed Firefly 'Ballymena'.
15 Knocked-out Sherman.
16 Infantry digging in.

17 Cpl Reg Spittles and crew.

18 Lt John Cloudsley-Thompson.

19 M. Jean Goubert, shot for aiding escapers.

20 *Obersturmführer* Werner Wolff.

21 GIs occupy Hebecrevon.

22 Shermans stuck in mud.

23 Engineers clearing mines in Lessay.

24 Infantry support 'Rhino' Sherman.

25 Animals at risk in battle.

26 Camouflaged Sherman liberates village.

27 Maj Gen Marcus Rose.

28 Gen Fritz Bayerlein.

29 Louis Aubert, French guide.

30 The public image – Bradley and Patton.

31 The hidden reality – Bradley and Patton.

32 FM Hans von Kluge.

33 Polish crew in Firefly.

34 Tanks escort prisoners of war.

35 Shermans roll off the assembly lines.

ACKNOWLEDGEMENTS

Operation 'Cobra' was an American concern and I was at a loss to know how to start a search for American reminiscences. Then I thought of my old friend from the Public Relations world, Hal Steward, also a retired US Army colonel from the Second World War. Hal opened up for me a chain of excellent contacts, starting with Jim Cary, veteran and historian.

Jim passed me on to that peerless collector of reminiscences, Aaron Elson, and that led to a journey across those emotive fields where Jim Flowers and the platoon suffered such agonies. American friends were most helpful in wanting to share: Tom Gillis, Tom Raney, Joe Solarz, Arte Krenn and many more whom I cannot thank enough.

Over the border in Canada I learned that Denis and Shelagh Whitaker, with Terry Copp, were working parallel to me in their research and again were only too willing to share. It has been a great shock to learn that Denis, hero of Dieppe and other fields, has been taken from us before I could send him the draft of my text for his acute comments.

Institutions in the States were also most friendly, especially Candace Fuller at the Patton Museum in Fort Knox and Randy W. Hackenburg at the US Army Military History Institute, Carlisle Barracks. In the UK my first call is always on David Fletcher, at Bovington, and he had bartered with visiting American tank men to obtain some precious documents. The Imperial War Museum (IWM) staff, as always, were most kind in helping with books, photographs and now their excellently indexed tapes of interviews obtained by Conrad Wood. An interesting discovery was the small but fascinating library at the RAMC Museum in Ash Vale.

Major Bill Close, MC, is the first call on anything to do with the 'sharp end' in Goodwood, and we should be glad that the battering he suffered on the slopes of Bourguebus Ridge has never affected his memory, nor that of another adventurer on the ridge, John Cloudsley-Thompson. The regimental adjutants of the Guards all opened up sources which responded with the crisp discipline of guardsmen, such as Major F.A.O. Clark and Laurie Lacey. To the many others mentioned in the text I also extend my thanks in this limited space, and apologies for any omissions – blamed on septuagenarian memory lapses, of course.

In our own Northamptonshire Yeomanry Association we have constant conversations with survivors, including Sid Jones, Reg Spittles, Bill Mosely and two sadly departed during the writing of this book, Keith Jones and Sandy Saunders. My 8.8.44 St-Aignan crew colleague, Rex Jackson, MM, is always ready with advice on sources and loans of books. It was also a privilege to stand with Sid Jones and lay a wreath on the slope of the embankment of that third railway at the spot where he first buried poor Niblock.

The Bundesarchiv and some German 'ex-enemies' displayed their customary courtesy and forgave my appalling German. My French is a little better but still required patience from several mayors who advised me. Resident and knowledgeable on the battlefields, Messieurs Pinel, Lefauvre and Lechipey guided me both geographically and in matters of fact.

A special 'Mention in Despatches' is due to my good friend Mrs M.C. Beech, Air Photo Archive Manager at Keele University. She had barely escaped alive from a car crash quite as appalling as a Sherman brewing up. With numbers of bones still mending she insisted on going into the archive to enable me to identify, out of hundreds of thousands of photographs, the aerial shot of Soliers, required for this book.

Jonathan Falconer at Sutton helped me to distil the present book's theme from the simmering broth of ideas which I poured out before him, and his staff have always been most encouraging. Although I have long experience of my wife Jai's patience, it needed full exercise as I commenced research on this book before finishing the previous one, while moving office within the home at the same time.

Some of us veterans are already planning that in 2004 we will return, after sixty years, to those remembered slopes, with a rendezvous around André Lechipey's reconstructed Firefly. And there perhaps I may even meet, for the first time, one or two of the survivors of Flowers' platoon. Undoubtedly 'Hell on Wheels' will be rolling again!

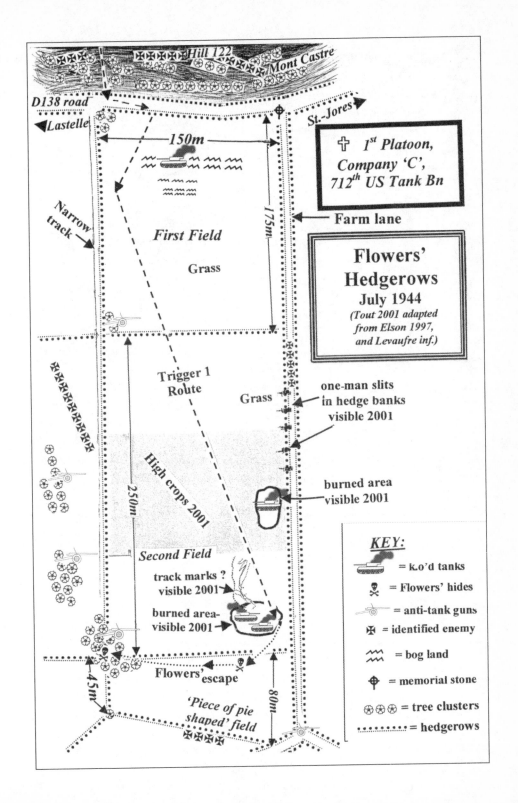

Hill 122 · **Mont Castre**

D138 road

◄ Lastelle

St.-Jores ►

150m

175m

Narrow track

First Field

Grass

⊕ **1ˢᵗ Platoon, Company 'C', 712ᵗʰ US Tank Bn**

Farm lane

Flowers' Hedgerows
July 1944
(Tout 2001 adapted from Elson 1997, and Levaufre inf.)

Trigger 1 Route

Grass

one-man slits in hedge banks visible 2001

High crops 2001

250m

burned area visible 2001

Second Field

track marks ? visible 2001 ➤

burned area visible 2001 ➤

Flowers' escape

45m

80m

'Piece of pie shaped' field

KEY:

= k.o'd tanks

☠ = Flowers' hides

= anti-tank guns

✠ = identified enemy

〰〰 = bog land

⊕ = memorial stone

⊛⊛⊛ = tree clusters

············ = hedgerows

NORMANDY
June-August 1944

Cherbourg

US VII Corps, 27 June

Utah

Omaha

Landing beaches

Gold Juno

Sword

Mont Castre

Bayeux

R. Orne

EPSOM

CAEN

GOODWOOD

Tilly-s-S

Cagny

Lessay

Periers D900

COBRA

Hébecrevon

ST.-LO

Bombed Carpet

Chappelle-en-J

St.Gilles

ATLANTIC SPRING

Bourguebus

Lisieux

Coutances D902

St. Canisy

Marigny

Villers-B

St.Aignan

TOTALIZE

Roncey Pocket

BLUECOAT

N158

Original plan= wide encirclement at R. Seine

Grimesnil

COBRA

TRACTABLE

Falaise

Vire

Falaise pocket

22/8

Chambois

GERMAN

Avranches *River See*

Flers

Argentan

BRITTANY

COBRA

Mortain

GERMAN

US XV Corps

[kjt2002]

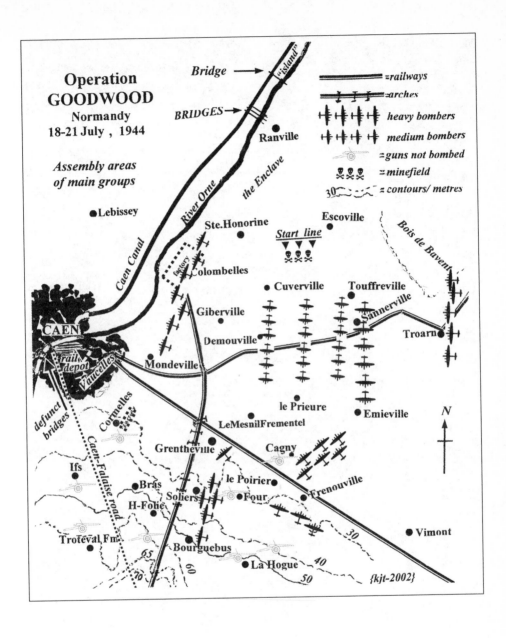

Operation GOODWOOD
Normandy
18-21 July, 1944

Assembly areas of main groups

railways
arches
heavy bombers
medium bombers
guns not bombed
minefield
30 — contours/ metres

Bridge →
BRIDGES →
Ranville
"island"

Lebissey
Ste.Honorine
Escoville
Bois de Baventi
the Enclave
River Orne

Caen Canal
factory
Colombelles
Cuverville
Touffreville
Sannerville

Giberville
Start line
Demouville
Mondeville
Troarn

CAEN
rail depot
Vaucelles
le Prieure
Emieville

defunct bridges
Cormelles
LeMesnilFrementel
N

Grentheville
Cagny

Ifs
le Poirier
Four
Frenouville

Bras
Soliers
H-Folie
Vimont

Troteval Fm.
Bourguebus
La Hogue
30
40
50

65
70
60
{kjt-2002}

16/727:18JUL44:F20"/K28.

Aerial photo taken during first day of Goodwood

Photo 4077- 18.7.1944- about midday, flying
south to north. The 'Third' Railway north of
<u>SOLIERS.</u>   Location verified by pilot's map
of each photo run, archived with the photos:
Keele Univ. Archive @*Crown Copyright/MOD*

towards Bras
across country

to Cornelles (D229)

Enlarged area

Tanks

Tanks

Railway

Tanks

Farmhouse

tank tracks
over lower
embankment

Railway

ighest embankment

broken arch

Area now
built up

Enlargement

SOLIERS.
(much smaller
1944 than 2002)

Grentheville

Tanks

Tanks

Fron...

Farmhouse
Maisonnette
de Soliers

INTENTION

Every good battle plan needs an 'Intention'. That of Montgomery and Dempsey for Goodwood was over-optimistic and ambiguous. Bradley's for Cobra was clear but not optimistic enough. I am optimistic, hoping that my intention will be understood.

This book has an axe to grind, or maybe two axes. Like untended weeds, two Second World War myths have grown and spread as wild vines do, and thickened into stout trees of history. The axes are intended to do some damage to those arboreal myths.

The first myth is about the supposed superiority of 'the German soldier' and the equally supposed inferiority of 'the Allied soldier'. I am not a military historian but a collector of reminiscences, so I am not qualified academically to refute the entire doctrine, although Terry Copp does so in my last chapter. But what I can do, from both a tank gunner's seat and a tank commander's perch, is to agree with the theorists that there were indeed some very good German soldiers. Too many of them. Men like Gerhard Stiller were superb tank crew members. But there were also some abysmal German soldiers, mainly unwilling conscripts from occupied lands, but still wearing the German uniform, even to the collars with SS runes on them.

We all knew useless Allied soldiers, not too many of them. But even the 'elite of the elite' Wittmann crew could not shoot better than Joe Ekins, the rookie shoe-clicker from Northamptonshire. If they could have done, they might still be alive. And Joe did not get a Knight's Cross with oak leaves, or even a mention in despatches, because he was only doing his duty. He was an average Yeomanry shot good enough to dispel the myth of total Allied inferiority for ever. It was often simply a matter of who had the best gun and the best location.

Flowers and Bill Close and Marcus Rose and Radley-Walters (all in these pages) were good, even excellent, soldiers. I saw them in action or others very much like them. The 'caged historian' (see the Aubrac controversy in Chapter Twelve) does not have that advantage.

My second myth relates to the war of words, with Montgomery and Patton among the prime culprits, which has been pursued by historians and the media over the years. The reader might almost be forgiven for believing that the average 'Brit' or 'Canuk' hated the average 'Yank' more than they hated the average 'Kraut' and vice versa. One book entitled *The War between the Generals* deals quite legitimately with the war of ambitions and suspicions between generals who were supposed to be on the same side.

This aspect looms so large that I believe it is necessary to emphasize the commonality of the 'sharp end' experience. The 'Pommie', Canuk or GI facing a Tiger or Panther at 50 yards range, and equipped with a gun which was little more use than a tin opener against the massive German tanks, in many instances had more in common with his front-line colleague of any of the nations than he had with his warring commanders.

The battles along the roads leading to the Falaise pocket have been acknowledged by several of my German informants as some of the worst fighting they endured, including their most terrible experiences on the Eastern Front. I had selected Operations Goodwood and Cobra as illustrating how the 'failure' of Goodwood and the 'success' of Cobra meant little in the heat of battle to Laurie Lacey or Joe Solarz. They were both surrounded by bloody death and blazing tanks and waiting for the bullet with their name on, unable to do much about it except obey orders, and hope that someone lower down in the command structure had got it right this time.

My previous books have dealt with Operations Atlantic, Spring and Totalize at some length, and where the present book dovetails into those operations I would ask the reader to forgive some brevity of information. Not being a professional military historian, as some critics like to assure me, I do take notice of criticism and trust that such comments are well founded. Two are relevant to this book.

One critic mentioned that my sudden first-person interruptions of a third-person story, in which I was part of the action, impeded the flow of the narrative. In this book, I have written my own experience, where pertinent, in third-person style and indicated myself as the source in the notes. Another critic suggested that some reminiscences did not fit directly into the flow and sequence of the narrative. But I believe this is in the nature of reminiscence, and that it is not always necessary for the author to top and tail it to fit precisely into his text.

So, then, this is a patchwork quilt of remembrance, with larger and smaller patches, some frayed by age. Such historical matter as intrudes, in Chapter Three for example, is simply intended to guide the reader new to Normandy 1944, and does not pretend to be exhaustive.

I dedicate this book not only to the fallen whom we always remember, but also to those who returned home, weary and wasted, from performing mighty deeds, only to find themselves written off as inferior. They're sorry! They apologise! They thought they had won the war.

Note: In the four chapters dealing specifically with Cobra I have retained the American spelling of 'armor' to avoid the confusion of two spellings.

CHAPTER ONE

FLOWERS IN THE HEDGEROWS

They lay shrugged down deep into the roots of the vast hedgerow, the two Jims, one the tank commander, the other his gunner, and an unknown infantry boy. Out in the Forbidden Zone.

One Jim had a foot amputated by an armor-piercing (AP) shot. The other Jim had a leg so shattered that he could pull his foot up to touch his knee. The infantry boy had wounds in both legs and his stomach slashed open. Then, Jim the gunner remembered:[1]

We were cut off there, quite a ways out there from our own lines. The Germans were lined up there and our people knew they were lined up there where our tanks were burned out. So they laid the hell of an artillery barrage, not knowing that we were there. It just practically plowed up that field. And one of them landed between Jim and the infantry boy.

I heard Jim scream. He let out a hell of a scream. And I looked over there and, Jesus Christ, his other leg was gone!

The four tanks of 1 Platoon 'C' Company (Coy), 712 US Tank Battalion (TB), had lived up to the Sherman tank's reputation – according to the Germans' own jibe, the 'Tommy Cooker', and to another description 'a self-igniting crematorium . . . a self-sealing mausoleum . . . or a self-igniting bomb'.[2]

As the tanks burned through the night, their thick grey-green armor-plate heated to a translucent orange glow. Some of the crews had fared even worse than the two Jims, and some others hardly better. The lead tank, the platoon command tank, code sign Trigger One, had exploded and flashed into torrents of fire. The two crippled Jims ejected fast with burns to hands and face. Ed, the loader, his clothing on fire, was lying on the ground crying, 'Momma! Momma!' Driver and bow-gunner had escaped through the small hatch under the tank. Even as they ran for shelter one of the myriad hissing bullets, criss-crossing the field like a whirling fiery spider's web, bored through the bow-gunner's skull.

As Trigger Five 'brewed', the loader was third man out of the turret but by that time his clothing and flesh was a ball of flame and he fell to the ground in his last impulses of escape. The driver had a large gash bleeding into his eyes. The bow-gunner jumped free but was hit in the chest by a grenade which miraculously did not kill him but filled his body with splinters, so that he ran and fainted and fell, ran and fainted and fell. The commander received two iron splinters as big as thumbs in his leg. They were splinters of the turret's own armor-plate as the cast-iron turret exploded. Emerging, the commander found himself surrounded by enemy infantrymen. His gunner did not emerge. The 88mm armor-piercing shot, the size of a small marrow, had crashed through his throat, scattering his brains over the commander's helmet.

Trigger Four had been bogged down and was a sitting duck for the enemy gunners. Trigger Four's commander had a large piece of shrapnel lodged in his cheek. He pulled the slug out and was left with his jaw flapping loose. His gunner had the right eye hanging out of its socket and deep cuts in his arm. Three other crew members, bruised, scratched and burned, jumped to the area of safety which beckoned them. The driver was immediately shot by a German patrol.

It was the fourth tank, Trigger Two (Trigger Three was absent) which fared worst. It had run on, burning fiercely and out of control, and crashed into its neighbour. None of the crew survived. Next day a sergeant was sent to investigate the wreck when it had cooled somewhat. He found of the gunner only a pile of black ash with one small solid hip joint like, he thought, a morsel of burnt turkey. Another pile of cinders he identified because under it he found the High School graduation ring of the loader. 1st Sgt Bucky Spearman drew this loathsome duty and when he returned he was black all over.

The few infantry who had kept pace with the tanks also suffered commensurately. Bob Levine was carrying the breastplate shield of a mortar projector. He owed his life to the fact that the sheet of armor served as his own personal breastplate. A row of machine-gun bullets stencilled a line of dents right across the breastplate. But a piece of shrapnel found Bob's unguarded thigh. He looked down and could see his main leg artery pulsing away in the gaping hole. It would cost him his leg.[3]

But now the two Jims from the forward tank were isolated under the Normandy hedgerow. They had experienced one of the two most feared scenarios of the 1944 tank crew, the sudden shock of a high-velocity projectile bursting through the armor-plate, detonating dozens of high-explosive (HE) shells and the belts of machine-gun bullets stored within the tank, and igniting a hundred gallons or more of high octane gasoline. The tank crew had three seconds, if lucky, in which to emerge from such an inferno.

And now occurred the second most feared scenario of the tank man: to bail out and find himself isolated in the Forbidden Zone. In July 1944 in the thick Normandy *bocage* of tiny fields and immense hedgerows there was no distinct unoccupied territory such as the No Man's Land of the First World War. There were no solid, deep-dug, continuous trenches running the entire distance of the war's battlefields. There were no enemy positions painstakingly marked on maps after months of observation. There were no goal lines across which to mark a victory or behind which to find safety.

The *bocage* zone was a perilous jungle of constantly shifting enemy pits and slits in hedgerows, abandoned as soon as identified. A nightmare of lurking, crawling, sniping marksmen or small patrols. A true trench map, if there had been time to make one, would have been a virtual reality film of shifting patterns, immediately breeding new patterns, like the writhing fertility of anthrax spores seen under a microscope. For all this the infantryman was well prepared. It was his element. For the tank man it was a largely alien environment.[4]

The tank man thought, spoke and acted in terms of spark plugs and track links, radio valves and telescopic sights, gun velocities and breech blocks, of screwdrivers and spanners, sledgehammers and towing cables, pull-through rods and wireless netting procedures. His military skill was in a clear shot of 75mm armor-piercing rounds at 800 yards or a patient 'brassing-up' of hedgerows with belt after belt of bullets at 100 yards. Outside the tank there existed a different, primeval world of murderous creatures inhabiting the undergrowth and trained to kill, one to one at arm's length range, with stabbing bayonet, slashing knife, clubbing rifle or throttling hands.

In that world the despised 'poor, bloody footslogger' combined the snake's slithering movement, the tiger's quickness in pouncing, the gorilla's awareness of the entire thesaurus of jungle sounds. And, in the *bocage* the human hunter was more lethal than the animal. A snake has only one tooth, but the snake-like patrol would sting with knife, throttling cord and rifle butt. A tiger's paw packs power but, in the time it takes a tiger's paw to strike, the Schmeisser m-g could spit out twenty iron claws, each more lethal than the tiger's. Marshland undergrowth can hide snapping alligators, but the marshland grasses of the *bocage* abounded with Schu mines, just as hungry for human flesh.

The infantryman knows this. The tank man's orders are not to stray into the infantry domain but to get back rapidly, collect a replacement tank and 'Driver, advance!' – back to the attack. Now isolated under their hedgerow in the Forbidden Zone, Lt Jim Flowers, tank commander and platoon leader, and Cpl Jim Rothschadl, tank gunner, must stay frozen as still as hares caught in a car's headlights. The night is full of mysteries. It seems that every living thing about them has become the enemy or traitorous collaborators – ferns, blackberries, sparrows, thorn bushes, flies.

When the wind whispers, is it an enemy uttering orders? While the rain patters on leaves, is it hiding more ominous noises? As the moon breaks through, is it deliberately exposing their cover? That dull croak of a frog, was it instead a sniper's cough? The tiny scream of a mosquito, was it a bullet passing the ear? A swish of an owl's wing, might it be an enemy hand pressing aside the lush ferns so that eyes could peer through?

Then the barrage: silver fantasies of lightning, thunder like rolling empty barrels in the room upstairs, tetchy grumbling of more distant storm echoes, or 'friendly fire' killer shells blasting the earth to seek them out and destroy? Because they are in the Forbidden Zone.

To stop the blood issuing from his left leg Lt Jim had contrived a tourniquet from the lace of the one shoe of the one foot with which he had extricated himself from the blazing tank. After the scream, the searing second amputation and the soothing touch of shock, Jim removed the tourniquet, the bleeding partially quenched and, wrestling with cramp and weakness, applied the lace awkwardly to the stump of the other leg. Jim the gunner ripped pieces of shirt from the anonymous infantryman's uniform to stuff into the wounds from which the lad's life blood was draining so rapidly.

It had all been so different when reading the battle plan. It had all started so optimistically, occasionally even with a touch of humour. 712TB would have a lead part in the vital battle. One month after D-Day and contrary to expectations, the Americans were still held outside St-Lo while the British and Canadians still struggled to enter Caen. It was necessary to break out of the cramping *bocage* so that the armored divisions could race across the open country to the south. But before that, the British and Canadians must cross the River Orne in the southern suburbs of ruined Caen. And the Americans must establish a firm front-line base along the highway west from St-Lo.

So there were still mazes of *bocage* to be flushed free of enemy troops in those tiny fields with their seeming endless series of huge hedges. Ah, those Normandy hedges! The reaction of Sam Cropanese, an 'A' Company gunner, 712th was typical of many:

Before St-Lo I never really knew what a hedgerow was. When I saw those hedgerows I said, 'My god, no wonder nobody can see anything'. They were taller than the one-story houses, and the hedges were so close together that you couldn't see nothing. My god, traveling down those roads, all of a sudden, Bam! A shell would smack one of the lead tanks.[5]

Each hedge was like a miniature moated castle wall, deep ditch usually flooded, two to three ft high bank, then, with roots growing densely out of the bank, a thorn hedge maybe ten feet high and so tightly compressed that barbed wire could not have served better. And beyond each hedge yet another small field, perhaps 100 yards in extent before arriving at another hedge.

Most of the time the eye was mystified and betrayed by the profusion of dense foliage within the close boundaries of the hedgerows. But in the country of the July 1944 battles certain low hills stood out like mountains, looming even above the hedges, and giving the owner of the hill a clear view for miles around. The military map-makers named these hills according to their height. The British had their point 112 (112 metres, only just over 340 ft) and the Americans their point 122 (122 metres, only just over 370 ft), Not the Rocky Mountains. Not even Snowdonia. But those points dominated the landscape and the shape of the battles.

The American 122 was known to civilians of the day as Mont-Castre.

It was also known to the ancient Romans. In 56 BC, precisely 2,000 years before 172 Battalion's battles, Julius Caesar's general Titurius Sabinus had camped there against the rebel Venelli tribes under Viridovix. Sabinus had cunningly enticed the rebels to assault the hill, thinking his forces weak. The Venelli had accepted the challenge, carrying bundles of brushwood up the hill to fill in the Roman trenches. But, up the steep gradient, by the time they reached the top of Point 122 they were so out of breath that the counter-attacking Romans easily routed and slaughtered the rebels.[6] The 1944 Germans were also known to be good at counter-attacking.

Not having heard of Mont-Castre the modern 712 had landed in Normandy with great enthusiasm. Their new Sherman tanks had smooth-running tracks, a reliable engine, highly sophisticated turret traverse and gunsight systems, well-stocked ammunition racks and apparently solid armor-plating. In their first attacks near Pretot things went reasonably well. But there were shadows under the Norman sun.

They saw their first Sherman erupt in a volcano of fire. The commander of Trigger Five, Sgt Kenneth Titman, gave his impression of such an event:

When the shell penetrated it exploded right inside. You take, oh, about 100 rounds of armor-piercing and 100 rounds of high explosive and about 4,000 rounds of ammunition going off, that looked like a popcorn factory going up through the turret. [Your own] shells bursting right out through the top. That's the way it looked.[7]

Some of the men of 'C' Coy had the duty of checking the fatalities. Lt Jack Sheppard told Aaron Elson:

I had the shitty job of going back to those four tanks and getting the dog tags of those that had died. I had to get in the tank and dig these . . . look for the . . . well, these guys had all been incinerated, because the tanks were like a furnace. I'd go where the tank driver was supposed to be sitting and I'd find a dog tag. I wouldn't even find the body. This is the way it was. It was a horrible experience, especially when you're gonna get in a tank yourself next day.

Even if you did not land that horrific job you saw plenty of destroyed tanks, enemy and your own, dotted around the landscape. And even if you shut your eyes to the sight you could never escape the smell, which drifted distances and penetrated every type of cover. Jack Sheppard again:

I'll tell you something you'll never forget, is when you smell the smell of one of those tanks. Barbecued people. You could smell it a long way. And it is horrible. It's worse than burning chicken feathers, if you know what that smells like.

Soldiers deal with such experiences in two ways. Some, a very few, lapse into an inarticulate state of mental paralysis, unfit for an intelligent action. The majority file the incident away in the mind as a piece of cautionary information, and press on with the ordered action, supported by the moral solidarity of the group. 712 pressed on, Jim Flowers leading his platoon of five Shermans. But tanks are huge and somewhat clumsy monsters, much subject to accidents, human and mechanical. It was two such accidents which meant escape from death for several men and an unlucky demise for others.

Humour turned to misfortune. Jim Flowers and his friend Judd Wiley were fascinated to see an extraordinary vehicle stranded between the two armies. Its front portion was a motor bike, minus the back wheel. Its rear end was a kind of tractor, steered by the motor bike's front wheel and driven by the motor bike's engine system. The tractor had a rack for carrying goods. Both men were motor cycle enthusiasts, so they had the mad idea of rescuing and 'liberating' the machine with a view to shipping it back to the States by some means or other. They dashed out along the road and were fired at both by their own m-gs and by German mortars. Reaching the machine they started it up and then dived for cover. When the friendly and hostile fire had died down they again ran to the contraption and started to drive it back. The camber of the road was bad, the machine unfamiliar and unwieldy and, as it were, they fell at the first ditch.

Flowers scrambled home unscathed but Wiley caught his ankle in the pedal and limped back with a rapidly swelling leg. He had already suffered a common tank accident. The Sherman turret opening was guarded by two semi-circular flaps which closed down for safety. Normally the commander had the flaps up and looked out between them. The flaps were held up in position by spring bolts. As Wiley's tank crashed through a particularly belligerent hedgerow, a spring gave way and the armor-plated flaps came crashing down on his fingers. Flowers now insisted that Wiley go back for surgical attention to his fingers at an aid post.

This was only one incident in a series which disrupted the first-line team of tank crews and caused substitutes to be called onto the field. In Flowers' absence one badly scared tank driver refused to drive any more. He was hustled back to rear areas (although Flowers would have been firmer) and Lt Sheppard's jeep driver, James Bailey, fatally volunteered to substitute for the missing driver in the next action. Jack Sheppard himself, although temporarily commanding 'C' Company, volunteered to take the place of Wiley for the day. The company commander, Capt James Cary, had got out of his tank to open a gate. The Germans had booby-trapped the gate and Cary was now back, wounded, at the aid post.[8] Maurice Elson had also been wounded nearby.[9]

The driver of Trigger Two had refused to come out of his tank at all, even in rest situations. He was obviously in an extreme state of fear, but only minimally more than everyone else. Soon comrades gave up the task of persuading him and he stayed in the tank. He would never leave. Meanwhile, Trigger Three had developed a transmission problem and would be a non-starter for the day.

In one of the brief moments of respite from battle the Catholic padre held an open-air mass for the front-line troops. Two good pals Louis Gerrard and Gerald Kiballa had lived near each other in Scranton before war service. From time to time they had attended mass in the home church together. As the padre and the faithful knelt in the mud in a nameless Normandy field, the two pals once again sought the consolation of religion together, for the last time. Only Gerrard would survive the coming battle.

The mission of the platoon was complicated. American infantry had partially encircled Mont-Castre and occupied part of the hill summit. The Germans, with typical tactical skill, had left many of their paratroopers (of the 15th Regiment of Fifth SS Parachute Division) scattered among dense trees, bushes and interwining undergrowth about the hillside. Others of the paratroopers moved back to turn the low rear fields into traps for advancing American troops. Although the Americans would seem to be winning the action, their 3rd Bn of 358th Inf Reg, under Col Jacob Bealke, was effectively cut off high on the hill. An encirclement within an encirclement.

Flowers' platoon was now sent with a dual mission, first to take supplies up the hill, risking the steep gradients and packing vital ammunition on the rear decks of the Shermans. The high design of the tank gave it a high centre of gravity and it could topple over on steep inclines.[10] Then the tanks were to act as battering rams to open an escape route through the impossibly thick brush, so that the infantry of Bealke's battalion could descend and join up with the main force once more. The terrain on the hill was a veritable jungle where the silent, patient, immobile defender held all the winning numbers in the lottery of death. The very few tracks up the hill were little more than animal runs and constituted suicide routes for men on foot.

The first part of the mission went like a troop of elephants rampaging through a village of mud huts. None of the Shermans toppled and none of the enemy infantry seemed disposed to get involved too closely. Flowers rounded up a group of young German lads in uniform (he himself was an 'old man' of twenty-nine) and drove them in front of him as he advanced along the track. He suddenly realized that he might be contravening the

Geneva Convention by putting the prisoners at risk in that way. Still a little naïve perhaps amid the brutality of modern war, he ordered one of his crew to de-bus and point the prisoners back towards the American infantry forward locations. After consultation with Bealke he then went on foot to reconnoitre the escape route, which lay behind the hill in the space between the two American infantry advances, instead of back down the safe side of the hill.

From the fearsome, treacherous terrain of the steep wooded hillside, the fields beyond looked benign and attractive in their soft green midsummer vesture – this was now 10 July. Immediately below the mount, as though afraid to try an ascent, a tarmac road gently curved around the foot of the hill and turned left towards the village of Lastelle. Where the platoon tanks had to descend, the tarmac road was guarded on its far side by a brute of a hedge in the extreme Normandy tradition. From the hill it was possible to see that two parallel tracks ran from the hill towards distant farms. The lane on the left was a passable dirt track for wheeled vehicles. The track on the right was little more than a narrow bridle path.

Beyond the first immense hedge, Flowers could see three more hedges lying across the tank route between the two tracks. The first hedge was about 100 yards into a field which produced a profusion of reeds or similar plants, suggesting very marshy land. Beyond that the second hedge stood at what Flowers first estimated 800 yards but was actually half that distance. And way beyond that was a field shaped like a piece of pie, narrow on his right and wider on his left. At the intersection of the various hedges grew confused clumps of high bushes where guns or infantry might shelter. On that stage nothing moved. Which did not mean that nothing existed.

There could be no hesitation. Bealke's infantry crowded behind the four Shermans. Again the wild rampaging herd of mechanical elephants crashed down the hill, their straining engines bellowing out animal challenges. Down that brief mountain-style slope the tanks speeded, each 30-ton vehicle powered as much by the force of gravity as by its own engine. The infantry had problems in keeping up with the tanks, although a clear avenue was now opened through the jungle. The scattered paratroopers in their hides were powerless to do much other than loose off random and fairly ineffectual fusillades. Bealke's men suffered casualties but ran on.

Flowers' tank bounced down on the tarmac road. At one place the hedge was less dense and he smashed through. A glance at the first narrow field and he was yelling a warning into the radio that there was a stretch of bad marshy land central to the field. He ordered his driver to do a mad swing to the right, along the right-hand edge of the field. Next in line Sheppard's tank burst into the field but did not turn quickly enough and drove deep into the bog. It stuck there, tipping slightly to one side, its tracks thrashing impotently and tending to sink the tank deeper.

'I'm bogged down. Stuck. What can I do?' reported Sheppard, who, although senior, was acting as a tank commander under Flowers as platoon leader. 'Stay there and fire at the hedgerows ahead', replied Flowers.

The other two tanks swung left and avoided the bog. At the first hedge they followed the platoon leader's tank as it crashed through the obstacle. Now there was a clear field of fire towards the next hedge and a fast run across a level solid field. The gunners began to fire both 75mm HE and belts of m-g from the three Brownings placed one on top of the turret for the commander to use, one inside the turret and working coaxially with the big gun, and the third m-g, the bow gun down in the front driver's cabin. The breathless infantry tagged along as best they could, all loaded with equipment like Bob Levine with his heavy mortar breastplate.

In the hedges the support line of paratroopers waited. With them were anti-tank guns carefully screened and camouflaged, guns capable of knocking out any Allied tank at far greater ranges than existed in those fields. Not far behind them were the inevitable Nebelwerfers, the multiple-rocket-launch tubes familiarly known as Moaning Minnies or Screaming Meemies with a strident siren attached to each rocket. And many of the paratroop infantry were equipped with the Panzerfaust, a one-off, hand-held, rocket-launcher to fire and throw away, an early and dangerous manifestation of the disposable society. Its projectile could stop a tank by smashing the track or killing the commander. A lucky shot could even set a tank on fire.

But this was where the brave man must go. None of the tank platoon was feeling particularly brave or heroic. They were caught up in a momentum which had some elements of excitement tempered by the underlying fear. The forward drive of the tank did not allow for diving into cover in mid-field, infantry fashion. There might be some hope of refuge in the shadow of the next big hedge. To halt would be to expose the tank, as had happened to the bogged-down vehicle behind, to a careful and repeated shot from a hidden anti-tank weapon. So the sensible thing to do was to 'bash on' at 25 mph on the easy run of 2–300 yards to the next hedge. Most of the infantry were hopelessly outdistanced.

A tremendous bell-gong-bang rang off the turret of the lead tank and reverberated through the tank. Flowers described it as having heard the Liberty Bell. An enemy hit. The first. And many to come!

As he manoeuvred his tank to move out of a potential pre-planned enemy line of fire, Flowers ordered his crew and supporting tanks to search for the anti-tank gun. The gunner thought he saw the dimming glow of a gun flash and fired at it. All tanks poured fire in three directions at the three tall surrounding hedgerows. From behind, the bogged Sherman also joined the firing, most of it geared to hope rather than calculated assessment.

Again the deafening crash of solid shot impacting on armor-plate, the flash of steel on steel, the scream of the shot hurtling into and through the tank turret, the searing heat of its passage, the shock of blows to human limbs and instant chaos. Stored ammunition starting to explode. The engine transmuted into a vast firelighter for the hundred gallons of gasoline to burst into soaring, singeing, skin-flaying flame. Three seconds: and Death would wave his fiery flag triumphantly, high above the doomed Sherman.

In the narrow confines of the tank the knees of the standing commander were normally jammed into the spine of the crouching gunner. Now Jim the commander must vault free first. Jim the gunner must join him as close as a Siamese twin, clutching the turret opening with upstretched hands and leaping into the open air. In that particular Sherman the loader had his own narrow hatch through which he could squeeze while the fires engulfed him. Down below the two drivers could loosen a hatch in the floor and drop to the ground if the tank was suitably positioned. They had a moment longer in which to survive.

The first physical action was for the commander to lodge his foot on the protruding turret ring inside, where the turret joined the hull. This gave him purchase to leap. Jim Flowers trod and leapt; but he didn't. Instead he collapsed into the turret on top of Jim Rothschadl.

As often happens with serious wounds, the solid shot, heavy and super-heated by its own friction through the air, and trailing its slipstream of sharp, red-hot turret splinters, had anaesthetized and amputated in the single act. It was not until Flowers, desperately pivoting on his hands, had again vaulted and fallen to the ground that he realized that a shoe was missing, and with it most of the foot. As gunner Jim landed close by, both men had suffered severe scorching of the fingers in pushing on the turret roof, already unbearably heated by the ascending fires.

The lead tank had hardly erupted into flame before other enemy weapons focused on the next two tanks. One blew up and shuddered to a stop. The other caught fire but continued running until it collided with a mate.[11] Back across the two fields and up the side of the hill, 80 per cent of Bealke's men had become casualties. The rest were speedily seeking cover. And back in the first field a camouflaged German anti-tank gun calmly set about the elimination of the bogged-down Trigger Four. Astonishingly, according to the infantry watching, the gun missed with its first two shots. The third shot succeeded. 1 Platoon had ceased to exist. For that day.

Up front the larger field had come alive with awesome anger. Batch after batch of screaming mortar bombs descended vertically, spewing up great blotches of earth and spawning spinning wreaths of shards and stones. Single shot and automatic weapons poured thousands of bullets into the confined space (one German m-g alone could fire more than 1,000 rounds a minute), until the air was alight with tracer and explosive bullets. The warp and woof of the traversing bullets produced an almost solid weave of killing missiles, blanketing the field.

Jim Flowers clutched at the earth with burned fingers and crawled to the farther hedge, which was now only about 10 yards away. Jim Rothschadl, tenaciously remembering his training not to panic, was on fire yet saved by wearing three layers of clothing. He could see no available water, but there was a muddy cattle wallow nearby. He rolled into the sump and gratefully covered himself in mud which doused the flames and cooled his aching body. He lay there content for the moment, at the disposal of tending friend or imprisoning foe. At least he was well beneath the blanket of fire.

Commander Jim had crawled through the hedge into a pie-shaped field where the ditch along the hedgerow gave cover. Recovering a little from his state of shock, he pulled the lace from his remaining shoe and began to tie a tourniquet around the stump of his leg. At the same time he called back through the hedge to his gunner. 'Cpl Rothschadl! Cpl Rothschadl! Come up here. Through the gap in the hedge.'

The younger Jim had started to wriggle away in the other direction, but now, reassured by his lieutenant's voice, he too moved up to and through the hole which appeared to have been made by a tracked vehicle. But no sooner was he through the gap in the hedge than the two tank men were assailed by a small group of paratroopers who evidently coveted the same refuge. The sorely wounded, crippled and even dying Americans responded, wielding their personal weapons with such a frantic will to live that the less enthusiastic enemy youngsters reverted to the traditional tactics of withdrawing and re-forming, with the option of counter-attacking later on.

Although the main body of friendly infantry had been left far behind, one lone infantry lad had kept pace and been mortally wounded for his efforts. He too managed to get through the hedge to join the tank men. The lead tank driver, Horace Gary, also located the group. Guided by the lieutenant he extracted some of the morphine syrettes that crews carried, and gave the wounded men an injection each to ease the pain which was overcoming the initial numbing shock. Then the platoon leader gave Gary firm instructions, in spite of the driver's wish to stay and guard the wounded men: 'Everybody that you can find that's ambulatory, with or without some help, get them the hell out of here. Go on back where we came from, get back towards the hill. Get back and fetch stretcher-bearers.'

Darkness began its advance across the land but met fiery resistance from the burning tanks which would continue burning through the night. Visibility was marred rather than aided by the brilliant, flickering and flashing light from the tanks, dimming a little with time but then flaming afresh as other ammunition stocks in storage bins exploded. In such a menacing atmosphere the jungle of the Forbidden Zone began to stir and its denizens to move furtively about their killing business.

Three now drugged and helpless survivors waited for the death thrust from prowling patrols. Silently the subtle enemy approached, halted, studied the ghastly nature of the men's wounds but decided not to risk the shots or screams which might give away their own position. They nodded, with the front-line soldier's sympathy for fellow sufferers, then stealthily continued on through the undergrowth. One medic stopped and examined the three men. He bandaged each of Jim Flowers' fingers individually with dry gauze. Did what he could for each. They pleaded for water. The medic reached for his water bottle, unstoppered it and then dramatically turned it upside down. He had no water. He in turn merged into the darkness and they were alone.

The brief July night seemed to last for ever in the gloom and gleam, the gloom of top-heavy hedgerows and the gleam of the still burning tanks, seemingly polished to a solid bronze by the intense internal heat. And if the brief night seemed an eternity, the long summer's day was like a series of eternities, each with its catastrophic climax.

Try as they might, the American infantry, so near on three sides, could not enter the box of death which the enemy m-gs and mortars fixed around the Forbidden Zone.[12] From the angle of the tiny nest in the bushes where the three survivors lay, any occasional movement dimly discerned was imagined to be in enemy uniform. American observers could also spot such movements and responded with barrages of heavy shells which descended about the three men like the end of all things. It was during one of those unnumbered, unplanned, unrecorded barrages that a shell fell in their midst, an American shell, and amputated Jim Flowers' other leg below the knee.

The young infantry boy who never told his name was also hit and visibly began to fade from life. Jim Flowers' only concern now was to nurse the lad until help arrived, sometime during the long, long day. Or the following night. He put his arms around the dying boy but was astonished when the lad uttered faltering words asking for the last rites.

Jim was not a Catholic and only vaguely understood the implications of a Protestant trying to imitate such a sacred act. All he could do was to speak a hesitant but heartfelt prayer. It seemed to comfort the infantryman as he died.

At last 12 July dawned. There was less furtive movement in the hedges around and behind the two Jims. There was more intense small arms firing back towards the hill. The German paratroopers were sneaking away quietly before becoming totally surrounded. The two badly wounded men were now in a state of confused pain. The eternity of waiting continued relentlessly.

Voices! Flowers roused.

'Well, here's some more of 'em. Wait! Here's another one . . . I think these are still alive.' Then a Texan voice of authority. An officer. Lt Claude Lovett held a wonderful canteen of glorious water and carefully allowed the two Jims to wet their mouths, to drink a little, while Claude sent out a radio call for stretchers and a jeep. Eternity had ended.

In the first moment of horror and happiness on hearing the American voices, Jim Flowers had raised his head and saw his amputated foot lying on his stomach. He did not remember putting it there. He also saw his tin helmet placed defensively over his groin. He did remember putting it there. It was the most important part of the body to preserve for posterity if he was to undergo more amputations by friendly shellfire.

Now, in a few minutes tank commander and tank gunner were strapped on stretchers on the roof of a jeep and bouncing, painfully but contentedly, down the rough track into the battalion surgeon's care. It was a regime of care, treatment and rehabilitation which for Jim Flowers would last three years before he was fully mobile on two artificial feet and able to resume a career. Denying himself the riches of continuing his pre-war life in the oil industry, he devoted himself to working with veterans who faced the traumas of rehabilitation and adjustment to prosthetics as he had done. He served many boys coming back from the Korean War. They were inspired to be counselled by a man who had 'seen it all' and who had been awarded the high honour of the Distinguished Service Cross, and who many believed should have received the ultimate Congressional Medal of Honor.

Meanwhile, in the constantly shifting patterns of the Normandy battlefield, Trigger Five commander Sgt Titman had been taken prisoner by the enemy. Then the surge of American advance rescued and released him. Gangrene had formed in his wounded leg and he was shuttled back to aid posts and to hospital in England in time to save his life.

On the other hand Michael Vona, bow gunner on Titman's tank, fainting and falling as he tried to escape, woke up to find himself on a stretcher being carried by four German soldiers. Sadly, he resigned himself to life in a prisoner-of-war camp for the rest of the war. Then, with immense joy, he realised that it was the Germans who were the prisoners of war and he too was on the way back to England and the States.

Bob Levine, leaving his mortar breastplate discarded in the field, was able to walk back at first with his paratrooper captors. Then they were caught, as the two Jims had been, in a sudden barrage of very unfriendly friendly fire in which Bob was flung across the road and his ankle badly shredded. And like Sgt Titman he was being treated by the Germans in hospital, in Rennes, when the tide of Operation Cobra liberated the hospital. After undergoing a second amputation on that leg back in the States, Bob was gallant enough to return years later and stump up to the top of the steep hill in order to help with identifying the sites of the 1944 battle.

His recollections are as graphic as any: 'Hill 122 . . . it was real wild, sheer chaos. Going through the woods, down the hill, was like that. Shellbursts, and guys yelling and screaming, then I heard, you could hear the tanks of course, crashing down, it was like, I don't know how they did it. I mean looking from the top, how much room could they see, what tree to hit, what not to hit?'[13]

For one of the survivors a part of the hospital experience was, in retrospect, perhaps the worst moment, worse even than lying out there with little hope of surviving through another day and night. Jim Rothschadl's burns included serious damage to the skin of his face. When he arrived in a main hospital his face was in such a terrible state that he heard someone say, 'They must be using poison gas over there'. He was told that they were going to put a plaster of Paris mask on his face. They did not tell him that they were then going to insert masses of live maggots inside the mask.

He recalled, 'Maggots eat up all the dead flesh. . . . They left them there for eight days. I nearly went nuts. About the second or third day they started to crawl . . . and it stunk awful. They grew, and I suppose they knew how many to put in, and they ate up all the dead flesh. I don't know what they did with my eyes, but I couldn't see. They must have taped them shut. I had a little hole in the mask, with a little glass tube. Anyway, when the eight days ended, they took this mess off.'[14]

Nine men of 1 Platoon are remembered on a modest but beautiful stone plaque at the top of the farm track on the left of the fields, on route D138 between St-Jores and Lastelle. Included on the list is the name of Harold A. Gentle who should have been going to officer training school but insisted on staying with the platoon. Also on the list is James A. Bailey who should have been driving a jeep rather than the doomed tank. It is a sobering thought in these days when pardon is sought for those who were shot for cowardice in the earlier war. James Bailey died because another driver refused to do his duty. In 1944 the dissenting driver was smuggled away in disgrace, but his life was not in jeopardy. It was Bailey who was shot.

As the two Jims and others were treated at the nearest aid posts, the way was now open for the American infantry to establish a firm line along the St-Lo–Periers–Lessay highway. This step was necessary to enable the heavy Armored Divisions (AD), the 2nd and 3rd, to break out into wider fields and begin the great encirclement which ended the Normandy war.[15]

CHAPTER TWO

THE SADNESS OF SERGEANT SID

Sergeant Sid had no aspirations to becoming a medic, a psychiatrist or an undertaker. He was a fitter, a mechanic, a handyman commanding a small group of technicians. They were available to render first aid to vehicles, guns, wireless sets and electrical systems.[1]

Their orders were simple. Just drive through that railway arch at the tail of the squadron. You, in your fitter's half-track following nineteen Cromwell tanks through the railway arch into the green fields beyond. Hot summer's day. Beautiful countryside. Acres of standing corn ripening towards gold. Seen, as though framed by a camera, through the narrow gap of the railway arch in the high embankment. Ah, that railway arch!

Across the 18 July battlefield of Operation Goodwood south of Caen ran a narrow-gauge railway track designed to carry iron ore from the mines on the ridge to the steelworks and quays around Caen. The line sometimes ran across high embankments, as at Soliers, sometimes through deep cuttings, as in the vicinity of Hubert Folie, and sometimes on the level of the fields, as around Tilly-la-Campagne. Sid in his half-track, a very adaptable vehicle with easily steered wheels in front and earth-gripping tracks at the rear, waited near Soliers where the lanes pierced the embankment through lofty arches.[2]

Through the archway to the north lay open fields in which their Cromwells could speed up to 35 mph and dash for the objective, the highly visible ridge village called Bras. This was country which the high command considered 'good tank country'. You had proved that you could drive around at high tank speed all day during exercises in this kind of country on Salisbury Plain, where the toughest opposition to be encountered might be an angry farmer with his pitchfork. This was obviously the place in which to encounter an enemy whose tanks were generally slower, massive 54-ton and 40-ton leviathans prone to breakdown. Not reliable, like Cromwells.

So here was a railway arch which gave access to this ideal tank terrain. A railway arch much like any other railway arch anywhere in the world. But this was an arch of destiny. As the first Cromwell tank revved up and slithered around and squared up to the narrow arch, Sid thought 'Simple!' Things had gone well so far, capturing those two villages almost without casualties. Today near Soliers was much better than terrible Cheux or Brettevillette. No high *bocage* hedgerows here. Just rolling fields of waving corn and pleasant copses of trees beyond.

Tanks commanders waved and grinned at Sid as he waited his turn. Then, because the great bass drum roll of engines and side drum rattle of tank tracks became deafening, he had to yell 'Driver, advance!' Trooper Cook went smoothly through the gears and the White half-track, much slimmer than the Cromwells, eased through the archway.

It was all so simple. Through the narrow archway one at a time. Then, 'Bras, here we come!' Bras pronounced soldier fashion of course, with that final 's' as in a button which you polish rather than an article a girl wears. Bras, precisely 1,500 yards away now, at, say, 30 mph, less than a two-minute drive over level fields. And nineteen Cromwells with nineteen big guns to fire back at any enemy that dared betray their presence. Simple!

The first tank moved cautiously forward from the arch. Halted. Waited. Watching. Tactically sensible. The other tanks hanging back. And nothing happened. Simple!

The lead tank moved forward, a hundred yards or so. The second Cromwell emerged from the archway. And a third. Still nothing happened. Tentatively, but gaining in confidence with every yard, the lead tank grumbled on in low gear as the rest of the squadron moved through, out into the fields, accelerating to spread out into open order, normal drill, plenty of room in the spacious fields, the lead tank and lead troop sniffing ahead, commanders ready to cry, 'Driver, speed up. GO!' Easy! Simple!

Tpr Cook drove the half-track 50 yards into the field and then halted behind the last of the Cromwells. At that moment neither Tpr Cook nor

Sgt Sid Jones could know or imagine that a German commander, way ahead on the ridge, patiently watching, was thinking, 'A half-track. Fitters or medics. No more tanks. The entire squadron now in view'. And his thought fathered the command, 'All guns . . . fire! Fire at will!'

Sgt Sid heard the sudden 'Blam-whizz-crash' of a high-velocity shot, the report of the gun and the report of the impact on target almost simultaneous. A brilliant red star sparked off the front of one of the nearest Cromwells and wisps of smoke lazily arose from the ghost of the star. Bodies seemed to be flung out of the turret and rolled into the corn.

There was a moment's stillness in which to stare and gasp and stifle the automatic reaction of horror. Then, from all points of the compass it seemed, enemy guns began to fire. High-velocity shots travelling at thousands of feet per second and heating the air through which they passed. Huge 88mm armour-piercing solid shot which pierced tank turret and driver's cabin and sent sharp shards of the tank's own armour-plating flailing and ricocheting around inside the close confines of the turret above and the compartment below. Simple, now, for the enemy!

It was indeed a matter of simple arithmetic. The lead tank had still perhaps 1,300 yards to go to reach the enemy lines. Experience would tell that at more than about 200 yards a Cromwell's gun could not hole a German Tiger's turret. And the lighter tanks were now totally exposed on the open fields thought to be so favourable to rapid movement. The enemy only a couple of minutes away. But in those minutes just one enemy anti-tank gun could fire a many as ten well-directed shots, seldom missing a target. And on the ridge there were guns, and guns, and even more guns now opening fire. Tank commanders had only a moment in which to curse, 'Who the hell sent us into this death trap?' Hardly time to fire their own gun once. At what remote target? Barely glimpsed gun flashes among the trees on the ridge?

Tanks in the lead troop began to pay for their temerity. Tanks in the middle of the squadron started to turn, churning up clouds of dust, seeking shelter but finding their way impeded by other tanks now on fire and belching clouds of confusing smoke. Cromwells did not flame as quickly as Shermans, but flame they did, sending up a cumulus of acrid smoke and shooting killer fireworks in all directions as their ammunition exploded in the turrets.

Several tank commanders fired off smoke bombs and flares to hide their retreat. Smoke and flame and dust and enemy shells exploding. The confusion not sufficient to hide them from the enemy but sufficient to cause danger of collision and delay in retreating and peril of being crushed under milling tank tracks for those now ejected onto the ground, some with clothing on fire, others with disabling wounds. Confusion. Chaos. Catastrophe.

This was no case of minor engine trouble or simple electrical breakdown. Nothing that Sid and crew could do for the moment except fly for their lives. Cook swung the half-track around in its own length and swept through the archway, the nearest and fastest survivor of the rout.

Some of the Cromwells continued to fire obstinately at phantom flashes. A gun on the ridge blew up. Meagre cheer. Drivers reversed. One tank slewed to a halt with a broken track. Another exploded again and again until its turret was flung awry, gun pointing brokenly at the sky. Another crawling round and round like a cockroach with back legs broken. Men vaulted free, dived, stayed still, jumped up, ran, staggered. Some lay smouldering on turrets, on the back deck, on the ground alongside, their blazing overalls serving as firelighters for the wounded flesh, skin peeling from the flesh, the flesh from the bones.

And all the while the pitiless, remorseless fire poured from enemy guns, solid shot to wreck the tanks and swirling masses of m-g bullets to scythe down escaping bodies.

Seeing the enemy gun flashes, hearing the explosions, feeling the concussions, sensing the panic, Cromwell gunner Bill Mosely thought to himself, 'These are angry men and they are firing at US'. He and Dougie his commander had already seen something of what the enemy guns could do to another unit nearby:[3]

The whole area was strewn with smoke-blackened carcasses of the 29th Brigade's Sherman tanks which had 'brewed up' and burned out, some with their turrets blown off, others still brewing with gouts of orange flame shooting skywards from turret hatches as the ammunition exploded, dead bodies hanging from escape hatches at grotesque angles; dismounted crews were glimpsed trying to rescue wounded comrades from the wrecked vehicles amid the stinking black smoke from burning fuel and the flashes of mortar bombs raining down – it was a scene from Dante's *Inferno* brought vividly to life. With difficulty we threaded our way through the carnage, under another arch in the railway embankment towards some farm buildings concealed in an orchard.

But by now the enemy, forewarned by the morning's advance, had saturated the area with anti-tank guns, mortar crews, snipers and men handling the lethal hand-held Panzerfaust rockets. There was less and less room for shelter on either side of the railway embankment. Dougie needed to think fast, as Bill remembered:

No sooner had we emerged from the arch than we came under heavy fire from the direction of the orchard. They had the advantage of concealment – our only hope was to keep on the move until we could find a hull-down position[4] from where we could observe their muzzle flashes. Dougie ordered me to plaster the orchard with HE fire while he directed our driver, Albert Cunningham, into a suitable position. With my eye glued to the telescope, left hand operating the gun elevating wheel, right hand operating the turret traverse spade-grip, I struggled to keep the gun on target against the bucking and rolling of the tank, while stabbing my foot on the firing-button as fast as loader Dickie Dixon could punch shells up the breech. The turret was soon filled with cordite fumes and the temperature rose even more as each burning-hot empty shell case was ejected from the breech.

For a while commander and driver successfully manoeuvred to avoid the horrific fate to which each Cromwell in the squadron seemed doomed. But it was a truly hopeless situation which no mere commander or troop leader had power to solve. Sooner rather than later it happened:

Abruptly Dougie ordered, 'Driver, reverse! Reverse!' – apparently realising that we were still too exposed. The tank had reversed only a few yards when it suddenly shuddered to a stop with the engine dead. Dougie yelled, 'Bale out!' Looking over my shoulder I was just in time to see his feet disappear through the turret hatch. Wrestling with my Sten-gun as I jumped I got hopelessly jammed in the tight turret hatch. After an age I abandoned the gun and hauled myself up, standing upright on the turret roof. 'Where the bloody hell are they?' I thought. There was no one in sight. Then realizing what a target I made, took a flying leap off, landing among the others who were flat on their faces in the corn, was greeted with a few choice Anglo-Saxon expletives as we disentangled ourselves. Dougie decided to make a dash for another of our tanks still mobile some distance away.

A few Cromwells still survived as the smoke and dust of the disaster served also to hide the survivors to some extent from the German gunners. Whatever the skills of individual tank commanders and gunners, their regiment (2nd Northamptonshire Yeomanry (NY)) had been sent into a Balaclava situation, with enemy guns left, right and centre trained on them. Higher commanders would squabble later about the reasons for the catastrophe. They would blame the battered regiment itself for having gone too far west or too far north, to the right or to the left – even the critics could not agree. But for Bill and the rest of the crew their objective was in full view and they had been heading directly for it. The enemy gun flashes were now visible south, west, north and north-east. Almost a closed box. A vast coffin with the lid almost shut.

Now their only objective was to sprint and leap onto that surviving tank which might then ferry them to safety. One man commented that, jumping out and running about the fields like a scared rabbit, the only thing he could think of was a line of the old hymn, 'Other refuge have I none'.[5] Again it was a vain hope, as Mosely experienced:

We made our dash for the other tank, that of Sgt Tite, and climbed aboard the outside. The turret was traversed to the rear with the gun blazing away – bad medicine for ear drums. The tank moved off towards the railway embankment to our rear and the next thing I knew was a frightening thud – an AP shot had ploughed through the armour-plate, shattering the idler wheel, missing the co-driver's and my feet by inches – we both felt the heat generated as the shot sheared through the metal. Another thud bringing the tank to a halt minus one track – and Sgt Tite's cry of 'Bale out!' sent us all running like 'the bats out of hell' for the cover of the railway embankment with m-g bullets zipping around us, kicking up the dust.

Other British regiments were enduring similar travail on that sultry afternoon of Operation Goodwood, south of Caen. But a single tank crew knew little of other regiments' problems and had no time to care. The crew was totally dedicated to the troop and squadron, totally enshrouded by the squadron. Even regimental headquarters had become merely an occasional squawk on the wireless net. Voices from other fighting squadrons snapped and snarled, cajoled and screamed. But the visible reality was just one squadron wide and deep.

Reg Spittles was only a corporal but, as a tank commander, he had experienced the weight of German anti-tank fire. The regiment's morning attack on two villages among the orchards, Cuverville and Demouville, had gone well. They had then moved out into that open country which senior commanders had promised would be good tank land. The corporal had no such illusions:[6]

The two villages were taken without any particular trouble and we continued down into open country. That meant that the Germans with their 88mm guns could hit us long before we could even see them, let alone shoot back. Previously [in the *bocage*] we had got as close as 30 yards without being aware of each other, sometimes so close they couldn't bring their guns to bear on you. Now we came into a broad valley with a railway running across the centre of it, built up on an embankment, and this proved a bit of a saviour to us. We were on a sticky wicket in open country, and Jerry was holding the Bourguebus ridge ahead. It was not much of a ridge if you were there for a holiday, but we were not there for a holiday and it was a devastating situation.

Like so many others Cpl Spittles now had to risk his tank, his life and his crew along that Via Dolorosa, through one of the railway arches, following the Cromwell of Sgt Jack Mann, whose misfortune it was to have the lead duty:

> There were two bridges through the embankment and my troop was sent through first. Sgt Mann took the lead and we came out onto some rough ground with scrub. We went a few hundred yards and then stopped to survey the ridge with binoculars. It was obvious to me that I was unsighted to whoever was shooting because Jack Mann's tank was about 50 yards to the right of mine and suddenly there were big clods of earth flying up in the air about 30 ft. It was AP shells going into the ground with such force. I saw Jack put his head out of the turret further so he could look behind, and the enemy put about 5 shells right into his engines. Immediately the tank started to brew. Flames were pouring from the engine and the crew baled out.

By a freak of fortune Reg Spittles' tank had not been chosen by the German gunner for destruction. It might have been that a slight undulation of the ground or drift of smoke had left Mann's tank more plainly visible to the gunner. Spittles decided to chance driving the 50 yards to the stricken tank in case any of the crew had been wounded:

> Sgt Mann was obviously having trouble with someone in his tank. It turned out that Bill McCool from Bedford had been hit. He was the gunner, down on the left side where the shells had come in, and one had taken off part of his left thigh. We helped get Bill out of the turret and on to the back of our tank with blood everywhere. The back deck of the Cromwell was good for taking casualties, a large flat area with plenty of handles and things to hang on to. We backed through the bridge and had a look at Bill McCool's condition. We had very good medical stuff inside the tank including a tin of morphine injections. There was a little phial like a cigarette lighter. We knocked the top off and stuck it into their wrist and squeezed the liquid in, and then threw it away.

Reg's tank had been fortunate in that cauldron of catastrophe. When fate did at last strike it sneaked up, as it were, on tiptoe. It was four in the afternoon, 1600 hours military language, on a very hot day. The thirsty crew learned that their tank was to be pulled back. Reg was watching out of the turret. Like the Sherman, the Cromwell's turret hatches opened in two halves which then protected the sides of the commander's face. Reg also had a couple of sandbags on the turret as further protection from snipers. Once again enemy shells began to fall around the surviving tanks:

Suddenly I felt as though somebody had tapped me on the head. With the noise of the engines and the firing going on, you can't hear much so it was possible for someone to climb on the tank. I turned my head and couldn't see anyone. I went to ease myself up on the sandbags but they weren't there. I thought someone was playing around. There was no aerial. I got back into the turret and pushed Baggeley, the operator. He looked up and I saw there was blood on his face. The gunner was sitting crouched down with his head in his hands. A shell, perhaps a mortar, had dropped on the back of the tank, blowing all the covers off with everything moveable outside. Tool boxes, the spare bogey wheel, the camouflage netting, the lot. And wounded all three of us in the turret.

The tank engine was OK but we had no wireless communication with anyone, not even within the tank itself. I ran across to the troop leader's tank and informed him of our position. He told us to go down the valley where we could see tanks of the 7th Div. As I could not transmit orders inside the noisy tank I showed Bill Benmore, my driver, where to make for. And off we went. Eventually we arrived and a 7th Div MO took care of our wounds.

Such occurrences, freakish or foreseeable, so many personal tragedies, so many blazing vehicles, were visible to Sgt Sid Jones and his fitters as they watched through the railway arch from their tiny area of comparative safety. There was no call for their technical aid for the time being. Apart from commander Sid there were Cook the driver, Lee Whitewood a mechanic, and 'Gerry' an electrician. Sid had a Smith and Wesson .38 revolver and the others held .303 rifles, not much armament with which to face the German guns. The half-track was equipped with tools and spare parts to complete repairs up to a certain standard. After that the Sgt had to call up the Armoured Recovery Vehicle from the A echelon. But they had only the normal first-aid box in case of medical emergencies.

Feeling both apprehensive and inadequate they walked back through the infamous arch and found themselves to be the first line of medical aid for crew members struggling back through the corn. The medical half-track with a trained medic on board was still some way back treating other casualties. The fitters took out their few bandages and morphine syringes and did what they could.

People were coming through the arch with a variety of wounds, including severe burns. In many cases the crews had needed to abandon an exploding tank without rescuing their first-aid box. Sid and the others used skilled fingers in an unaccustomed task. They were fairly pleased with their work until one soldier appeared, drenched in blood and with the side of his mouth hanging loose. Sgt Sid then learned that a wound of the lips is one of the worst bleeding injuries of the human body. Whatever they tried, they could neither staunch the blood nor manage to fix a bandage to the contour of the face to seal up the wound. The only thing to do was to lift the soldier into the half-track with one or two other badly wounded men, wheel about and dash full speed back to the medical half-track. It was only after they had delivered the injured men that Sid realized the badly bleeding man, who happily survived, was the major, their squadron leader Stancomb. There was no time or need to look at rank badges when the flesh was so badly mauled.

Whether wounded physically or not, most of the men hurriedly retreating through the archway were in a state of shock, some with faces rigid in disbelief, others volubly cursing their luck, others trying hard to look unconcerned. It would have needed a complete psychiatric unit to deal with that stream of shocked survivors under the railway arch. Again Sid and Tpr Cook and Tpr Whitewood and Gerry turned their hands to an impossible task.

The experience of baling out of a tank was unique and produced an entire range of conflicting passions as the 'dehorsed' crew member rushed for physical shelter where no psychiatric help could exist:

I called myself 'Coward! Idiot! Useless tool!' as I ran, almost crying with frustration. I was sure that another commander would have done better, done the right things, got his crew out of trouble. All the while I was looking for my crew in the corn. I thought I had counted them all as they bailed out, but had I left one inside to be grilled alive? It was useless with the tank exploding, all that ammunition blowing up and if I had gone back the explosions would have blown me bodily out of the turret before I could rescue the one who was there or who wasn't there. But I couldn't reassure myself.[7]

Then other thoughts crowded in. Hating the enemy. 'I'll murder the next bloody Hun I meet even if he has given himself up as a prisoner.' And hatred and disbelief of the generals. 'They must have known what they were sending us into. If they didn't they shouldn't be wearing generals' badges. Bloody staff!'

And then you see some echelon wallah waiting to meet you and say stupid words like 'what happened' or say they're sorry that your gunner didn't make it, got his head blown off. And you want to say 'What the bleeding heck do you know about it?' And then you realise that the echelon wallah had probably been sitting all day in a lorry with his ass up against thousands of gallons of petrol or thousands of rounds of HE, with fire going on all around him and what if that little lot went up? Worse than a brewing tank!

So Sgt Sid and crew performed their task of support and reassurance. They carried a keg of rum for such moments, and perhaps a tot of rum is more acceptable than a psychiatrist at crisis time. A pat on the back and a word or two – 'I saw your gunner and driver just go through' – were better than a Harley Street consultation. But there was another task still waiting to be performed, the worst of the lot.

Behind the embankment, in that somewhat safer zone, a Cromwell had been abandoned. It had not burned. On the tank sprawled a body, the body of a man who had been beheaded. The driver of the tank. It was not decent to leave him there, splayed in that undignified posture as rigor mortis set in. It was doubly horrifying for brewed-up crews passing by, a decapitated body of a good pal. So this one more duty awaited, a duty for which the fitters had not been trained.

Sgt Jones squared his shoulders. At twenty-eight he was an older man than the average crew member. He had been serving in the army since 1940, more than four years. After basic training he took fitter's courses, was promoted and in June of 1944, just before embarking to sail to Normandy, he was made up to Sergeant. So it was his responsibility to show his less experienced crew how to perform this most harrowing of duties.

It did not have the mitigating effect of being an anonymous body, always easier to dispose of. No, they had recognized it as being the mortal remains of Niblock, Tpr Jock Niblock, a quiet man, an excellent tank driver, a popular friend to all, just a 20-year-old Scot from Dunbartonshire. How did they know it was Niblock? Well, they knew. They just knew. It was his tank. And there were features about the body's shape, the way of wearing the uniform, the boots or shoes.

If it was any consolation to them, they knew he could not have suffered. They dug. Sometimes the Normandy soil was hard and difficult to dig. Here a foot or two up the embankment the soil was soft. They picked up the normal tools of their trade and dug the grave. Beyond the role of undertaker lies the role of priest. Sgt Sid could only mutter a few words of farewell before they filled in the hole and marked the place. Niblock's body was safe at least from the continuing rain of explosives as the battle raged on. One day the War Graves people would come and take him to Ranville for more permanent rest and remembrance.

Meanwhile the knocked-out tanks stood scattered around the good tank countryside, the heavy barrages and the chattering of m-gs continued. So Sgt Jones in his half-track, after the journey back to the medics near Demouville, could not yet move safely out into the open fields to render assistance, mechanical or medical, which might be necessary. A phase of the battle had ended, but the regiment and the division and the entire corps would still endure further similar suffering as Goodwood continued with ever less hope of success.

Sgt Jones and Cpl Spittles and Tprs Mosely and Cook survived the day, as did also the badly bleeding Major Stancomb, winner of the Military

Cross. Sid's electrician, 'Gerry', never came to terms with the awful experiences of helping others and burying Niblock. He himself became a case in need of prolonged psychiatric treatment. Sid Jones continued his mechanical interests throughout his life, becoming a motor cycle enthusiast. In his 80s he was still performing duties as marshal at the TT Races in the Isle of Man where he lives, a task calling for much agility when the bikes speed round the narrow corners at 150 mph or more.

The fortunes or the misfortunes of war are as difficult to predict as a national lottery. Reg Spittles, his minor wound duly bandaged, was now well back from front-line danger. During the night a German plane dropped bombs and German guns shelled on the echelon. A nearby lorry was hit. Its ammunition was set on fire. Loaded with 25pdr shells it exploded in a huge conflagration as bad as any Sherman tank brewing. Bits flew everywhere. A piece of the lorry drove straight for Reg, hit him in the back with a tremendous thump and knocked him to the ground struggling for breath. Reg described his subsequent experience:

> I was gathered up and despatched to a field hospital. This was a marquee which was in a hole dug out so that only the top was above ground with the soil banked around to prevent blast in case of shelling. I had been struck by a piece of flying debris from the lorry which had almost broken my ribs and my right forearm was swollen up like Popeye in his cartons. This on top of my earlier shrapnel wound, which our own MO was intending to deal with, meant I was in dock for about a week. Then I returned to the same crew. And we went through the same experience of all being knocked out together twice at later battles, away up in the Netherlands.

The war diary of the regiment involved, of Sgt Jones and Cpl Spittles and Tpr Mosely,[8] provides scant corroborative detail of the events here described. The reason becomes evident in a war diary entry later in the month to the effect that the existing war diary had been destroyed by enemy action and the officer who was compiling it had been killed by the same shell.

CHAPTER THREE

HALT! WHO GOES WHERE?

Like a tense chess game: 'check!' Again 'check!' And then 'stalemate!' The story of the month following the glorious, triumphal, deceptive optimism of D-Day. After the 'Longest Day', the longest month.

The Allied pawns had moved slowly and cautiously across the Normandy chessboard up to D + 30, 1944. The black knights of the SS Panzers had made their violent moves but to no avail. There had been no catastrophic gambit. The black knights even had their kings: Wittmann cruising the Villers-Bocage countryside in his Tiger tank one fine afternoon and knocking out a couple of dozen British armoured vehicles in an area not much bigger than an athletics field and in less time than it would have taken for an athlete to run the 5,000 metres. Wittmann and Barkmann and Panzermeyer and others. But to no avail.

In the words of one chronicle, 'The advance came almost to a halt. Indeed it needed a careful examination of a large-scale map to discover the places where territorial gains had been made. A sense of despondency and frustration was in the air.'[1] In 1944 there was no force called, as in 1914 or 1939, the British Expeditionary Force. Proudly the invaders had been termed the 'British Army of Liberation', the BLA. But to some it seemed that the British Army of Liberation, after liberating just one significant city, Bayeux, had become the 'British Army of Hibernation'. The Americans and Canadians seemed to be doing not much better.

The target on D-Day for British troops surging off the beaches was the city of Caen. For five weeks that vital centre proved impregnable. Then on 9 July, after a massive RAF bombardment, Caen was said to have fallen. True, the city centre had been occupied. The Abbaye aux Hommes, which sheltered 16,000 refugees, had been liberated. But the pivotal city was so ruined that no vehicle could pass through it. The enemy still occupied the southern suburbs and industrial zones beyond the River Orne. Over on the Allied right wing towards St-Lo American troops were both metaphorically and literally bogged down in the flooded *marais* and the mazy *bocage*. The enemy pushed and prodded with crumpled horns and would never drive the Allies back to, and off, the beaches.

Stalemate! Such high hopes. Such low achievement. Such disillusionment.

An official historian's eventual verdict was that the stalemate was more apparent than real:

The Allies were now so strongly established in Normandy that they need fear nothing that the enemy might do to prevent their continuing the attack, but the German forces were stretched to the limit in their attempt to prevent a break-out from the lodgement area . . . while the Allied strength increased daily the German strength daily diminished. And neither at sea nor in the air were their efforts to hamper Allied operations having any significant effect.[2]

That was the confident voice of hindsight. But, at the time, for many on the Allied side it was a situation like that of a heavyweight boxer in the fourth or fifth round of a long bout, assured by his seconds that he would win in the end but meanwhile being hit, left and right, with crunching, energy-sapping blows.

While the Germans appeared to be able to continue, absorbing knock-down blows, round after round, without visibly wilting, many of the Allied troops were already tiring and loath to submit themselves to further punishment. Three of the British divisions had already fought arduous campaigns in Africa and Sicily, their infantry tramping a thousand miles or more. They were not too pleased to find themselves selected for the spearhead honour in Normandy when other units had spent years unbled at home in Britain. One tank troop leader remembered that, as early as D + 24, his supporting infantry (D-Day veterans) refused to cross the start line until the tanks (a fresh unit) were already almost on the objective.[3]

For the Germans, punching hard, the boxing metaphor had another significance. Their opponent's reach, like Mohammed Ali's, was so long that they could not get close enough to land the final knock-out blow. Knockdowns, yes. Knock-outs, no. In military terms Field Marshal (FM) Gerd von Rundstedt advised Hitler that, 'the guns of most enemy warships have so powerful an effect on areas within their range that any advance into the zone dominated by fire from the sea is impossible. The ships keep constant watch on the coast inland, up to the limit of the range of their guns.'[4] And the big battleships and monitors could fire over, and well beyond, Caen.

Two of the greatest German commanders had been detailed to defend occupied France against the Allied invasion. At first they had disagreed on how to do this. Rommel, the immediate commander of the area, wished to place his main forces right up to the beaches in the hope of preventing an Allied landing. Von Rundstedt, his superior, planned to hold back strong reserves and then counter-attack, perhaps driving the Allies out from a precarious beachhead. Historians have tended to favour Rommel's view, forgetting that the Allied command of sea and air made a landing almost inevitable. German elite forces crowded up to the beaches on D-Day (even if they had known which beaches to defend) would have suffered incalculable losses from sea and air bombardment.

Now, facing the *fait accompli* but unable to call up large reserve forces at will, due to the Allied command of the air, von Rundstedt planned a more modest but quite effective strategy, saying later, 'If I had been given a free hand to conduct operations, I think I could have made the Allies pay a fearful price for their victory. I had planned to fight a slow retiring action exacting a heavy toll for each bit of ground that I gave up.'[5]

As usually happened in the German High Command, Hitler had other ideas. His will prevailed. He insisted that not a yard of ground could be conceded to the enemy. He seemed to have succeeded in the month since D-Day. The 'give no inch' strategy 'seemed to be on the verge of stabilizing the whole Normandy front altogether'.[6] Hitler, the Grand Master, had provoked the stalemate, if such it were. In fact, reverting to the boxing metaphor, he was saying to his champion in the ring, 'Stop dancing around like a butterfly. Stand still and let yourself be hit by all your opponent can muster.'

On the Allied side the plan of Montgomery, the overall land commander, was to use the city of Caen, which led along the direct route to Paris, as a bait to entice elite German forces into that area so that the Americans could break out through slimmer defences farther west. More than once Montgomery's reluctance to communicate and his genius for obfuscating issues meant that other commanders came to varying views of what he really intended. Biographers of Gen Patton assert that 'the Allied military leaders had planned to control the whole of Normandy and Brittany by July 6 . . . access to more than 500 miles of French coastline . . . suitable terrain for at least twenty-seven airfields.'[7]

The Germans were equally confused. This was understandable because the Allies had carried out a brilliant campaign to persuade them that the main landing would be in the Pas de Calais, a short crossing area. The Allies even invented an extra army waiting to make the crossing, commanded by senior American Gen McNair and with the redoubtable Patton as a corps commander. As late as 26 June Rommel, the arch proponent of fighting them on the beaches, was still hedging his bets expecting 'a thrust from . . . Caen towards Paris' but in coordination with 'a large-scale landing between the Somme and Le Havre'.[8]

Opponents of Montgomery considered that 'the general's pre-invasion master plan is a fiction. In fact, General Montgomery envisioned quickly seizing the city of Caen with British and Canadian forces and then rapidly expanding the lodgement area. When that failed the Allied offensive bogged down. The rest of the campaign . . . was a makeshift attempt to make up for Montgomery's failure to take Caen. No one has found a historical "smoking gun" to resolve the debate.'[9]

The Germans had been equally as unable to break the stalemate as the Allies. As early as D + 1 and D + 2 the fresh and formidable 12th SS Panzer Division Hitlerjugend (Hitler Youth) was attacking towards the beaches. Throughout the month other fierce counter-attacks followed. On 11 July another elite division, Panzer Lehr,[10] hit the American 9th and 30th infantry divisions. British code-breaking had learned of the attack before it started and the GIs were able to inflict heavy losses on the attackers. And so day by day the movements back and forward would normally be indecipherable on a map the scale of a motorist's touring atlas.

By 7 July the Americans were holding a front 61 miles long, while the British and Canadians held 44 miles. However, in several places along that front the line was still only 5 miles from the beaches. Cherbourg had been captured but its docks were so badly damaged that they would be out of service until September. By mid-July the Americans had landed 770,000 troops while the British and Canadians had 591,000 in the beachhead.[11] The liberated area was becoming seriously overcrowded, as can be imagined if the masses of vehicles, stores, workshops, hospitals and other 'army tail' are added to that armed population.

Indeed a joke prevalent in the bridgehead proclaimed that, 'If we do not push inland shortly, we shall have to build skyscrapers to accommodate everyone.'[12] One Highland Division battalion, unable to find a firing practice area in the beachhead, dug and piled up earth at the end of the field to serve as butts. However, when the riflemen fired their 'overs' landed among a sister battalion in the next field. The sister battalion responded in like currency. Some Sherman Firefly gunners, needing a clear space of 1,500 yards to check and correct their gun sights, could find no such open ground and had to zero by guesswork until they moved into the front line.

The spectre of a prolonged and bloody trench warfare, as in 1914–18, began to loom over the Normandy battlefields. Certainly both President Franklin D. Roosevelt and Prime Minister Winston Churchill saw this as a distinct and horrifying scenario at this time.[13]

Such a presentiment was sustained by the casualty lists of all the Allies, and these losses themselves, together with reinforcement problems, contributed considerably towards the stalemate. Already, only one month and 5 miles along the weary road to Berlin, still some one and a half million 30-inch paces away, for some infantry divisions it was as though they had only two pawns left to patrol the entire chessboard.

Of the 770,000 Americans put ashore 73,000 had become casualties in the month. When it is realized that only one in seven soldiers actually carried a 'rifle' (or other battle weapon) into direct action that percentage of casualties becomes highly significant. The British and Canadians had lost 49,000 out of the 591,000 landed.

This rate of loss becomes even more significant when extrapolated from division or battalion statistics, where the 'tail' of relative non-combatants is smaller. In the much maligned 51st Highland Division one battalion with an establishment of thirty officers had lost forty-four. In two days' fighting to liberate Caen some infantry battalions lost a quarter of their strength. At the same time around Hill 112 the 43rd Wessex Division lost 2,000 men in two days. The loss of tanks was equally high, although tank crew casualties were somewhat lower than the infantry. Throughout the campaign the American 3rd Armored Divison, with a complement of 234 tanks, was to lose 580 per cent of that number in a continuous wasting process against more powerful enemy guns.[14]

A worrying factor for higher commanders was the incidence of what was known to the troops as 'bomb happiness', but by 1944 classified as 'battle exhaustion'. Medical officers had been trained to distinguish between malingering and genuine exhaustion. By the middle of July more than 2,000 casualties had been diagnosed and treated as psychiatric cases. A few days of rehabilitation was considered adequate treatment.[15]

A Canadian psychiatrist who has studied the problem of 'burnout' cases (that is, psychologically 'burned') found that in Normandy in 1944 'powerful defences that produced crippling physical casualties also starkly demonstrated the variable limits of individual tolerance to the terror and chaos of a modern battlefield'. He identified two main types of collapse: frightened, inexperienced young soldiers who lost self-control briefly at a moment of crisis, as opposed to older soldiers who burned out after long periods of unrelieved stress.[16]

His researches showed that:

In 1914–18 shell shock was thought at first to be caused by *physical* damage to the brain. In time, psychological explanations, only very reluctantly received, came to supplant physiological ones. . . . Field psychiatrists found that there was no practicable way to predict beforehand which individual would make an effective soldier, especially an infantryman. They also concluded that, although timing and circumstances varied, *virtually every soldier* had his own breaking point, the defining features of which were the combat situation, motivation and morale.[17]

In spite of more informed and tolerant attitudes to such defaulters, the losses due to non-enemy, self-inflicted action were so high that Canadian Army Commander, Gen Crerar, not having the death penalty available, invoked a standard sentence of from three to five years' imprisonment, with hard labour, as a tourniquet to staunch the bleeding manpower. Among the ploys used by malingerers to leave their units were plain desertion, self-inflicted wounds, feigning 'battle exhaustion' and deliberate VD re-infection.

Looking ahead, the Supreme Commander, Eisenhower, was having qualms about the possibility of reinforcements, knowing that 'August would be a lean month for infantry reinforcements. No more British divisions would be available. . . . Infantry divisions direct from the States would not begin to arrive until September, and he feared that . . . the enemy would gather sufficient strength to contain the Allies [in Normandy] throughout the winter.'[18]

The response of the men on the other side, von Rundstedt, Rommel and then von Kluge, who replaced von Rundstedt, might have been, 'If you think you've got problems, look at what we have to contend with.' Already on 17 June, after only ten days of counter-attacking the beachhead, SS corps commander Sepp Dietrich, the toughest of the tough, was informing Rommel that, 'I am being bled white and am getting nowhere.' When ordered to continue the counter-attacks, he responded tartly, 'With what?'[19]

A week later a Panzer Lehr report, captured by the Allies, revealed that the division had lost 160 officers and 5,400 men, while only sixty-six of its original 190 tanks were ready for action. 1 SS Panzer Division strength report for 1 July reported 2,769 personnel as being absent from division more than a year (non-leave). By 1 August that figure had risen to 3,783.[20]

As to equipment, on 7 July 17th SS Panzer-Grenadier Division had available a mere seven out of their establishment of twenty-five armoured cars, forty-five out of ninety of their self-propelled guns and 676 out of 1,105 cross-country trucks. Probably the most powerful unit at war, 102nd heavy SS tank battalion started the month of July with forty-three Tigers (twenty-five available, eight in for repair and another ten in transit), but by the end of the month only thirty remained, after reinforcement. And these were the 'invincible' 54-ton monsters which were not easily replaced from the factories in Germany.[21]

One day before Operation Goodwood, on 17 July, the total German casualties in Normandy passed the 100,000 mark. Of those, 2,360 were officers whose experience and skill would be harder to replace than Tiger tanks. The German commanders had analysed that they could replace only about 12 per cent of their casualties. The problems posed by these shortages were exacerbated for the higher commanders because the constant pressure exerted by the Allies on the outnumbered German defenders meant that each German unit had to be constantly in action, with the mobile units dashing from one danger point to another without respite. As a result it was impossible to build up a strategic reserve with which to launch a decisive offensive against the invaders.[22]

As the human players called on all their resources of will and determination, guile and deduction, endurance and initiative in an endeavour to get going, two new unwelcome players entered the game. Scorning human arrogance they proceeded to dominate the exchanges. Their names were Weather and Terrain.

The weather had already intervened to rule that 6 June rather than 5 June should be celebrated for posterity as D-Day. Now it decided to play an even more dominant role. As no great ports were immediately available in the Caen area the Allies had decided to build prefabricated docks just off the landing beaches. This project was given the code name of Mulberry and required the component parts to be towed across the Channel and joined together like Meccano sets. By 18 June the new installations were already functioning, although not yet totally completed.

Against the predictions of meteorologists, who had forecast fine weather, a gale blew up on D + 13. It was of such violence that elements of the Mulberry docks still being towed across the sea were broken up and sunk as effectively as if the German Navy had acted. Two days of errant ocean storm lashed the gentle beaches, the worst storm to hit the area for forty years. Ships were driven ashore, parts of Mulberry smashed and convoys outward bound from England had to hurry back to port for shelter. Weather had shouted 'Halt!' or at least 'Slow march!' to the hosts of puny soldiers equipping themselves for battle. The prefabricated harbour was planned in two parts, one for American landings and one for British and Canadian. It was the American section that suffered most.

All the Allies were affected by the loss of ships and docking space. The three days prior to the storm the number of troops landed daily averaged nearly 35,000 and about 25,000 tons of stores unloaded: during the storm days the average fell to under 10,000 with about 7,000 tons of stores.[23] In the prior days nearly 6,000 vehicles came ashore daily: during the storm 2,400. By D + 13 the British Army unloading schedule for troops was running two brigades late. By the end of the storm this had increased to a shortfall of three divisions (nine brigades).

Human ingenuity responded to the challenge of the gales. On the American beaches it was found possible to run coasting ships ashore, unload them and then eventually float them off again. There was an increase in the amount of supplies being airlifted in. During the same period, the enemy, not being dependent on the whims of the sea, took advantage of the lull in the battles to do valuable work on their defences.

By 10 July there was still only one of the Mulberry docks working. On that day the American Commander, Gen Bradley, advised Montgomery that delays in building up ammunition stocks meant that the intended major offensive would have to be postponed.[24] While the naval people were again pushing supply ships across the Channel, the aftermath of the storm, in the form of thick clouds and high winds, continued to frustrate the airmen for some time. Once the storm had ended and the supply chain had been stepped up into top gear again, the human commanders breathed sighs of relief and returned to their plans and projects. They were unaware that the gods of weather were also planning some more interference for Operations Goodwood and Cobra.

The terrain also had more influence on matters than was anticipated by the planners, judging by the apparent lack of technical preparation made before D-Day. Moreover there appears to have been inappropriate personnel training, which was often carried out in terrain in no way resembling the *bocage*. (This was a grave problem in wartime Britain, where many Americans and others had to complete their pre-D-Day preparations. Training areas were mainly located on uncultivable land because land resembling *bocage* was essential food-producing territory which had to be kept for that purpose.)

Most soldiers were taken by surprise on first sight of the *bocage* and the *marais*. In the former it was as if a team had arrived at a stadium to play a football game and found that a huge maze had been constructed right across the centre of the field. The attackers' tactics were rendered difficult by the many dead ends, while the defenders knew the maze well and could use it to reinforce their defence.

Each small closely hedged field was like a separate Roman camp or a Wild West stockade. A deep ditch had yielded soil to provide a high bank behind it. On top of the bank had been cultivated virtual bulwarks of intertwined bushes and trees up to an average height of ten feet. One tank commander was able to measure just such a hedge fairly accurately:

> We move into a narrow lane governed by some of the highest hedges I have ever seen . . . I climb onto the tank top. Here, when I am fully extended on tiptoe, my eyes probably some fourteen feet or more above ground level, I can just peer over the top of this Beecher's Brook *in excelsis*.[25]

In the British and Canadian zones, areas of *bocage*, or equally entangled ancient apple orchards, were spread haphazardly across the countryside, with wider open plains in between. In the American zone 'the hedgerows commenced right behind the original First Army landing beaches and extended up to 50 miles inland in some areas', providing for the defenders 'effective camouflage' and for the attackers 'obstructed observation, and hindered the employment of both artillery and tanks'.[26]

The *marais* (marshlands), and sometimes *marais salant* (saltings), particularly affected the Americans, and in contrast to the *bocage* were low-lying, open, treacherous stretches of land, often enshrouded in mist. The going was very bad as infantrymen squelched through thick stews of bog and tanks sank deep, often driving themselves deeper by the useless threshing of tracks. With typical attention to detail the Germans had flooded many of these marshes.[27] Normandy was certainly not what in later years became known in business patois as 'a level playing field'.

The lack of preparation for such country, and the tactical ineptitude in trying to penetrate it, have been commented upon by a number of critics. One unabashed American view comments:

> For a nation which prides itself on the ability to get the job done, the history of American tactics proves surprisingly dismal. . . . American tactics in the Second World War started off almost as poorly as Civil War tactics, but they improved rapidly. While inferior tanks and insufficient training certainly hurt the combat troops, the principal weakness was the army's lack of combined arms doctrine. Put simply, the military thinkers [some British also] assumed that tanks and infantry worked best separately, and did not prepare for a war in which the most successful attacks would be by combined arms.[28]

That writer goes on to support his contention by quoting two other authorities:

> Weigly ascribes 'more ingenuity' to the soldiers and combat officers on Omaha Beach than the planners of the assault; without their initiative in getting off the beach, Bradley might have been forced to evacuate. Before the landings, nobody seems to have recognized the problems that fighting in the Normandy *bocage* would present; if anybody did, he failed to inform the junior officers. Doubler, author of the most recent study . . . notes that the solutions to the tactical problem of fighting in Normandy came from the initiative of the small units themselves. . . .

This enshrines a good deal of truth but is a little unjust to some generals such as American Marcus Rose, Canadian Guy Simonds and the British inventor of 'Funnies' (armoured vehicles for specific purposes), Percy Hobart, who commanded an entire division (79th Armoured) dedicated to technological inventiveness.

Gen Bradley found it necessary to replace some unsatisfactory divisional commanders. He also instituted retraining of troops to cope with Normandy style fighting, insisting to Montgomery that there should be some delays in major American actions in order to do this. The British and Canadians were also finding the need to 'unstick' under-performing generals at corps, division and brigade level, not the most useful kind of change to ensure continuity of action or improvement of morale.

In another aspect of terrain the British commanders had shot themselves in the foot, as it were. A massive raid by RAF bombers had devastated the city of Caen, particularly the northern and western suburbs, in order to destroy the German defences. Knowing what was coming, the Germans had moved out of the area and suffered fewer casualties from the raid than did French civilians. The huge RAF bombs clustered closely had caused unimaginable damage to the routes through which large numbers of Allied tanks would have hoped to advance to the south. For the time being the raid had closed off Caen as a transit centre.

At 2300 hours on the night before the eventual liberation of Caen the first Sherman of the first troop from the direction of Lebissey in the north moved expectantly down into the summer gloaming:

We recognize the outskirts of Caen not by the houses but by the ruins. At one moment we are running through grassy open slopes, next moment the slopes have become uneven and mounded with rubble. Within fifty yards the rubble grows into mountainous proportions. Our progress changes into a series of thuds and crashes and tumbles as we climb over fallen houses and descend into interlinked craters. 'For what it's worth', comes the commander's voice, 'we are now in Caen.'

Ordered to get the tank down into the city centre by whatever means, the tank, now in darkness, crashed on at some peril to the crew. Then:

There is no more street. There are no houses. There is no Caen. Only a towering wilderness of ruins. . . . Now we are grinding up Everests of pounded rubble. And sliding and rocking down Wookey Holes of RAF excavation . . . before us lies a black void . . . even with tracks braked and halted the Sherman is toppling and sliding down into what seems an underground cavern . . . we crash with bone-shaking violence to the floor of the ultimate pit . . . the epicentre of the earthquake unloaded by the RAF last night.[29]

Part of the reason for the continuing stalemate was the need to plan and prepare some method for moving up to three armoured divisions with 800 tanks through that chaos in order to attack the Germans across a wide river where the bridges had been demolished. The only suitable site for rehearsing battle in such conditions might have been a blitzed area of London or Coventry.

A Normandy factor which is sometimes overlooked is that the region was not conducive to the type of major guerilla activity which could be conducted in the southern French *Maquis*. French Resistance activities had necessarily to be much more subtle and subdued than the open warfare which was conducted against the 2nd SS Panzer Division (Das Reich) on its journey from the south towards Normandy, action which drew from the SS a terror reaction, including wiping out Oradour village, which would later be treated by the Allies as a war crime.[30]

Because of the great productivity of Normandy in items ranging from dairy foods and cider to iron mining and building-stone quarrying, the Germans had been particularly careful to treat the population with stern but fair civility. There was a superficially adequate system of charging for requisitions of goods by the army. Strict behavioural discipline was imposed on German soldiers of the occupation force. The sanction for even trivial misbehaviour was transfer to the Eastern Front and the horrors of the Russian winter.[31] It might even be said that some Allied soldiers behaved less well than did the average German ranker in dealings with the civilian population, particularly its women. So resistance work in Normandy tended to be channelled into providing information and guides for the Allies and helping Allied prisoners of war to escape.

The Allies had one undeniable advantage in the poker game of guessing and double-guessing, deceit and counter-bluff. This was the Ultra system, with the supreme tool of the Enigma code-breaking machine at Bletchley Park in England, which could pick up and translate German High Command messages without the enemy being aware of the procedure. When von Kluge took over from von Rundtstedt he was alarmed by the resources he had inherited. He sent back to Hitler, in code, a complete list of the units under his command. Ultra read it, as it read so many other vital messages, enabling the Allied command to know the colour and value of the enemy's cards.[32]

What was not so pleasant about Ultra was that it conveyed not only the good news but the bad news too. At this time of stalemate Ultra picked up the fact that, in spite of all impediments such as Allied air bombing and French resistance, new German units were managing to approach the Normandy battle front. Ominous message followed ominous message. First that two front-line German infantry divisions, 271 and 272, were about to arrive in Normandy from the south of France. Then 5 Parachute, and 16 GAF (Luftwaffe), 276 and 277 infantry. And not far behind them 326. There was need to break the stalemate before these fresh divisions could give it much more permanence.[33]

The Germans' major problem was in bringing such reinforcements quickly up to the line of battle when the Allies dominated the air. One staff officer reported:

> The effect of Anglo-American air supremacy on the Normandy front and as far as Paris is so great that all convoy traffic is restricted to night time and even single vehicles are only used by day in the most extreme emergencies. The main highway . . . is ploughed up. The losses in motor vehicles in some units is as much as 40 per cent of the original strength and at the same time large quantities of reserves of munitions and fuel were destroyed.[34]

Some impression of the impact of this supply starvation on the Germans is reflected in the amount of artillery fire the two sides could employ. On 10 July the Germans were able to fire only 4,500 rounds as compared to the British who alone fired 80,000 rounds. German fuel shortages were running at 200,000 gallons a day, and only 400 tons of other supplies were getting through out of a requirement of 1,250 tons.[35] An RAF pilot described how during a night attack he had seen columns of German trucks driving with headlights on, so desperate were they to speed up deliveries. The result was that the planes were more able to discern and target the convoys.[36]

The German High Command also suffered from personality clashes. When von Kluge took over as Rommel's immediate superior his first act was to quarrel with his formidable subordinate. 'On July 5, Kluge greeted

Rommel with the words: "Now you, too, will have to get accustomed to obeying orders!" Rommel did not take this insult lying down, and a terrible row ensued. . . . The marshals' argument became so personal and insulting that Kluge ordered everyone else to leave the room.'[37]

On 17 June and again on 29 June von Rundstedt and Rommel had journeyed together to see Hitler in the hope of persuading him to allow them to make tactically preferable retreats as the situation demanded. 'Hitler looked pale and sleepless, playing nervously with his glasses and an array of coloured pencils which he held between his fingers. He sat hunched upon a stool, while the field marshals stood.'[38] However, Hitler continued to insist on a total non-retreat strategy. It was two days later when, asked his opinion by the High Command as to what might be done, von Runstedt uttered his famous retort, 'Make peace, you fools!'

At the sharp end of battle many German soldiers also felt frustration but had no idea what to do about it. Even the fanatically loyal Hitler Youth commander, Panzermeyer, admitted that 'we had often talked of the futility of conflict during the last few weeks and cursed this horrible inhuman war. Why do we not put an end to it? . . . [we] clearly see defeat. . . . The political aims of the Allies are felt to be even more awful than the cruellest death.'[39]

A German mortar crew corporal, Karl-Heinz Decker, scurrying from hide-hole to hide-hole like a weasel in the night, could see no future at all because his home province, East Prussia, was to be occupied by the Russians, as decided in the Allied plans for the postwar reorganization. He would have nowhere to go. The Allied aim of total surrender had a boomerang effect. It made the enemy fight harder. Lt Wenzel Borgert declared that 'if the Allies had said, get rid of the Nazis, no one would have objected to that. But none of the Allies said that.'[40]

If anything, backbiting and bickering may have been more widespread on the Allied side than among the Germans. The first month of invasion had bred many frustrations and rebuffs. These in turn had spawned misunderstanding and cynicism, often along nationalistic lines. A Canadian described it as 'an already sulphurous atmosphere, the American press . . . complaining that Americans were dying while Britons and Canadians loafed'.[41]

Not to be outdone, when the British suffered a reverse in Sicily in 1943, Gen Patton, who beat Montgomery in a race to capture Messina, remarked, 'our cousins got a bloody nose'. To some Americans Montgomery was 'a Gilbert and Sullivan caricature. If it rained, he carried an umbrella onto the battlefield.' On the other side the normally strait-laced BBC allowed a comment that, 'Patton's Seventh Army was eating grapes and sitting under the pine trees of Sicily.'[42]

Churchill himself was sometimes indiscreet. When disagreeing with the Americans on 30 June he took the attitude, 'All right, if you insist on being damned fools, sooner than falling out with you, which would be fatal, we shall be damned fools with you, and we shall see that we perform the role of damned fools damned well!'[43] Eisenhower felt that Montgomery needed to speed up operations. When Montgomery sent him a telegram on 13 July, setting out his strategy, Eisenhower replied 'describing how American troops were constantly fighting to give the British a chance to break out'.[44] All this caused Britain's top commander, Alanbrooke, to groan to his diary on 27 July, 'My God, what psychological complications war leads to!! . . . Will we ever learn to "love our allies as ourselves"??!! . . . "national" spectacles pervert the perspective of the strategic landscape.'

Not all bickering was focused by 'national' spectacles. There were internecine battles within nations. The British airman, Tedder, was Eisenhower's deputy and, in theory, senior to Montgomery. Tedder was rabidly angry about Montgomery's failure to capture country suitable for much-needed airfields, and after Goodwood would recommend his dismissal. 'Sir Arthur Tedder's fear, after only a fortnight's fighting, that the situation in Normandy "had the makings of a dangerous crisis", developed into a positive distrust of General Montgomery's leadership and outspoken criticism of his conduct of operations.'[45]

Among the Americans, top generals Everett S. Hughes, J.C.H. Lee and Bedell Smith were indulging in a running feud. 'In early June, Smith was still fulminating against inspector generals (Hughes) who . . . "delve too much into his affairs". On 22 June, Hughes chanced on another expenses scandal involving Smith. Six days later Hughes added ". . . Bedell don't like the way he has been investigated".'[46]

It is unlikely that the lower ranks knew much of what was going on, although not all front-line soldiers subscribed to the wartime 'spin' (to use a much later term) such as the myth that Montgomery was revered and respected by all British soldiers.[47] The rifleman and tankie might not have concerns about higher strategy but a feeling of discrimination could work its way down to the men who mattered. The war diarist of the Canadian infantry regiment, the Reginas, was understandably cynical as their brigade shed blood at 1914–18 rates. 'It was this unspectacular but vital role that Canadian forces carried on while the glamorous armored Spearheads spread their arrows over the front page of newspapers the world over.'

There was still room for a modicum of humour. One joke going the rounds was that by Christmas the Russians would be in Berlin, the Yanks in Paris and the Brits in Caen. A newspaper reported that in a briefing session for correspondents someone burst in and claimed that they had seen a German aeroplane and that it had dropped a bomb. Everyone immediately wanted to know where this strange event had occurred.[48]

On a more serious note, the newspaper which printed the joke also carried a learned-looking opinion from the military analyst saying that 'Russian Victories Are Magnificent, But – The War Will Be Won In Normandy'. This was based on the argument that, while the Germans could retreat for hundreds of miles on the Russian Front without a final disaster, a break in the Normandy Front would mean a total collapse of German resistance between the Seine and the Rhine – as happened within another month or so. And the less sustainable argument that the Russian advance would cause them to slow down because of supply problems, while the Allies, breaking past the Channel ports, would have all supply problems easily solved.

This kind of argument built up expectations which were not be realized by mid-July. The failure was made more humiliating by the vivid headlines from other sectors of war: Russians cross old 1939 Polish border (4 July); Leghorn and Ancona (Italy) captured; Russians within 9 miles of Lwow, 'the gateway to Berlin'; American troops land in the Marianas (Pacific); French *maquis* destroy 116-vehicle German convoy; Russians advance into Latvia; American heavy bombers hit German rocket and plane factories from two directions, from bases in Britain and in Italy.

It was time to get going in Normandy, but who would go, and where?

CHAPTER FOUR

WORLD'S WORST
TRAFFIC JAM

Frank Clark, rookie guardsman, sat in his tank, fretting and fidgeting. The war and the fate of the world bore heavily on his shoulders. But there was nothing he could do about it, except chew a finger nail or two. The worst scenario was being played out. The Guards, the elite, the royal, the infallible, the invincible Brigade of Guards, were going to be late on parade![1]

In all his training, the initial square bashing and ear bashing at Pirbright, the technical training for tank crew, the battalion and brigade exercises in England, Frank had been indoctrinated to one fundamental principle, more important perhaps than shining boots or well-oiled weapon working parts, that the Guards were never late on parade. Now he peered ahead from his place in the Forward Delivery Squadron (an urgent sounding title) and perceived the long line of Guards' tanks rumbling along at a maximum 2 mph. Which would never deliver them at the rendezvous on the stroke of the hour.

Little comfort to Gdsm Clark that the Guards were not to blame. Nor the tailenders of Canadians and 11 Armoured ahead. Out there under a dust-saturated night sky some 3,000 tanks and similar vehicles, the majority of them 32-ton monsters, and 50,000 men contended for the shifting ten-yards-a-time leap which this vast traffic jam permitted to each vehicle. From nameless sites all over the Normandy bridgehead, along narrow lanes and over open fields, they were converging on a narrow river crossing, the tanks, the ambulances, the bulldozers, the recovery vehicles, the towed guns, the outsize trucks (many carrying stocks of wooden crosses) and, as ever, the uninhibited motor bikes squirming in and out of the impatient queues.

If a satellite photograph of the Lebissey-Ranville area had been taken on the night of 17/18 July 1944, it would have been fascinating: dozens of lines of grey conjoined centipedes and millipedes wriggling across the dull gold of nocturnal cornfields, then converging and coalescing into a pulsating mass by the silver ribbon of the River Orne, sliding over the tight black bridges and then again bulging towards assembly areas.

In one of those centipedes was travelling Robert Boscawen, then a Coldstream Guards officer, who vividly remembers the eye-wearying, throat-rasping, nose-souring experience:

> It was an awful approach march, cross-country on a very dark night with only tail lamps, and, worst of all, a thick cloud of dust everywhere. The dust was appalling. I had made my co-drivers drive as I thought it would rest the first drivers, but this turned out to be a mistake. The visibility was so bad that it needed the best possible driving to keep going without running into everything. Because of this I lost one of my tanks [interestingly enough named] 'Cobra', which went into the ditch. . . . 'Cougar', Sergeant Emerson's tank with the seventeen-pounder, also broke down due to dust in the petrol filter.[2]

Three armoured divisions were ahead in the incredible circus procession, with a total of twelve armoured or reconnaissance regiments, not to mention the infantry contingents. To stand and watch just one of those regiments go by would give an impression of the whole. Leading the way was the Third Royal Tank Regiment (3 RTR) and they alone put on the road that night four scout cars, forty-nine Sherman tanks (75mm guns), twelve Sherman 'Firefly' tanks (17pdr guns), three Sherman recovery vehicles, six anti-aircraft Crusader tanks, two Stuart light tanks, five half-tracked vehicles, thirteen 3-ton petrol lorries, twenty-three ammunition lorries, thirteen admin lorries, two Light Aid Detachment (LAD, fitters) vehicles, two HQ trucks, two Base Depot (BD) tractors, and, in and out, four motor cycles. One regiment![3]

So, one by one, the regiments started up, and behind them the motorized infantry, the 'walking infantry', the echelons, the headquarters. Along unknown, dimly perceived routes, they crawled to the Orne. There they drove carefully over wobbling bridges with inches to spare on either side of a tank's tracks. On the other side, released into more open country, they found themselves surrounded by crashed D-Day gliders and, strewn between the gliders, long-dead, bloated bodies, animal and human, which, when crushed, emitted a further nauseating element into the existing brew of vehicle, munition and human stenches.

Beyond that hazard the military police, immaculately uniformed amid the thunder of explosions and clouds of tank dust, channelled the columns into the tight mouths of cleared passages, only four cleared passages, each not much more than a tank's width, through an extensive uncharted minefield. Beyond might be the open, typical tank country, the Promised Land of the Prophet Montgomery, where tanks might accelerate into a mad charge like the cavalry gallop at Balaclava – but not, of course, so ill judged and fateful.

In the long columns were Canadian infantrymen charged with one of the earliest and most hazardous tasks of the day among the steel mills and fortress-like chimneys at Colombelles. The men of the Stormont, Dundas and Glengarry Highlanders did not know that the world's worst traffic jam would mean that they would fight for twenty-four hours on one hard biscuit and one slice of spam as supply wagons were delayed.[4]

Even as staff officers and military policemen tried to keep the convoys moving there were inevitable breakdowns which exacerbated the problems. Some were individual, like Boscawen's 'Cobra'. Others were of more serious import. At about 0400 hours on 18 July, the unceasing traffic of massive tanks cut all signals wires on one route across the bridges. Until 0730 a divisional commander was having to talk to his brigadiers by patching through the army HQ system. And at 0857 a section of the road to which the division was restricted collapsed and caused a difficult time-consuming detour.

As the tanks rolled into the assembly area Lt Boscawen looked out beyond his troop of Shermans:

'Cougar' had turned up during the night, so I walked back down the column to look for it. There were tanks, guns, carriers, half-trucks and other vehicles as far as the eye could see, hundreds of them, tail to tail, rank upon rank, arrayed behind a small ridge. Beside each was a little petrol fire and around this a small group of men cooked or washed and shaved. . . . I found my lost tank 'Cougar' . . . but 'Cobra' had not yet appeared.[5]

A brief review of some of the factors outlined in the previous chapter will highlight the problems. The Allied bombing of Caen, thought very necessary at the time, had so devastated the city that the passage of thousands of tanks through its streets was impossible. Geographic factors meant that the only viable route was from the north of Caen, eastwards across the River Orne and then south, bending in to form a new forward line to the south of Caen. The bridges were restricted to the bridge captured on D-Day and two pairs constructed by the engineers since then. One writer has commented that this route was decided 'not because it was satisfactory, but because it was not quite so unsatisfactory as the alternatives. And the shape of the ground shaped the plan of attack.'[6]

Beyond the Orne the arriving legions would find themselves in a tiny enclave of about 4 miles by 3. This was secured on D-Day by airborne troops but was immediately closed off by vicious enemy counter-attacks. As early as 1100 on D-Day the German 346th Inf Div, according to its commander Gen Dienstl, was ordered from beyond the Seine for this action. There were few ferries across the Seine and a shortage of road transport, so a battalion mounted its bicycles and 'gaily' rode the 40 miles into immediate battle.

Striking south from the enclave the advancing troops nearest the Orne would soon find themselves in the Colombelles steel works, which had already become notorious to Allied soldiers. This was an area of about one mile by half a mile, boasting some of the largest mills and the tallest, strongest chimneys in France, amid marshalling yards and sundry workshops and warehouses, a ready-made redoubt, familiar to the defenders but for which the Canadian attackers would have no time to study and train.

A factor whose importance would not emerge until the second day of the anticipated advance was the strength of the German defences. The Allies had badly underestimated, for no apparent reason. Available for immediate counter-attack was 'Hitler's Own', the 1st SS Panzer Regiment

LAH ('Leibstandarte' (Lifeguard) *Adolph Hitler*), elite of the elite, with fifty-nine Mk IV tanks and forty-six Panthers ready for battle. These with other formations and vehicles in short-term repair gave a total of 377 tanks and self-propelled guns (very similar to tanks but with restricted traverse).[7] As by this stage of the campaign the Germans anticipated taking out five British armoured vehicles for every one of their own lost, their 377 guns in armour represented a terrifying potential for destroying British equipment and trained crews.

Fearing the stalemate referred to earlier, Eisenhower had written criticizing Montgomery for limiting the weight of British attacks to only two or three divisions when an attack by the whole of the Second Army might set the left flank (Caen area) in motion. He observed that 'we have not yet attempted a major full-dress attack on the left flank supported by everything we could bring to bear'.[8] Eisenhower's very diplomatic message to his irascible subordinate might be translated, 'Get your finger out!'

On 10 July Montgomery met Gen Dempsey, British Second Army Commander and Gen Bradley, US First Army Commander. The latter proposed an operation to reach and open up the Brittany ports from the Allies' right flank. Dempsey suggested a complementary major attack on the left flank. The objectives of this would be to clear Caen and its environs, to gain sites for airfields in the open spaces beyond Caen, and to draw German Panzer divisions away from the American breakout area. This was approved by Montgomery as the Allied commander in the field. The British attack was to be known as Operation Goodwood (another British racecourse code name, following Epsom) and the American endeavour would be coded Cobra (of the fastest sting).[9] In the event 'Sidewinder' might have been more appropriate. The horsey soldiers of the British household cavalry termed their operation the 'Goodwood Meeting'.

The British force, including the three armoured divisions, would be commanded as VIII Corps by Lt Gen Sir Richard O'Connor, a very experienced commander. O'Connor was two years younger than Montgomery but had on occasion climbed above Montgomery in career appointments. He had carried out a brilliant desert campaign in 1940–1 but had the misfortune to be taken prisoner. This formed a hiatus in his career, so that by D-Day 1944 Montgomery was commanding the army group while O'Connor, having escaped from a prisoner of war camp disguised in a costume from the camp theatre, was coming back into harness as a corps commander two rungs lower on the ladder.[10]

A serious disagreement arose almost immediately. Taking into consideration firstly the army's lack of infantry reinforcements and secondly the attractive open plains beyond Caen, Montgomery and Dempsey had decided to use three armoured divisions as a spearhead to charge through the German lines, with the infantry following on when able. O'Connor wanted to use armoured personnel carriers to deliver some infantry up front, a tactic successfully used by the Canadians three weeks later in the same area. Dempsey overruled the idea. Neither O'Connor nor Roberts, his lead division commander, protested vigorously enough. The British army was not yet ready for full cooperation of infantry with tanks, in spite of lessons learned in 1916, 1918 and 1940.[11]

On 16 July senior commanders were called to a conference at which the details of Goodwood were filled in. In view of later criticism of the intentions of the operation it is relevant to include some of those details at this point:

8 Corps to advance and establish themselves in the area of BRAS/ VARRIERS [*sic* = Verrières] – high ground North of CRAMESNIL 0857 – VIMONT 1561.
29 AB with u[nder]/c[command] 13 RHA, 1 sq and 1 trp 22 DGns, 119 A tk bty, 1 trp 612 Fwd sq RE with 1 trp AVRES.
159 IB with u/c 2 NY, 74 A tk regt less 2 btys, 1 tp 612 Fd Sq RE. Inns of Court after phase 2 (29 AB –Les Mesnil Frmeentil & 159 Cuv.Demou) recce towards St-André-sur-Orne/Bretteville-sur-Laize and St-Sylvain.

The gist of this somewhat garbled instruction is that 29th armoured brigade with added troops would lead. 159 infantry brigade with 2nd Northamptonshire Yeomanry would follow. When these troops had captured Le Mesnil-Frementel and Cuverville/Demouville area the Inns of Court regiment, in their fragile if fast armoured cars, would sally away towards fairly remote places in terms of what was being envisaged. In the event the killing ground of the largest British tanks would be the very area where the frail armoured cars were supposed to be roaming. Furthermore, code names were allocated for St-Aignan, Bretteville-le-Rabit, Soignolles ('Brain Fag'), Falaise ('Gastritis'), Potigny, the last three places still four weeks away in real time. Apart from an appalling taste in code names the planners appear to have been bitten by some mysterious optimism bug.

To be fair, the stated Phase 3 objectives were the somewhat more accessible villages of Bras, Verrières, Roquancourt and Crasmenil, the last two of these being liberated on 8 August. The optimism and false assumptions of open country are underlined by accompanying intelligence summaries as at 16 July which, for example, quote 1SS Pz LAH at 80 per cent strength with forty Panthers, sixty Mk IVs and seventy-five anti-tank guns available. The other divisions quoted are calculated to have thirty-three Tigers, five Panthers, 240 Mk IVs and 135 anti-tank guns available. And yet when the excuses for Goodwood's relative underachievement started it was stated that the strength of enemy forces was underestimated.

More than one historian has commented that Montgomery himself 'was perhaps purposefully vague about what the tanks should do when and if the breakthrough was achieved'.[12] Another writer perceived the intention as to 'race across the great sweep of open country beyond. The tanks would drive headlong for Falaise'.[13] Falaise was indeed mentioned as an objective when the planners were lobbying for massed air support. Eisenhower, the Supreme Commander and Montgomery's immediate superior, certainly took this view of the intentions, saying that the drive across the Orne 'towards the south and south-east' would then be exploiting 'in the direction of the Seine basin and Paris'.[14]

Montgomery had written more cautious instructions for Dempsey while inflaming expectations at higher levels of command. He had told Eisenhower that 'my whole eastern flank will burst into flames on Saturday'. He had assured his British chief, Brooke, 'that the time has come to have a real "show down" . . . loosing a corps of armoured divisions into the open country about the Caen–Falaise road'.

The objectives he set down for Dempsey were 'to engage the German armour in battle and "write it down" to such an extent that it is of no further value to the Germans', and 'to gain a good bridgehead over the Orne'. Yet instruction 5 suggested that 'armoured cars should push far to the south towards Falaise, spread alarm and despondency . . .'. Also, once the Canadians had cleared the industrial suburbs of Caen (achieved on 19 July), 'then VIII corps can "crack about" as the situation demands'.[15]

The force chosen to lead the attack was the 11th Armoured Division (AD), with its sign of the charging bull, specially formed for Normandy but already well blooded. It would be followed by the Guards, once simply the elite infantry but now supplying both tank and infantry battalions. Third in line would be the desert-tried, but also apparently desert-tired 7th Armoured, the 'Desert Rats'. Other infantry divisions would work the flanks.

Commanding the 11th would be a young general, 'Pip' Roberts, who since 1939 had worked his way up from the rank of captain. Another general described him as 'a man of superlatives. He was at thirty-seven the youngest divisional commander in the British Army. He was one of the most experienced. . . . He was the smallest and shortest by stature; the most boyish and benign by appearance, but the toughest by performance.'[16]

Roberts himself admitted that 'Falaise was in everyone's mind as a point to be aimed for' and O'Connor discussed 'the best formation . . . once they had broken through into open country', while Dempsey stated it was 'more than possible that the Hun will break'.[17] In any case the initial moves could only be slow. As the vast procession got under way the general speed was to be 10 miles in two hours up to the bridges and then a speed of sixty vehicles per hour passing over each bridge. Such instructions were sensible for the approach march, even assuming accidents and loss of direction in the night conditions. The night move was chosen in the hope of surprising the enemy. It was all 'one way', even ambulances prohibited from returning.

However, it was audacious to assume that the huge force would be able to cross the restricted bridge spaces, find its way through the maze of wrecks in the enclave, thread through the minefield and then dash through unknown territory under enemy guns with military precision and keeping to strict schedule. It was almost as though the planners were saying 'for the plan to work at all it must work this way, and so it will work this way, whether possible or not'. They could have added that 'missions impossible' and 'forlorn hopes' have been accomplished throughout military history.

In a further attempt to cause confusion in the enemy's mind feint attacks were planned around the centre of the Allied line. From 15 July two other British corps attacked towards strategic places like Esquay and Noyers. In addition to actual troop advances various types of deception were introduced to give the impression of even bigger operations there.

Lt Col A.D.E. Curtis of the Royal Engineers was working with No. 1 Light Scout Car Coy of R Force (the deception group) near Fontenay-le-Pesnel.[18] They had the dual task of producing tank noises through loudspeaker vans and also maintaining a busy and realistic radio traffic, three or four wireless sets simulating a large tank force preparing for battle. Two puzzled tank men on night guard imagined ghosts when they heard disembodied tank noises:

'Can you hear that noise?'
'Course I can bloody well hear it. But I can't see it, can I?'
'It's a bit spooky. . . . Bugger me if it isn't the ghosts of knocked out tanks come back to haunt the place at midnight. . . .'

A large van with loudspeakers projecting from it, brakes on the road, backs into our drive and then drives away . . . blaring tank noises into the still hours before dawn.[19]

Another tank man, Terry Boyne, well remembers the rubber tanks inflated and placed not too carefully under trees. 'We were told prior to moving off for the battle that rubber tanks would be placed in our positions [when we had left] to foil the enemy's air reconnaissance.'[20] Curtis felt justified but in some peril when the Luftwaffe attacked his fictitious tank brigade that night. Curiously, and relevant to later arguments about 'good tank country', in the Noyers feint one well-combined tank and infantry attack gained ground in the *bocage* with few casualties and took the largest number of prisoners (310) achieved by one limited attack since D-Day.[21]

On the larger canvas these conjuring tricks were of little avail. The Germans knew that Goodwood was imminent. About the only factor they were not aware of was its code name. German general Sepp Dietrich at this time initiated a Second World War myth when he claimed to have foreseen Goodwood by lying down, pressing an ear to the ground and listening for the rumble of tanks – a trick he had learned in Russia. The actual nub of the trick was the act of covering up the exposed ear so that all immediate sounds would be shut out and the rumbling through the cavernous, limestone Normandy underground could be more clearly discerned.

Every tank crew in the three British divisions had a fair idea of what was to happen. Former corporal Reg Spittles remembers that, even as the junior commander in his troop he was always called to 'O' groups, sometimes with the colonel, more often with the squadron leader major, and always with the troop leader. As the orders were given each tank commander drew the details on a large-scale map covered by a chinograph, showing the regiment's own orders and the known dispositions of the enemy. This map would then be kept on the tank and shown to the crew, as the rate of fatality among tank commanders was one of the highest in the army: at any moment a commander might literally lose his head and another crew member would have to take command. Sometimes tanks could be delivered back to start line with only one crew member surviving. So each of the crew had access to the local plan of action. The Germans sometimes appreciated such detailed plans found on knocked-out tanks.[22]

The lead regiment, 3 RTR, safely negotiating the narrow bridges and, given absolute priority, unimpeded by other troops, arrived in the 'Cone area' at 0230 on 18 July after their overnight journey. There was a brief opportunity for sleep, with réveille at 0430 and an 'O' group with Lt Col D.A.H. Silvertop, MC, at 0500 hours. The tank commanders would learn that they must move to the final forming-up area from 0610 to 0700, ready to advance at 0745.

Next behind them in the bewildering series of contractions and expansions of the traffic block came 2nd Fife and Forfar Yeomanry (2 F&F) under Lt Col A.B.J. Scott, MC. They had had to concentrate at

Gazelle, still on the wrong side of the river. At thirty minutes past midnight they had started to march, and, still relatively unimpeded, crossed canal and river at 0400. At 0545 they reported hundreds of aircraft overhead. 23rd Hussars (Lt Col R.P. Harding, DSO) started moving towards the Orne at 2300 on 17 July, following behind 2 F&F without too much trouble.

Unfortunately one of the bridges was unusable, damaged by a British soldier driving a captured German Panther back to HQ. This left only three Class 40 (prefabricated) bridges, each fed by one tank track (over open country) and one wheel track (an existing road), before and after the bridges.[23] It was hoped that the whole of 11th Armoured would be over the river by H Hour (when 3 RTR would already be in action). Until then there would be no room beyond the bridges for the Guards to start moving over 'York' and 'Euston' bridges. In the meantime Frank Clark and a few thousand other Guards shunted and fretted way down the queues.

Next it was necessary to insert two Canadian infantry brigades across 'Euston' and 'London' bridges with the mission of clearing the immense Colombelles factory zone and the fort-like château beyond it before the right flank of the great tank armada could be secured. Only then could the Desert Rats of the 7th begin to cross, at H Hour + 60 according to plan. This all involved about 6,000 vehicles, with many more shuffling up behind.

At this point the fragile wrapping-paper and loose knots of the overall plan began to unravel under the pressure of slashing tank tracks. VIII Corps reported damage to the northern bridge, resulting from several minor driving errors on 32-ton tanks, causing the northern bridge to be closed for thirty minutes, further causing the added concertina 'pile up' factor so well known to motorists encountering a crash on the motorways.

5th Guards Brigade, commanded by Brig N.W. Gwatkin, MVO, had been driven to the limits of discipline to assemble in time because the final components of the brigade had arrived on the Normandy beaches less than forty-eight hours previously. They departed from their location near the beaches at 2000 on 17 July and then had to halt and queue 5 miles short of the Orne. The Medical Officer (MO) of the Irish Guards noted their progress, or lack of it:

> We set out on the evening of 17 July, eastward across the beachhead to
> our start line 30 miles away in the region of the River Orne. We left
> St Martin des Entrées at about 8 p.m. travelling one vehicle behind
> another, each of us inhaling clouds of dust put up by the vehicles in
> front. . . . During the hours of darkness one had to try and follow the
> light on the back of the vehicle ahead. . . . Here and there, there were
> white tapes to help but without headlights they weren't a lot of use. Thus
> we travelled, stop-go, stop-go, until 4 a.m. We were all by then dog tired.[24]

The problems with radio communications were now being felt as urgently
needed messages, aimed at smoothing out the traffic chaos, failed to
arrive. John Yeburgh, with the 'Micks', was a very young liaison officer on
a motor bike and was sent by 5th brigade to the Irish Guards with a vital
message:

> No wireless would work, as there were three armoured divisions all
> trying to use the same frequencies. . . . I was sent by Brigadier Norman
> just before 0800 hrs to tell 2nd Battalion to move at 0800 hrs! Panic
> all round! – as of course there was no hope of finding the battalion in
> five minutes. I think I got there in about ten minutes. Then the
> difficulty was finding anyone who would believe a very junior officer on
> a motor bike, telling them they must start at once. The adjutant was
> still shaving, Col Kim was having breakfast . . . the air was blue with
> smoke . . . eventually it was the Signal Officer, Stephen Langton, who
> listened and persuaded them that . . . this silly officer on a motor bike
> was telling the truth.[25]

Behind the Guards and even more frustrated were the Desert Rats who
had been used to roaming the wide open spaces of North African deserts.
They were led by 22nd Armoured Brigade under Brig W.R.N. 'Looney'
Hinde, DSO. They were equipped with the somewhat lighter and faster
Cromwell tanks, rather than Shermans, but they had 139 of the British-
made tanks, plus twenty-five Stuarts, seventeen close-support guns and
thirty-six Sherman Firefly tanks to squeeze through the traffic jams, even
before the 'soft' vehicles began to roll.

Troops in the flanking divisions were held up even more than the priority divisions. The tanks of East Riding Yeomanry (ERY), starting at 1800 and crossing the Orne en route, could only make their 6 miles target after a hazardous six hours' shuddering travel. 'It was dark, no lights were permitted, and the dust created by the dry weather and churned up by the mass of tanks ahead made movement slow and difficult . . . two tanks were blown up by mines on the very edge of the track they had to follow.'[26]

Capt Charlie Robertson of 7th Black Watch was astonished when his company was actually ordered to withdraw. In the enclave beyond the Orne the Highlanders had been grimly holding on and responding to sometimes incomprehensible orders to attack through the almost impenetrable slopes of the Bois de Bavent. Now the armoured divisions would advance through the Highland Division's protective minefield. But first there would be a massive air bombardment. The Bomber Command chief, Sir Arthur Harris, insisted on a 6,000 yard safety zone in front of the British infantry forward positions. The events of Operation Cobra a few days later might indicate that this was sensible although Operation Totalize in August would show that 1,000 yards could be sufficient. Be that as it may, before H Hour on 18 July Charlie Robertson had to gather his men and move back to the 6,000 yard marker before the bombers arrived at 0545.

As the first sky-borne rumour of masses of heavy planes broke through the immediate ground noises, people were already getting hurt. ERY had lost two tanks on mines. There were vehicle collisions and minor accidents. Ambulances were prohibited from moving against the one-way traffic. At this point most histories leave the reader wondering what happened to the badly injured soldier in that tiny enclave with few major medical facilities. The DIMS (medical director) of VIII Corps knew that there was neither room for large installations in the enclave nor a route back down over the vehicle bridges. His staff moved quickly to sort a remedy.

The RAMC men noticed on the map that there was an island in the middle of the river and its canal. At the seaward end, Ouistreham, a lock bridge connected the island with the mainland close to the beaches. On the night of 15 July a small footbridge was slung across the river by the engineers, from the enclave bank to the island. Ambulances could 'retreat' as far as that footbridge without impediment. Teams of stretcher bearers waited to carry patients by hand across the primitive sagging bridge. On the island, cars of 16th Light Field Ambulance queued at the footbridge to rush casualties along the one-mile distance to the lock bridge. Enforced though it was, this route may well have been faster than a controlled stop-and-start route back over the main vehicular bridges.[27]

By 0545 the ominous 'noises off' of approaching aircraft was swelling into an overarching audio domination, and as the bombs began to fall, all other sounds seemed to be buried under the earth-rending weight of blast and reverberation hammering at frail human eardrums:

The heavy bombers . . . came lounging across the sky, scattered, leisurely, indifferent. The first ones crossed our lines and the earth began to shake to a continuous rumble of falling bombs. There were no individual explosions, just a continuous rumble . . . and at no time were fewer than fifty 'planes visible. The din was tremendous. We could see the bombs leaving the 'planes and drifting down almost gently, like milt from a salmon. . . . The Jocks were all standing grinning at the sky. After weeks of skulking in trenches, here was action.[28]

There was still some inter-service rivalry, and some air commanders (not to mention land generals) were very precious in their attitudes. VIII Corps had needed to negotiate a timetable and target allocation. At 0545 some 1,100 heavy RAF night bombers, Lancasters and Halifaxes, aimed at Touffreville, Sannerville, Banneville, Emieville, Cagny and Giberville for 45 minutes. By 0700 the skies were clear for 400 medium bombers of 9th USAAF to hit Cuverville/Demouville again for forty-five minutes. At 0830 in came the big 8th USAAF machines, Fortresses and Liberators, going for Bourguebus and Troarn during a thirty-minute period. Bombing of these sites was calculated to destroy the main German defences.[29]

An astonished journalist, watching with 50,000 soldiers, needed all his descriptive skills to report the awesome drama:

I noticed a speck in the sky. It was a Mosquito [fast fighter-bomber]. Directly afterwards it dropped a cascade of coloured lights . . . all fell on the factory, which, with its 14 chimneys has provided the enemy with perfect observation posts. Majestically, in a great cloud, the Lancasters and Halifaxes were approaching. Within a matter of seconds a mass of black smoke enveloped the factory. Into this smoke more and more bombs were dropped. It was like an eclipse of the sun. One Mosquito after another dropped fresh 'markers' of coloured flares.

My eyes were smarting, my face grimy, my nostrils assailed by the acrid smell of high explosive, and my head still buzzes from the noises of the bombs, the A.A., the unceasing hum of the aero engines, the swishing sound of the shells, just like that of a train travelling overhead and, above all, the sharp, ear-splitting crack of the batteries of guns that opened up immediately behind me when the turn of the artillery came.[30]

At 0645, as the waiting troops listened, 'the artillery started with a tremendous crash which merged into a steady roar. The 4.2 mortars were slamming away in a field behind us (they got rid of 2,500 bombs in that one field alone). I remember a flight of pigeons going up as the guns started.'[31]

To the almost unbearable cacophony of the British guns was added the competing tempest of Canadian corps guns to the right. Canadian gunner lieutenant, George Blackburn, described the artilleryman's burden of hard labour which lay behind the easy firework display from the gun muzzles:

Each six-man gun crew, slogging back and forth through the dark with 138 boxes of shells and 69 boxes of propellant charges, carries more than ten tons 300 yards. By now, when weary gunners try to pick up a box of shells it feels as though it is anchored to the ground. Scarcely have those men wrestled and stacked those 18.5 tons of shells and cartridge cases down in their pits before they are hauling them up again and shovelling them into the guns at such furious rates of fire, the barrels glow red in the dark like candles, and buckets of muddy water must be poured down the muzzles to cool them off, producing spectacular geysers of steam and water.[32]

Not all comments were entirely favourable to this apocalyptic doom of carpet bombing and carefully targeted gunnery. The official historian noted that in the heavy bomber plan 'the wood area near Garcelles-Secqueville was not included though it was known to contain a large number of enemy guns' and tanks. In spite of the 6,000 yard safety area 5 RTR squadron leader D.E. Cockbaine humorously says, 'I could not forget the 2 Goodwoods. (1) we were bombed by about 1,000 planes from the RAF and (2) we were bombed by about 1,000 from USAAF.'[33] A little exaggerated perhaps, but quite understandable if one was hit by only one or two bombs from what were supposed to be friendly aircraft. It was not the most nerve-soothing experience to be underneath so many free-falling bombs.

For wireless operator Terry Boyne in 2 F&F it was a rolling memory: 'At the start line at first light. Watched the massed bombing raid, 1,000 plus planes, the sky was thick with planes. When the bombing stopped we rolled forward with an artillery barrage in front at 3 mph.'[34] 3 RTR's Lt Philip Brookshaw saw that 'the sky was black with a combination of Halifaxes and Lancasters who laid a carpet of bombs. It worked extremely well – except when they ran out of carpet – and there were the inevitable 88mm guns and then the real casualties started.'[35]

For many Allied soldiers the exhilaration of watching the massed air fleets in the heavens was soon lost in the sight and stench of deadly reality upon earth:

After the barrage had ceased and the last of the bombers had departed there lay before us a wasteland, five miles of utter devastation; the trees blasted, the buildings shattered, the air foul with the death-stench of cattle and horses. There is a certain intangible nightmarish quality about such scenes . . . the acrid pungency of high explosive . . . for beyond and beside the fated acres the enemy waited behind his guns, and even within the dead land itself he began to emerge blinkingly from his foxholes ready to sell his life dearly to our troops.[36]

Commanding a Tiger tank company under the bombing was the then Capt von Rosen. Years later he described it as like hell and was still astonished that he had ever survived it:

I was unconscious for a while after a bomb had exploded just in front of my tank, almost burying me alive. I could see that another tank, about 30 metres away, had received a direct hit which had set it on fire instantly. A third tank was turned upside down by the blast. And when I tell you that the tanks weighed 58 tons and were tossed aside like playing cards, you will see just what a hell we found ourselves in.

It was impossible to see anything, as so much dust had been stirred up by explosions; it was like being in a very thick fog. It was impossible to hear anything; because of the unceasing crashing of explosions all around us. It was so nerve shattering that we could not even think. All one could say to oneself was 'will there never be an end to this?'

All our tanks were completely covered with earth and those which were operational had to be dug out. Engines were full of sand, air-cooling systems were not functioning, gunsights had been thrown completely out of adjustment. Fifteen men of the company were dead. Two soldiers had committed suicide during the bombardment; and another had to be sent to a mental hospital . . . the psychological shock of these terrible experiences remained with us for a very long time.[37]

Looking from the other side the infantrymen of 8 Rifle Brigade met with shell-shocked Luftwaffe men (serving as infantry in 16 GAF division) 'who were doing their best to give themselves up . . . one carrier of H Coy noticed activity in a nearby wood and fired a few shots into it; seventy-five Germans thereupon came out of the wood, laid down their arms and surrendered.'[38]

Reg Robbins was sergeant of 7 platoon in the Herefordshires. He came from sleepy Hereford where, before the war, if a single plane flew over everybody would go out into the streets to watch it. Now he had a view, 'from the front of the terraces' and was amazed at the size of the bombardment. 'But it made you feel good to see so many of our planes.' The Herefordshires had to clear a fortified village, Demouville, early. Fortunately the enemy were still dazed. 'They looked as though they had drunk too much Schnapps the night before. So due to the bombing we had light casualties.' There was still plenty of action in the surrounding woods but with artillery support they took the first objectives on schedule.[39]

It was fortunate that the bombing was so effective as, in spite of all the attempts at secrecy, on 15 July the German intelligence report warned that:

According to information derived from photograph reconnaissance of the lodgement area the enemy command is planning to start a major operation across the Orne towards the south-east from about 17 July onwards . . . the [British Second Army's] intention is to push forward across the Orne in the direction of Paris.

The bombing had been sensational and terrifying in its impact, but in the miles of reserve defences behind von Rosen's men the bombing had accomplished either insufficient damage or nothing at all (as at Garcelles-Secqueville). Forewarned by their intelligence the enemy had now been fully alerted. Less well served by their intelligence, the British troops, unaware of the depth of German defences, now had to cross the hazard of the extensive Highland Division minefield before fanning out to the attack. Canadian troops in the meantime were preparing to attack the Colombelles complex and also had to find ways of crossing the destroyed or badly damaged normal road and rail bridges south of Caen.

Still greatly enthused the men of 3 RTR crossed their start line at 0745, advancing due south behind a barrage of 25pdr shells. But the war diary notes almost immediately 'owing to speed of barrage and nature of country tanks begin falling behind line of barrage'. What the RTR men did not blame, but which was of great significance was the funnelling of the approach lanes down into narrow cleared gaps through the minefield. This had been laid at a time when no such massed advance was anticipated. There were no charts. The time for clearing the minefield was insufficient. The situation was exacerbated by the growth of corn to the height of a man so that even loose mines lying on the ground could not be seen.

Maj Gen Roberts commanding the 11th later confessed that he had not anticipated mines and had not intended to ask for flail tanks which beat the ground with chains to set off mines. However he was visited by the commander of 79th AD, Maj Gen Hobart, who was senior in age and had

once been Roberts's commander. Hobart recommended using the flails of
the 79th, saying, 'Dear boy, if you are the leading division and got held up it
would be a disaster.'[40] Hobart was right. Already by 0830 2 NY had lost
four tanks on British mines at map reference 104713, near the start line.

John Wallace Bell, an officer with the flail regiment, Lothian and Border
Horse, was one of those sent forward to flail the cornfields. He found
crops up to 7 ft high. In the hot midsummer sun the huge chains of the
flails reaped and threshed the corn, sending up huge clouds whose
spectacular golden glow belied their fatal density. John Bell's troop tanks
were soon out of sight of each other at a few yards' range. Their usual
exact formation of two flails up and three spaced behind, to provide an
entirely cleared channel of ground, broke up. Working gingerly forward
and relying on radio communication they noticed the infantry firing at
something ahead. The flails traversed and tried to fire in that general
direction. But their guns and gunsights were covered with 'hay and
straw'. Reaching the far edge of the minefield they turned and flailed back
the way they had come, at least leaving ruts for others to follow. They had
blown forty-one mines in 100 yards.

When Bell arrived back at his starting point his tank was loaded down
with a 4-ft-thick mass of straw and corn. What then annoyed the flail
men, having dangerously flailed a corridor which was marked with white
tape, was to see careless infantrymen stepping over the tapes and being
blown up on Schu mines. It proved the lack of infantry training in
walking through minefields.[41]

The Shermans of 2 F&F followed 3 RTR through the minefield. They
recorded that they were hampered in their scheduled progress by being
forced into four tank-wide lanes by the minefield bottleneck. Each regiment
found its way through, four abreast, in three waves. 2 F&F's A Squadron
(19) tanks took the right two lanes and their B the left lanes. Then followed
Regimental Headquarters (RHQ) and recce troops on the right and part of 8
RB's F Coy left. Finally the ill-fated C Sqdn took the right lanes and the rest
of 8 RD F with a battery of mobile artillery left. As they made their exit
slowly but safely from the minefield they opened out to a 700 yard frontage.

It has sometimes been said that there was no infantry up with these
spearheads. In fact the motor companies of the Rifle Brigade (RB) went

through with the lead tanks. 8 RB G Coy went with 3 RTR, F Coy with 2 F&F and H Coy with 23 Hussars. In spite of all the difficulties 23 Hussars followed through into the open with little delay on schedule. But again the concertina effect was taking its toll, and without undue enemy interference, small delays at the head of the advance would magnify into crucial delays at the tail.

In the words of one divisional history, 'The debouchment from the bridgehead may be likened to the nozzle of a shower-bath fed by a pipe so small that the volume of water which can flow through it is sufficient to serve only two or three of the apertures [of the nozzle] . . . to achieve saturation the shower-bath has to work properly, and it didn't.'[42] Put in more technical terms, 'The axis of advance was much too narrow for effective fire and manoeuvre by three armoured divisions within space [normally] allocated to a single armoured *brigade.*'[43] And it was the gaps in the minefield which most restricted and compressed the jet of advance, leaving the nozzle spluttering too slowly.

As yet these reservations and premonitions did not affect the forward Goodwood troops. 0800 hours saw them bypassing the critical village of Le Mesnil-Frementel, which was reported clear. In spite of some difficulty in crossing a railway line, due to the unexpected depth of the cutting, Major Bill Close's lead tanks of 3 RTR had bypassed Grentheville at 0830, having already achieved an advance of some miles, which was astonishing by Normandy standards. The barrage had paused at 0800 so that 2 F&F could come up level with 3 RTR at the railway. They found much enemy equipment abandoned and enemy soldiers surrendering quickly. 2 NY with the Herefords and Monmouths had been sweeping through Cuverille and heading for Demouville.

On the extreme left the Highland Division moved forward through the thick woodland and encountered many frightened prisoners. Some were afraid of being shot by their enemies until one battalion padre intervened, shouting in his best German, '*Ich bin Pastor, Kamerad!*' The Canadians were slogging away, with an impossible schedule, in fortress Colombelles. Around the equally problematic château with its walled orchards, the CO asked for tanks. When he was refused he walked out into the passing masses of tanks and negotiated the aid of two willing tank commanders as the Canadians fought foot by foot through the orchards.[44]

It was only farther back that doubts began to arise. 5th Guards Brigade was beginning to move tanks up, and these met dazed enemy crews out of their tanks and quite willing to surrender. But the main groups of Guards vehicles still struggled through the various obstacles from the bridges onwards. At 0900, 22 AB reported 'advance very slow owing to congestion'. 7th Armoured reported only half 1 RTR over the bridge and movement very slow. Yet probably for most rank-and-file soldiers the greatest worry was the mosquitoes.

Nobody seems to have anticipated the counter-attacks by these insect nuisances which bred so prolifically amid the *marais* along *La Grande Ruisseau* stream past Demouville and on to the Orne. The ERY found that 'there were a lot of flies and mosquitoes around which didn't help comfort at all'. Heading for Troarn across country, 'this created its own dust clouds and made people even more uncomfortable and dirty, with their faces and arms and other exposed parts of the body already swollen by constant "dive-bombing" from mosquitoes.'[45]

Surprisingly the veteran Seaforth Highlanders found that the local mosquito 'was far bigger and more inquisitive than any we had encountered in Africa, and its powers of penetration were phenomenal. Battledress was no bar: if a mosquito decided it would dine off your knees, then dine it would; and as it dined its friends would be wriggling happily inside your gaiters to nibble your ankles, while others clamped down in hordes upon your wrist and face. . . . On average each of us had twenty [stings] on the back of a single hand. . . . They caused us more discomfort and loss of sleep than ever shelling did.'[46]

Yeomanry Tpr Ralph Hill also remembers that 'mosquitoes were our main misery, rising at dusk in vast clouds'. He continues:

Applications of anti-gas ointment proved to be useless and hiding in the tank with hatches closed provided no escape. My commander, Ossie Porter, was so badly bitten about the eyes that he could hardly see at all. I took a dixy of boiled potatoes to some infantry lads dug in nearby and far worse bitten than ourselves. One of the soldiers had said to the company commander, 'The mosquitoes were certainly busy last night, sir.' To which the captain had replied jokingly, 'Oh, really? I didn't know they were operating last night' (meaning Mosquito planes!). I didn't think it at all funny at the time.[47]

Those who were bitten, and those who made jokes about the 'mozzies', might have been much more worried if they had been aware that in 1944 malaria was still endemic in the *marais* areas of the Orne lowlands. Cases of malaria would occur in due course, some with a longer recurrence cycle over the years than most wounds.[48]

CHAPTER FIVE

THE BULL MEETS THE MATADORS

When all the talking and planning had ended it was people like Bill Close who really mattered. A major commanding a squadron of 3 RTR Shermans, he was to be the very sharp tip of the spearhead as the great mass of tanks filtered through the minefield and spread out to head for Bourguebus Ridge.

On his upper sleeve Maj Close wore the badge of a black charging bull on a yellow background, the emblem of the 11th AD. Everyone in the division from Maj Gen 'Pip' Roberts down thought it was the finest armoured division anywhere, and now, in ideal tank country at last, they were going to prove it. No real qualms so far, towards midday on 18 July, for Bill Close. He had seen the devastating bombing and felt its hot wind. He had driven safely through the minefield. Now, apart from a railway or two (or three) to cross, there were no great obstacles ahead. The artillery barrage ploughed ahead of him like some monstrous invisible combine harvester slashing through the corn and sods. True, he was not entirely happy with his orders just to 'bash on' without pausing for the normal bound by bound tactics. But that was what charging bulls do: bash on![1]

His tank commanders and tank crews were equally proud and confident. Sgt Jim Caswell felt the importance of their mission:

Our objective was about 7 kilometres ahead and once we had captured it, the other regiments of our Division, following the corridor we marked out for them, had to make a dash across the plain in the direction of Falaise. The aerial bombardment and the artillery barrage had completely demoralized the enemy and our advance was easy. Hundreds of German soldiers surrendered and many tanks and guns were destroyed. However, the most serious obstacle was the Caen–Troarn railway line and crossing a very deep ditch at this place proved to be difficult for our tanks.[2]

The artillery barrage continued to roll according to VIII Corps instructions '300 yards deep at 300 yards in 2 minutes [5 mph] with two stop lines' at which the OC of 3 RTR could, if necessary, call 'Stop!' in order to let the tanks catch up. The tumult of the ground artillery was made even more impressive by the regular passage overhead – frequently likened to express trains in the sky – of shells from naval guns out at sea. These included the veteran monitor, HMS *Roberts*, whose guns had not fired in anger since the First World War, but those guns were now firing 15in shells, sounding more like heavy freight trains in the sky.

Some tanks of the second regiment, 2 F&F, had now caught up with the leaders. The extensive farm buildings of Le Mesnil-Frementel loomed in front of them like a ready-made tank obstacle. 3 RTR were ordered to pass on one side and 2 F&F on the other, leaving the farm to be dealt with later. And bash on!

Already the tanks had bypassed two strategic villages, Cuverville and Demouville. Roberts had been ordered to leave his 159 Inf Bd to deal with those villages, but he was not happy with those orders. The divisional armoured reconnaissance regiment, 2 NY, with 3 Monmouthshire infantry, had moved on Cuverville at 0830 and quickly cleared it of enemy soldiers who had been bombed into a total mental and physical paralysis. 2 NY moved on to Demouville with the Herefords at about 1100 and the units engaged reported little real opposition. Two self-propelled enemy tanks had survived the blitz and opened fire but were quickly destroyed by the Cromwells of 2 NY. By 1400 the tank regiment was able to be released to support the attacks further forward.[3]

On the vital right flank of the attack the Germans were comfortably installed in the industrial suburbs of Caen and would be able to rake the flanks of the massed attack with their anti-tank guns. The Canadians had been charged with clearing these suburbs, but the orders given to them seemed to assume that, after the air bombardment, the infantry would be able to walk through the Colombelles factory as though on a Victory Parade. Some planners had apparently been looking at maps and not at the skyline. The chimneys!

One tank gunner recalled how, a few days earlier, his regiment of sixty tanks had fired fifty rounds each at the chimneys from 2,000 yard range 'but inflicting only tiny, distant sparks of wrath on the immovable gargantuan chimneys . . . the massive chimneys remain erect, for all our pounding. The 75mm shells bounce off those reinforced layers of brickwork.'[4] The Canadians had to fight their way from the start line for three hours to get into the Colombelles complex and then 'like beaters at a shoot had to work methodically through the wrecked buildings and large bomb craters where the enemy held out well into the night'. The ferocity of the defence is illustrated by the log of final messages from a defending battalion of 21st Panzers:

8.00 (p.m.)   Shall I withdraw?

8.09   Enemy already broken through in encircling movement.

8.19   Enemy has cut off this battalion.

8.20   Battalion HQ surrounded. Long live the Führer.[5]

As the sun moved past its zenith and the day grew hotter, tank crews sweated, endured thirst, suffered cramp but rejoiced in a fast advance beyond anything that had been known by British troops in Normandy. There was a kind of indolence, a kind of arrogance about the battle. Capt Lemon of 3 RTR had 'a wonderful feeling of superiority as many Germans, shaken by the preliminary bombing and shelling continued to give themselves up'.[6]

The men from Fife and Forfar and all points south (regiments were now reinforced beyond regional recognition) bullied along, past the dimly discerned village of Cagny, which was being left for the Guards to assault. A and B Squadrons of 2 F&F, up exploring a route somewhat left of 3 RTR, rolled happily onwards. RHQ followed, anxiously awaiting some word of negative import. C Squadron, commanded by Maj C. Nicholls, at the rear, were not prey to any apprehension except perhaps that an odd

German infantryman might have awoken from his bomb-delivered knock-out and decide to be a hero. Bashing on. And then!

A bright red spear seemed to impact on Major Nicholls' turret.

A gusher of flame rushed up from the turret and human forms leaped for safety. No time even to guess what had happened when the tank of Capt J.E.F. Miller, second in command, seemed to shudder and burst into flame. Gordon Fidler, driving a 2 F&F tank, commented on the velocity of 88mm shots, for such they were: 'You could literally hear the 88mm fire and it would be there in your lap.'[7]

Another Yeoman, Geoff Hayward, could not believe what he was seeing:

I could actually see the German guns firing. I could see the muzzle flashes in the woods. And I could see one by one these Shermans of ours going up in smoke and it was really a terrible sight because at the end of it when you looked round there wasn't a single tank moving. They'd all been evacuated, blown up . . . some tanks were rescued later in the darkness of the night.[8]

L/Cpl Ron Cox watched the first two tanks blow up. 'Other tanks I could see were stationary and some were beginning to brew. Dust and smoke were combining with heat-haze to make visibility more and more difficult. I watched through the periscope fascinated as though it was a film I was seeing.' It was no film, for an almighty crash almost deafened him, the tank shuddered, and the commander shouted, 'Bale Out!' Even as they vaulted out and away and ran into the corn the tank was hit again and began to spew smoke and flame.[9]

The indolent afternoon had been transmuted into a horrifying fiery carnage with not the slightest warning. As eyes watched, minds like automatic calculators tallied only two men emerging from that tank, only three from that, five from that, but one tumbling figure like a bundle of firewood ablaze. Spectacular firework displays of exploding ammunition seemed to be a devilish mockery, celebrating the slaughter. Not so much spilled blood was seen, for blood which spurted could fry instantly amid spatters of human fat along the red-hot walls of furnace Shermans. Not so much screaming was audible, as some bodies afflicted by 100 per cent third degree burns had their screams cut off by the swift scalpels of steel splinters. Solid shot bludgeoned other brains into merciful unknowing.

Wounds were painful, but often shock countered the immediate pain. There was no relief from the psychological trauma. Gordon Fidler wanted to sympathize with his petrified colleagues, to comfort them somehow. But 'seeing these people coming back, you could not talk to them. They didn't want to talk to you about it. They were in a state of "I don't know where I am". It was really frightening. Their tanks were burnt out, flaming, all over the place. Nobody could have trained us for this.'[10]

Shocked survivors were at a loss to explain this sudden disaster, way back from the spearhead in the regiment's formation. It was a classic surprise action. But the survivors would have been even more surprised if they had known that the enemy's evil genius out there across the fields was fighting dressed in the full trimmings and regalia (including red trouser stripes) of a German staff officer. Or that the guns which hit them so accurately had been aimed to shoot down Allied planes.

Colonel Hans von Luck was surely one of the most experienced soldiers of the Second World War. He remembered that on 1 September 1939, during exercises on the Polish border, he had been ordered to unload his guns of the blank ammunition which they contained and reload with live. The regiment was about to fire some of the first shots of the war. Although a fierce enemy, von Luck was a strictly correct soldier who would eventually gain the admiration of his enemies. On the night of 17 July his rectitude had wavered a little. He had taken advantage of an apparent delay in the start of Goodwood to dress up, drive to Paris and spend an evening and most of a night savouring the heady pleasures and luxuries of that famous city.

Guardsman Frank Clark, by then a major, well remembers von Luck lecturing in Britain and telling against himself the story of how, 'a little under the influence,' he arrived back in the firing line to see hordes of British tanks streaming across his front. For a moment it seemed a dream induced by indulgence in Paris. It was real enough and von Luck's command was not ready for the sight. The only warlike Germans he could see were the crews of four 88mm anti-aircraft guns, aiming at the sky, with one eye on the look-out for Allied bombers and the other eye watching the British tanks.[11]

Von Luck approached the lieutenant commanding the battery and commanded him to lower the guns and use them in an anti-tank role, in which they were equally efficient. The lieutenant, whose authority derived from the Luftwaffe, not the Wehrmacht, refused.

Von Luck was being frustrated by one of the inherent weaknesses which dogged German forces throughout the war, the plethora of 'private armies'.

In Normandy, Gen Sepp Dietrich commanded the Panzer Army but Luftwaffe Gen Pickert commanded the anti-aircraft units, enjoying a good deal of independence. Dietrich complained, 'I constantly ordered these guns to stay forward and act in an anti-tank role against Allied armour.' Pickert would allow the guns to be moved to Dietrich's orders and then would immediately move them back again and point them at the sky.[12]

The very senior and influential Field Marshal von Rundstedt also complained about the machinations of the divided commands. Goering with the Luftwaffe, Himmler with the SS, Doenitz with the Navy, and other lower commanders in the hierarchies insisted on the right to reject Army orders. 'While the army formations were constantly told that equipment and reserves were scarce,' observed von Rundstedt, 'the SS units received the latest weapons and best clothing, the Luftwaffe field and parachute divisions were supplied with constant reinforcements, and the Navy was stocked with better rations. This created resentment and suspicion among the men who had suffered the brunt of the fighting in France and Russia.'[13]

So on 18 July SS Dietrich's von Luck confronted Luftwaffe Pickert's anonymous lieutenant. With the decision and resolve which had brought him through many battles, von Luck pulled out his revolver and tersely offered the lieutenant the choice between being a live hero or a dead lieutenant. The lieutenant angrily told his guns to lower their sights and it was the rear squadron of 2 F&F which caught the full blast of the lieutenant's ire. It has been said in jest that the SS Colonel's presence at that moment was 'a stroke of Luck' for the Germans. In fact, it was not just luck. The battle was swayed by the appointed presence at strategic points of experienced skilled soldiers like Hans von Luck, and also, along the first stage of the Goodwood trap, others such as von Rosen and Becker.[14]

Although an outstanding soldier himself, von Rosen was quick to pass the credit right down the line:

A word about the crews. They were all men who had had considerable experience of tank fighting in the East. Everyone in a Tiger battalion was specially trained and understood every aspect of their jobs. Everyone had already served in a normal tank battalion. Looking back, the type of man we had at our disposal was certainly better than in normal units.[15]

Becker was another extraordinary German soldier. In civilian life he had already been a successful industrialist and engineer. As a reserve officer he became interested in adapting captured armoured vehicles as the German armies conquered other countries. He saw that it was possible to mount anti-tank guns in various types of chassis. His first 'self-propelled guns' were used in 1940 before Dunkirk. Hitler was impressed and arranged for him to mount an exhibition of his ideas. The 21st Panzers utilized Becker as an engineer to adapt outmoded tanks from French factories.

With the rank of major he was now offered the chance to demonstrate his ideas in the firing line in Normandy. He developed batteries of six guns of 75mm bore (the German 75 was much more powerful than the Sherman 75) plus four guns of 105mm. These vehicles were rather clumsy in the open, but carefully located and camouflaged they provided an overwhelming concentration of fire when commanded as a single firing machine. Becker himself was commanding five batteries along the left flank of the British march. He had also cleverly worked out a system whereby the battery commander gave orders on a very low frequency radio signal, relayed from tank to tank. This meant that the British monitoring of German radio signals was not able to locate the Becker batteries, which could therefore fire on the British tanks with their weaker guns with a certain impunity.[16]

At this point Roberts intervened. Not always sympathetic to the problems of his subordinates, he could sympathize with the colonel of the F&F, saying:

I would like you to visualize what you would do if you were CO of Fife and Forfar in these circumstances. Your leading squadron is ahead, you are just behind it with the Motor Company. Your rear Squadron is behind you. You hear nothing on the wireless. You look back. You see all your rear Squadron in a sheet of flame. What do you do? Do you say, 'Oh to hell with that, I'll get on', or do you get involved in another battle to destroy your attackers? . . . I happened to hear the CO telling his Brigadier that he was going to attack Cagny. I countermanded that order as I thought adequate forces were on the way, so Fife and Forfar should get on.[17]

The battered 2 F&F complained to their war diary, 'It had been stated that Cagny would be "hamburged". But it did not happen – bombing insufficient.' (Hamburg had been devastated by a fire storm during an RAF raid – hence 'hamburged'.)

While 3 RTR had enjoyed a fairly easy ride there had been some delay in crossing one of the first two railways encountered, which ran straight across the front of the advance. The artillery barrage had rolled on ahead and the careful coordination of the advance began to unravel. Signs of resistance became more ominous. At 1000 anti-tank guns were reported firing from Hubert-Folie. Bill Close, on the regiment's right, saw tanks brewing in the neighbouring squadron. Then, near the village of Grentheville, three of his own tanks were hit. Becker's No. 3 battery was well ensconced in the hedges and trees around the village. Close also saw enemy gunners running to man static anti-tank guns.

By this time the advance had reached the vital third railway 'emanating from Colombelles that turned south, crossing over the other two lines to climb into the hazy high ground. This line divided Bourguebus from Hubert-Folie and disappeared into the upper distance. . . . This was the most embankmented line of them all . . . [giving] cover to troops on either side of it. . . . As we were to find, however, the enemy had both sides raked with fire most of the time.'[18]

Well aware of the danger, Bill Close ordered his tanks to use the cover of the embankment and put down HE fire on the village. Meanwhile he sought artillery support:

I had an OP [artillery observation officer] right from the start who was in a sawn-off Honey and I had given him instructions to stick close to me. He was a splendid chap. So I tucked myself just behind a little ridge and called him over and I said 'For Christ sake put something down on this village quickly'. All the time I was being told by my CO to get over the other side of the embankment. I was extremely reluctant to turn the back of my tank to this strongly held village, so I said 'Wait out until I get a stonk down on this village!'

The CO was undoubtedly being pressed to speed things up by the 'bash on' commanders farther back who seem not to have known of the tactical problems associated with the highly embanked third railway, although this was clearly shown on the French maps of the time. Close would have been a fool at that point to try to take his tanks over the accessible part of the embankment. His tanks had also spotted a number of Nebelwerfer crews in the cornfields, firing over the tanks at the infantry behind. The tanks responded by running over some of the mortars and blasting the others with machine-gun fire.

Following the artillery stonk, Close needed to move his troops over the embankment:

I took off my beret, waved it round my head and said 'Conform to me' over the air. There was a gap in the embankment and as I approached my feelings were extremely mixed. I was not quite sure what to expect. I shot through the hole like a rat up a drainpipe. I emerged on the other side to see this beautiful countryside looking perfectly peaceful. There was no sign of movement whatsoever. We tucked ourselves in along a line of hedgerows just short of the Cormelles factory area . . . and I had a jolly good look through my glasses at Bras, Hubert-Folie and Ifs.[19]

Then followed one of those extraordinary ploys at which the Germans were masters. Lt Col Silvertop decided that it was necessary to have a closer look at the apparently peaceful village of Hubert-Folie. He decided to send Lt D.M. Stileman of the supporting motor infantry (8 RB) to look. Stileman was to take a couple of the speedy carriers and drive through the village. If he survived, the village was unoccupied. If he did not return, hard luck! Stileman set off to 'belt hell for leather down the main thoroughfare' of the tiny village. A cluster of shells was dropped on the village, followed by a smoke shell. Aided by this Stileman's little group raced through the village, out the other side, circled and then, with some sighs of relief, headed back to the waiting tanks. Obviously the village was unoccupied. But, in Stileman's own words, 'How wrong can one be? As we discovered later, the village was groaning with enemy.' They were simply 'lying doggo'.[20]

This heartening prospect, the peaceful countryside and an empty village, now enticed Bill Close forward, as much as the incessant orders chivvied him on. There still remained an uncomfortable feeling that a classic bound-by-bound advance with infantry would be more sensible. But 'bash on' was the gospel of the day. There were other reasons for uncertainty. 3 RTR was now going to roll out beyond the edge of the bombing carpet and beyond the reach of the majority of supporting artillery guns.

The earliest divisional history records that 'owing to the congestion in the original bridgehead most of the guns had to be sited west of the Orne. This fact both limited the distance over which we could be supported and entailed considerable delay before the guns could occupy more advanced positions east of the river. However, the greater part of the artillery was able to support the attack as far as the [second] railway line . . . since this was 5 miles forward of our start line it was felt that by the time we reached it we ought to be through the worst of the enemy positions.'[21]

Beyond the bombing carpet, beyond the reach of the big British guns, the enemy came out of the cellars of the evacuated houses in Bourguebus, Bras and Ifs and sighted their well-camouflaged guns. The leading 3 RTR Shermans moved forward so near to the objective. As they moved across the open ground, anti-tank fire poured, as at a single signal, from the villages and connecting woods. Four or five tanks went up in flames. And then it was Bill Close's turn:

I felt a hell of a crack on my own tank and a stentorian voice yelled out, 'Bale out, sir!' I hopped out and saw the crew out. The left rear [track] sprocket of my tank had been shot off completely. I waved my crew back down towards the embankment. Two other squadron HQ tanks were nearby. One had been knocked out. I jumped into the other and resumed command of the squadron.

There was considerable fire coming from Hubert-Folie [the 'empty' village]. We at the time were broadside on to the village and it was extremely dangerous. Every time we tried to move forward we lost more tanks. The squadron on my left had moved two troops forward from their hedgerow, but all those eight tanks were brewed up in a matter of seconds. As soon as you exposed yourself above the line of the embankment you received casualties from Bourguebus.

Fortunately the infantry carriers were doing absolutely sterling work, going up to the burning tanks, helping any survivors of the tank crews out of the flames, putting them in their carriers and rushing them back to the regimental aid post down along the embankment. So in an hour or two this beautiful, peaceful scene had been transformed into a hellish battlefield.[22]

Close and his comrades had been the victims of a gross failure by the British commanders to estimate correctly the extent and strength of the German defences. To anyone standing in the plain south of Caen it should have been inconceivable that the enemy would not fortify strongly the most visible and strategic feature in the area, the Bourguebus–Verrières ridge. And, if they did, then the charge of the outgunned Shermans would be another charge of the Light Brigade. Perhaps the most amazing outcome of the day is that any British tanks sent out as targets for the more powerful German guns survived to fight again.

The Noyers feint had been briefly successful, for there the '1st SS, 10th SS and 2nd Panzer Divisions had been kept in the battle, and 9th SS Panzer Division from corps reserve had been called in to help with counter-attacks. The fighting had served . . . to disguise the intention to attack on the east of the river.'[23] Unfortunately this 'turned out to be one of the few relatively lean periods for ULTRA in the west' and the system for breaking German codes was not able to advise of the rapid German response to Goodwood.[24]

By 14 July most of the villages to be fought over in Goodwood had been evacuated and turned into strongpoints.[25] Gen Eberbach had set up four defence lines to a depth of some 10 miles, with a fifth line possible in reserve. By 0930 on 18 July orders had gone to 21st Panzer, with 503 Tiger battalion under command, to counter-attack from the south-east, and 1st SS Panzer received orders shortly afterwards to attack from the south. These units, and others later, were able to use the wooded and undulating terrain alongside the attackers' 'open plain' to move into position virtually unobserved in spite of Allied command of the air. Most of the weapons of these defenders were much more powerful than the guns of the attacking divisions. Even German crews who fought in the smaller, less well armoured MK IVs felt confident that their skills and experience, often of nearly five years' fighting, would offset the Allies' superiority in numbers.[26]

The disparity between the Tigers and Panthers on the one hand and the Shermans and Cromwells on the other, that huge fatal burden which Allied tank crews had to bear, is well known but needs reciting again. In sheer weight of massive armoured steel, the Panther tipped the scales at 50 tons, the Tiger at 54 tons, the Royal Tiger at 68 tons, compared to the Sherman at 32 tons. The muzzle velocities which drove solid shot at and through opponents' armour gave the Tigers an advantage at 3,186 ft per second, and the Panthers at 3,070 ft per second against the Sherman's 1,950. The Tiger MK II had 150mm of front armour compared to the Sherman's 75mm. Any of the named German vehicles could knock out a Sherman at 2,000 yards but a Sherman might see its rounds bounce off a Tiger at as close as 200 yards.[27]

It is no joke, following these statistics, that the Sherman was regarded as the main Allied 'heavy' tank, while the Cromwell, used by several regiments in Goodwood was an even lighter 'medium' tank. These tanks had perhaps two advantages. The Sherman turret traverse system was much faster and more reliable than the enemy versions. And just before D-Day the efficient 17pdr gun had been mounted on some Shermans to produce the 'Firefly' variant. The Firefly could knock out Tigers and Panthers in equal battle but was still very vulnerable when moving around open country in its comparatively thin skin. And the

Germans quickly learned to knock out the Firefly first before the 75mm Shermans.

The German formations used in counter-attack during Goodwood were mainly SS, whose units were relatively more powerful than corresponding 'ordinary' Wehrmacht units. A comparison of certain establishment strengths, with SS first and Army Type 44 Panzer Divisions second, reveals: in total personnel 17,809 (SS) against 14,727 (army); in number of rifles 12,285 against 9,094; in heavy machine-guns 102 against 72; and in towed field guns 35 against 23. The theoretical strength in tanks was equal across the various divisions, but the SS received priority in replacements whereas Army Type 44 Panzers might be unable to obtain replacements.[28]

As the units of 11th AD spread out across the open plain, more and more found it to be a veritable 'Valley of the Shadow of Death', and knew reasons to fear evil. 2 NY was ordered to try and contact 3 RTR in the midst of the havoc. The regiment was equipped with the lighter Cromwells and did not receive one of the upgraded 'Challengers' with the heavier 17pdr gun, added road wheels and heavier hull (equivalent to the Sherman's Firefly variant) until 4 August.[29] Where the heavier Shermans with Firefly support were being annihilated, Cromwells were hardly the tanks to scare the SS away.

2 NY had suffered their first casualty before the battle began. In the dark night there had been confusion when assembling for the march to the Orne bridges: when James Packard jumped out of the slit trench in which he had been sleeping, a heavy truck ran over the slit trench and James, causing serious injuries. However 2 NY's advance through Cuverville and Demouville had been much less dangerous, and the crews were optimistic as they began to advance farther into more open country. They too came under the malevolent wizard's spell of the third railway embankment.

A present-day general has highlighted the importance of the iron ore railway. Noting that the first two railways on the Goodwood route were only minor barriers, he comments:

Much more significant, and usually not even shown on maps in most books, was the [third] railway line . . . for two reasons – one, it ran

along a high embankment (which still exists) . . . and was therefore a
serious obstacle requiring even tanks to use its underpasses; and two,
because it was, and still is, impossible to see to the west of it from the
villages of Le Mesnil-Frementel and Grentheville. In effect it divided the
battlefield into two quite separate parts.[30]

2 NY were now under orders to move up and try to contact 3 RTR. When
they came near to the cited map reference they found only burning tanks
or evacuated tanks smashed beyond repair. They themselves, happening
on one of the underpasses, were about to pass through what one crew
member termed 'those railway arches – portals to a cauldron of
destruction'.[31] It was here that the events recorded earlier as 'The Sadness
of Sergeant Sid' took place.

Sid Jones had been sickened and saddened to come across the body of
the popular Jock Niblock. Bill Moseley remembers the actual occurrence.
Bill and Niblock had been on those vulgar slanging terms with which
inarticulate young soldiers would disguise their extraordinary affection
for each other, born of shared dangers. For them such affection, in the
days when 'gay' meant just merry, was un-British, if non-sexual. It
was an emotion difficult to explain or exchange. So, in typical Tommy
Atkins style, Jock Niblock would address Bill as, 'Ye wee Sassenach
bastard, ye!', to which Bill would call back, 'You bloody heathen haggis-
basher', all of which meant among tank crews, 'I'll die for you if
necessary'. Jock did.

While Sid Jones was carrying out his first rescue forays into the
burning B squadron, Niblock's battered tank had managed to pull back
into partial shelter of the embankment, and anticipating an immediate
flash fire and explosion, the crew aborted. As they scrabbled for shelter in
the undergrowth Jock Niblock realized that one man was missing. He ran
back through the wild mêlée of armour-piercing ricochets and overs,
climbed on the tank and saw his mate, wounded or dead, still in the
turret. Standing exposed 9 feet above ground level, he was about to
attempt to discover if his comrade was still alive. One of the 88mm
armour-piercing rounds, which were coming from all directions, simply
smashed his head from his body. No medal was awarded.[32]

As Mosely and his crew retreated they had an encounter which typified
the strange empathy which existed between most fighting troops, friends
and foes alike:

A little later we fell in with a couple of dazed and 'bomb-happy' Jerries
with their hands on their heads who shouted 'Kamerad! Kamerad!'
Someone said, 'I'll give 'em effing Kamerad, the bastards were trying to
kill us not so long ago'. Someone else said, 'Well, so were we, it's the
same difference'.

Then, to the Jerries, 'It's allright for you, Fritz, your krieg is bloody
kaputt! Fini! Ja?' To which they replied 'Ja, allus kaputt. Uns
kriegsgefangen [prisoners of war] in England, ja?'

We felt sorry for them. They look as 'knackered' as we felt. We gave
them some cigarettes and a light and said, 'Nein hende hoch, you komme
mit uns, right?'

One said, 'Jawohl! Krieg nein gute vor allus soldarten, nein?'

'Ja, you can bloody say that again, Fritz!'

Sid Jones and so many others had agonized to the point of involuntary
vomiting, over the state of badly burned crew, as yet an unfamiliar sight.
During the period from D-Day to 1 July, out of 20,492 cases admitted to
British medical units, only 331 were burns cases, some accidental. The
afternoon of Goodwood saw the first major plague of tank-brewing burns
in the armoured divisions.[33] Treatment was still rather primitive. The 23rd
Hussars' regimental MO had, from knocked-out enemy vehicles, 'collected
a lot of German burn dressings – impregnated gauze packed in small
round tins – and these were found most effective' and better than
anything the MO had in his own issue kit.

There was a strict order that major burn cases should not be undressed
while the victim was in primary shock, which could last for a considerable
number of hours.[34] This conformed to best practice but ignored reality. As
happened in the Jim Flowers incident, when a man baled out with
clothing and skin ablaze the immediate action had to be simply to roll him
in the dust, unless a pond or rainwater was available, ripping off the
gasoline-soaked clothing, and with it sometimes the blackened flesh, in

order to quench the actual flames. In some cases a harassed survivor might turn a fire extinguisher on the human body. The sheer intensity of flame and the immediate burn wounding was such that no leisurely training with uninjured models in a British Nissen hut before D-Day could in any way simulate reality.

While the tanks probed well ahead, behind them the few but stout buildings of Le Mesnil-Frementel proved to be a nest of enemy resistance. All the motor companies of 8 RB had been allocated among the tank groups, but the 8 RB CO, Lt Col J.A. Hunter, MBE, MC, was ordered to do something about the nuisance farm. He assembled a hasty task force of odd units which had adhered to RHQ, including a squadron of flail tanks which had completed their mine-clearing task. Supported by the 75mm cannon and Browning m-gs of the flails, the HQ infantry dashed into the farm buildings. Fortunately its garrison was too dazed to respond to the challenge of hand-to-hand fighting and quickly surrendered. The colonel and his men counted up 134 prisoners, most of them the normally aggressive Panzer-Grenadiers.

On the extreme right of Goodwood, the Canadians were having no such easy fortune. (Even further right, in the ruins of Caen railway station, more Canadians were advancing, but in the simultaneous 'Operation Atlantic'.) More than one British regimental diary stated, unfairly, that the Canadians were advancing too slowly. The British units had not been asked to conquer the Colombelles rolling mills and furnaces or take the fortified château beyond. Again the impractical demands of the master plan tended to reflect adversely on the troops who were obliged to try to keep pace with it. These targets were allocated to the Canadian Régiment de la Chaudière, which lost 50 per cent of B Coy rifles and 25 per cent of each of A and D in the battle.

The Queen's Own Rifles of Canada, with tanks of 1st (Canadian) Hussars suffered seventy-eight casualties but took 600 prisoners around Giberville. The Stormont, Dundas and Glengarry Highlanders (the Glens) came up to reinforce the Chaudière men at the château, where 'there was a walled orchard with enemy defence posts dug deep in craters and pits between the trees, which were thick with lush leaves and ripening fruit'. Strangely, in that vast procession of a thousand armoured vehicles, not a single tank had been allocated for the Glens' unenviable attack. And when they did break through the château grounds into full view of the notorious open plain they were not encouraged to see 'some hundred or so wrecked British tanks and only fifteen derelict enemy Panzers'.[35]

Looking in the other direction the Canadians might have been able to discern that the incipient traffic jam of the dark hours had solidified into an almighty insoluble impasse. The Guards still champed at the bit, trying to get to their task of capturing Cagny, where the 'screening' units of the 11th had learned that 88mm guns could fire through screens. The knocked-out tanks added to the traffic block. Behind the Guards the diaries of the 7th and its 22nd brigade aptly illustrate the problems:

0857   section of road collapsed.

0900   advance very slowly owing to congestion.

1057   half of 1 RTR over bridge but movement very slow.

1130   5 RTR completely held up. Roads too full of chaps.

1219   1 RTR still going over London Bridge

1345   2 sqdns of 4 CLY not over bridge. No movement at the moment as no movement over the other side.

1440   3 tnks attacked by AIR. 1 k.o'd.

1442   APM [police] – 2 miles block East of river. All traffic stopped.

1530   22AB unable to make any progress owing to congestion of troops on the ground.

As a result of this 'mother of all' traffic blocks there occurred another of those freak incidents which could only happen in battle. Brig 'Looney' Hinde was ordered to get some of his 22nd brigade tanks up to support the forward units. Himself a DSO with a formidable reputation for daring, Hinde barged and harangued his way forward through the obstructions. He could see further masses of tanks of 3 RTR and 2 F&F ahead. There would be no room for his own troops to filter through those manoeuvring regiments. He stalled, waiting for an opportunity to direct his own tanks with a chance of success. Only later did he realize that all the tanks he saw were abandoned. His military mind could not immediately identify such a catastrophe without precedent in warfare. (He was later axed as one of the scapegoats.)

Like the Canadians at Colombelles, other units of the British 3rd and 51st infantry divisions were fighting hard to secure firm flanks, away to the far left. Not all experiences were fatal. Caprice could sometimes save lives. Berkeley Meredith was a trooper with 13/18th Hussars. His tank had just crossed a railway embankment when it was hit by a solid shot. It went through the side armour, missed the stacks of 75mm shells and the crew, pierced the diesel engine and started a fire (which in a diesel burned more slowly than in a petrol engine). However, the shot had also hit the fire extinguisher, which was immediately set off and automatically put out the flames in the engine.[36]

Two German grenadiers on the other side of the embankment were lobbing grenades over the slope, trying to drop them straight down into the tank's turret. The 75mm would not depress sufficiently to fire down at the enemy. Meredith tried to fire the Sten gun but, not unusually, it jammed. So he fired the next weapon to hand, the Verey light pistol. A couple of blazing flares at a few yards' range discouraged the Germans, who fled.

Two troop leaders of another Yeomanry regiment, the East Riding, were not so fortunate as they skirted the thickly wooded slopes of the Bois de Bavent. Sgt Moverley, of A Sqdn, ploughed through high corn and was then in the fringes of woodland. Enemy infantry with the hand-held rocket launchers were everywhere. Moverley's tank was knocked out and flamed. He escaped and took over another tank. Again a rocket homed in on the tank. The serjeant was badly wounded and had to be evacuated. Nearby, Lt Chris Moreton of B Sqdn, out on foot, trying to find a way for his tanks through the woods, was gravely wounded. A patrol of the Royal Ulster Rifles tried to reach him but lost several men as the enemy mounted an impassable barrage of m-g fire, each Spandau (MG42) spouting twenty rounds per second. Moreton's body was later found decently buried by the enemy.[37]

The Highland Division had been opposing the German 858th regiment for some time and had discovered that there were festering sores of unreliability in the enemy formation. Now radically reduced to a strength of about 350 men, the regiment consisted of only 60 per cent reliable Germans. Twenty-five per cent were conscripted Poles, and 15 per cent Russian. Few of these men from occupied areas had any desire to suffer further in the Nazi cause. As the Highlanders advanced one of their most baneful tasks was moving through the noxious reek of dead animals. 'There were nineteen dead cows in one farmyard and eleven in another, killed by shelling. . . . They had lain there in the sun for twelve days. . . . Hens were plastered on to the walls like pats of mud. The place was a shambles. With a bulldozer we scooped forty-seven beasts and countless hens into three gigantic graves', done not only to respond to finer susceptibilities but also in the urgent interests of hygiene.[38]

At 1350 hours on that fatal day one humble tank gunner looking up was puzzled by a multiplicity of boots and shoes in the turret opening. He was amazed to find that three generals were sitting on his turret, O'Connor, Roberts and Erskine of the Desert Rats. It seems that in the prevailing situation three brass-hatted heads (although two were in black berets and the other in a cap) could think of nothing more subtle than setting up more targets for the enemy anti-tank gunners. The Desert Rats were to hurry up and mount an attack while the devastated units of the 11th dared the open plain once again.

2 F&F were launched at the thirty or so houses, one farm and a château which constituted the village of Soliers, then with a green strip of fields between the houses and the railway embankment. Up on the ridge Rudolf Ehrhardt of 1 SS Panzers was noting 'there was no life in the ghost town, except for an occasional dog or cat or perhaps a few chickens and rabbits. . . . The field in front of us is even, open, ideal for Panzers.' He meant for the guns of the hidden Panzers.[39]

On the about-to-be-receiving end, Terry Boyne scanned the land through his Sherman periscope:

We then had a stretch of open ground to cover and the unit fanned out moving across it as fast as possible. Viewing the scene through the visor periscope I could see Shermans slowing up and falling back behind us in flames, left and right, Targets appeared everywhere, Tigers, Panthers, SP guns and towed 88s. Progress was slow, breaking through one hedge line to be met with enemy fire from the next. My commander reported we were running out of ammunition and we were told to return to a knocked-out Sherman which we had passed earlier, its drive sprocket smashed.

On the return run we picked up a number of bailed out crews – some badly burned. That returning run gave us a sight of what we ourselves had been through – frightening – many burnt Shermans – cornfields on fire – hedges and trees ablaze from the knocked-out vehicles under them. We dropped our wounded off at a railway embankment.[40]

Norman Habetin, a wireless operator with 8 RB, was impressed by the intensity and consistency of German artillery fire. He observed that the mortars only stopped briefly between 1400 and 1500 'perhaps only when the gunners were cooling their mortars'. Looking towards Bourguebus 'the whole hillside was a horrible graveyard of blazing tanks. Tanks were being used to take wounded back but they were never fired on. They [the enemy, the much maligned SS] left them alone. People have the idea of masses of infantrymen in grey uniform, but they [the enemy] were always hidden and rarely seen. We couldn't see anything at all when advancing – just smoke and mess.'[41] In fact 8 RB reported that for part of the day some of their companies simple kept 'out of the way of the tank battle that was raging'. There was nothing much the infantry could do at such moments.

As if the immolation of so many crews was not enough to satisfy the anger of the gods of war, 23rd Hussars were next fed into the hungry fangs of Bekker's guns, now withdrawn to Soliers, and the LAH gunners up on the ridge. It was the same brief story. Guns reported at Le Prieuré. Then 'with no time for retaliation, no time to do anything, almost in one minute, all the tanks of three troops and squadron HQ were hit, blazing, exploding. Everywhere wounded and burning figures ran or struggled painfully for cover, while a remorseless rain of armour-piercing shot riddled the already helpless Shermans. All too clearly we were not going to "break through" today.'[42]

2 NY were directed towards the more confused skyline of Bras. They moved cautiously now. A rear link captain saw two Cromwells and a Firefly, well spaced, moving in coordination, looking for targets and

supporting each other. He thought that 'their whole operation contrasted with the one which had seemed to characterize the earlier part of the day, that of whole squadrons charging along in formation or column, when anti-tank fire from concealed guns could kill off virtually every tank inside two minutes.'[43]

The same observant officer, watching tank after tank brew, wondered, 'Why was our division not using rocket-firing aircraft to break up the Panther counter-attack?' The answer was that the tank in which the sole RAF liaison officer was travelling for greater safety had been quickly knocked out, putting ground control of aircraft out of action. 'We only knew we saw no aircraft.' As his regiment approached Bras a massed counter-attack of Panzer-Grenadiers commanded by Maj Rettlinger swung around both sides of Bras and, supported by heavier guns from the ridge, subjected 2 NY in their inappropriate Cromwells to another bitter cup of slaughter.

3 RTR who had been the first sufferers were still hanging on and being made to suffer. Their diary recorded laconically:

2100	fired on by 4 Tiger tanks from area 083634 [500 yards north-east of Soliers] . . . engaged them with assistance from 2 NY.
2200	fired on by approx 3 Tigers and Panther from ridge
2215	6 Sherman tanks of unit knocked out
2230	Withdraw and leager. 12 tanks [out of 61] in leager.

Sgt Jim Caswell was one of those caught up in this grim epilogue. On the right of his regiment, he heard of three camouflaged Tigers in a wood on the ridge. He saw other tanks brewing up. He moved to find a better position:

Just at that moment I spotted an 88mm gun pointing at me. I saw the terrible flash of its muzzle and heard the shell whistle by. I ordered the driver to go into reverse. He did so, very promptly, but we had hardly gone a few yards when another shell hit us. There were three of us in the turret; the navigator [gunner] was killed outright and my wireless operator, seriously wounded, collapsed onto the rear of the tank. In a

Sherman it is difficult to see what is happening in the driver's compartment so, using the inter-com, I asked the driver and machine-gunner if they had been hit. I did not receive a reply.

I realized they had both been killed and that it was impossible for me to regain control of the tank. It was still going backwards and steering itself towards the enemy. I finally abandoned the tank. . . . I found the wireless operator in the wheatfield. I took him over my shoulder and headed for our lines. I had to walk and crawl 2 miles before finding a first aid station. After handing over my comrade to the doctor I collapsed.

In the darkest hours of the night survivors heard Caswell's tank, like a demented ghost, still reversing around and around. Later it was discovered that the driver had fixed a home-made gadget to keep the revs at speed without constantly treading on the accelerator. When the dead foot ceased to exert authority the gadget continued to dictate the unending quest.[44]

It was now apparent to even the most optimistic British commander that the ridge was strongly held by high-quality troops, while the four leading tank regiments had suffered disabling casualties. Those regiments were ordered to withdraw a short way to replenish and re-form after the village of Four had been captured by 2 F&F, the day's high-water mark.

In the night hours only the infantry continued to prowl. 8 RB's G Coy sent out a midnight patrol which managed to locate enemy tank dispositions around Bras. In spite of the general idea that the Luftwaffe was totally absent, some tank men still suffered that night from the depredations of the German airmen who took great risks in daring to fly through Allied airspace. Terry Boyne recalled German bombs falling among the wrecked gliders in the original enclave east of the Orne bridges. The diary of the much battered 2 F&F (whose MO had been a casualty) confirmed this, saying that several 'unhorsed' crews got back to A1 echelon in the enclave, but were hit by a bombing raid 'and lost 2 Ofs [Officers] and 4 ORs [Other Ranks] k., and 3 Ofs and 40 ORs w.' (more ORs wounded than in brewing up tanks during the day).

In the 18 July inferno it was difficult to keep proper records. 2 NY RHQ noted B Sqdn commander's message that two tanks had been lost, and then the wounded commander went off the air. That loss number stayed in the diary but the loss total was probably sixteen. One informed calculation suggests that the three regiments of the leading armoured brigade (3 RTR, 2 F&F and 23H) lost at least 125 of their approximately 180 Shermans.[45] Bitter medicine for the men who so proudly wore the black beret.

CHAPTER SIX

GRIM GUARDS AND HAMSTRUNG RATS

'It started as a shambles and it continued as a shambles, for it was not long before 11th Armoured, who were leading, were held up, and the Guards Armoured ran into the back of them. There were tanks to the right of one and tanks to the left of one, tanks in front, tanks behind. It seemed to me we were fired on from all sides and our guns and tanks were firing in all directions. I certainly remember throwing myself flat on my face by the side of my half track, only to find that it was not the enemy firing at me, but some comrades in arms pulled up behind me firing at the enemy.' So complained the MO with the Irish Guards.[1]

Some might respond, 'But what was the MO doing so far forward anyway, risking his life and skills? Should he not have been way back, awaiting the arrival of casualties in due course?' Captain Hujohn Ripman, RAMC, was in the right place. A 1943 review of Regulations for the Medical Services of the Army, 1938, observed that 'such a specialized military machine as the Armoured division needs a very mobile and adaptable medical organization in support. . . . It is essential for the Medical Officer to be provided with an armoured vehicle for his own personal use in battle', in order to keep up with the advance, and that 'he is in W.T. communication with all Squadrons via the regimental forward control'.[2]

So the proud Guards, now destined to be late on parade, rolled forward into the ever more confusing turmoil of their first big battle in Normandy. Maj Gen A.H.S. Adair's division would be led by its 5th Guards AB, comprising 2nd Grenadiers, 1st Coldstream and 2nd Irish, each with about sixty Shermans, of which twelve would be the Firefly variant. The motor battalion, 1st Grenadiers, would send a rifle company with each of the three armoured units. Following on would be the 32nd Guards brigade of infantry with the 5th Coldstream, 3rd Irish and 1st Welsh. The 2nd Welsh formed the division's recce battalion.

The very experienced 'Pip' Roberts of the 11th commented about the Guards: 'They were completely new to armoured warfare. I don't think they had anyone who had fought in a tank before. But they were enthusiastic about the chance of entering their first battle.'[3] Some soldiers were not too convinced of the wisdom of training some of the elite infantry troops of the Guards to fight in tanks, when there was a shortage of infantry and an excess of tanks.

But guardsmen like Frank Clark were very happy with the system whereby Guards tanks worked with Guards infantry. 'You might look out of the turret and the infantry soldier walking alongside you could be an old friend who had done initial training with you at Pirbright. Even if not, you had so many things in common with the walking Guards outside', in contrast to the average armoured regiment where your infantry might belong to a battalion you had never heard of.

The problems in switching Guards from foot-sloggers into mobile mechanics were often humorous, as huge men, especially selected for their size, were crammed into tiny light tanks. One Guards officer related an incident concerning a most efficient parade ground NCO who was suddenly transmogrified into a tank commander. It was noticed that he took an inordinate time to respond to wireless messages. Further investigation revealed that when he was addressed by his superior officers over the wireless, he first paused in the turret to come to attention and salute (Up-two-three! Away two-three!), before replying, 'Sah!'[4]

On 18 July, experienced or not, Brig N.W. Gawtkin, MVO, had split up his brigade into what might be called 'battle groups', a more sensible idea than some tactics which had governed armoured attacks in Normandy to date. 2 Grenadiers and 1 Coldstream would each have with them a motor company, an anti-tank platoon, a Royal Engineers recce party, a section of Field Ambulance and a battery of 153 Field Regt, RA. 2 Irish would be of similar strength but with a squadron of XXII Dragoons' flails added.

VIII Corps reported that at 1030 [18 July] the lead tanks reached a point 'between Le Mesnil-Frementel and Le Prieuré which is a slight rise hiding

Cagny. There – anti-tk fire from E, S and SW . . . tks k.o'd – so a more cautious advance required.' Grenadier Lt Col R. Moore hurried forward to get a better view and meet his lead squadron leader, Maj Sir Arthur Grant. A brief consultation and exhortation ensued. Sir Arthur returned to his tank. Moments later he was killed. An ominous beginning![5]

What the Guards did not yet know was that 'no less than 272 Nebelwerfer rocket launchers and 250 guns were untouched by the air and artillery bombardment'.[6] Nor did they yet know that, as O'Connor's own summing-up later admitted, 'Cagny was not obliterated by air attacks, so slowed the Guards'; nor that they were facing elite German troops, for they had been encouraged to believe that in front of them they would encounter 'only a few old men and boys with Spandaus' in third-rate units.[7] In Capt Lord Carrington's words: 'The Germans – allegedly now of poor quality because of their losses in Russia, bombed to distraction and outnumbered by enormous odds – had shown themselves pretty effective.'[8]

Laurie Lacey was a typical tall guardsman, squashed into a small Honey recce tank. The Honey, or Stuart, was fast but carried only a 37mm gun (as against the ineffective 75mm of the Sherman), and in terms of fighting 88mm guns, was so lightly armoured that the manufacturers might have economized and used cardboard instead of steel. Laurie and his commander, Sgt Dusty Smith, and his troop leader, Capt Webster, knew all about this. They knew they must advance quickly and be ready to reverse back even more quickly if they descried any danger ahead. Smith's code sign for the day was Baker One. Sitting a little bored in the tank during one of those monotonous waits which constitute much of a battle, Laurie was shocked into awareness as the wireless crackled and he heard the dreaded order over the air: 'Baker One, Baker One, are you receiving? . . . Baker One proceed ahead. Anti-tank guns are causing some trouble. Locate their positions. Over.' And Laurie, the overgrown, boyish rookie, would be transformed, within minutes, into a mature man who had looked Death in the eyes and who had witnessed the ultimate in human suffering.[9]

Sgt E.A. Smith gave the order, 'Driver, advance!' and, as they rounded a small copse, 'Gunner, traverse right!' While Johnny Mock was traversing and Ken Kent cautiously steering round the trees in low gear, all were on tenterhooks. Then, Laurie remembers:

> Suddenly there was a terrific crash on the side of the tank which seemed to leap three feet into the air, all 15 tons of it. Commander shouts, 'Reverse! Reverse! Throw out smoke!' The tank reverses a yard or two. Stops. Seems to shudder. Smith shouts, 'Bale out!'
>
> There was smoke inside the tank. I tried to lift my driver compartment top hatch. The gun had traversed over it and jammed it. One way out was through an escape hatch in the floor, but that would take time, unlatching clips. And on the uneven ground it might not fall far enough to let me squeeze through. I had to squirm up through the turret cage and then through a small gap between ammunition racks. Flames were issuing from the engine and I was surrounded by live ammunition, 37mm size, very explosive. It was jump or die. I scrabbled up inside the turret. Out through the top. Sgt Smith, two others and I had jumped into long grass or perhaps it was high green corn. We started to crawl towards safety. I was unhurt. But something far more horrible was to come.
>
> Staggering towards us came another Guards sergeant who was a stranger to me. He had been on fire. His clothing was all burned and in shreds. Worse, his skin was hanging from his body. Face, arms, naked bits of body, the black skin hanging away from the red flesh. I stood up and went to try to help him walk. He screamed with the pain of me touching him. I had to let him go, try to guide him towards the field dressing station. He just staggered and screamed.

Sgt Smith and Laurie managed to steer the burned man back to the medical officer and asked for water for him to drink. The MO replied that it was too late. Nothing could be done. Indeed, within minutes the burned man had breathed his last scalding breath. Death was the only surgeon who could help. They saw another casualty running across the field, screaming out in pain. He was holding his hands to both ears from which blood was pouring out.

Like so many tank crews, Sgt Smith, Laurie, Ken and Johnny then had to find a replacement tank, mount it and resume their place in the battle line, fully aware of the fate that might await them. Other men had equal fears about other of the dangers encountered. Laurie's friend, Gdsm Ace Diamond, had a particular dread of mines, having suffered from them:

> Suddenly there was an enormous bang and a cloud of smoke. One of the tanks had been hit, my first thought was 'an 88!' I started to turn round to pick up the crew but we were then blown up on the co-driver's side – mines had been laid along the side of the road. John Champken was badly wounded and Cpl Cartwright had wounds to his legs. Roy Galligher and I were very lucky not to be injured. Sgt Doug Tamblyn in the lead tank . . . appeared to be unhurt but Johnny Rigg (the battalion goalkeeper) was in a bad way, trapped inside the tank. Sadly he died after two or three hours, and we learned that John C. had lost a leg.[10]

Capt Lord Carrington, also of the Grenadiers, was at first encouraged to see 'disconsolate-looking German prisoners wending their way northward in sad little field-grey columns'. Then he was equally discouraged because on advancing 'the first sight to meet our eyes was a large number of British tanks blazing on the skyline'. Soon his own tanks had moved into the thick of the embroilment:

> Our own tanks were being hit by German dug-in tanks and anti-tank guns sited skilfully . . . on the edges of the villages, by the barns and in the coppices with which the open cornfields were studded. We saw very little of the enemy who . . . had recovered enough to be picking off British tanks with enthusiasm. What we did see was our own blazing hulls – our battalion lost over twenty tanks . . . in the first hours – and very soon we found ourselves halted while a more deliberate attack was put in on the village of Cagny.[11]

Grenadier Maj Ivor Crosthwaite, DSO, described 'being shot at by a German 88mm' as 'terrifying if one was looking in its direction as it fired. From 1,000 yards it took about a second to arrive. One saw the tracer all the way like a hose jet coming straight at one, as if a bayonet was about to be plunged into one's stomach. The pain was acute.'[12] 3 RTR's Maj Bill

Close had also remarked on watching the shot scythe through the corn, leaving a kind of 'wake' behind it. Another gunner saw it as 'a black object like the head of a seal speeding through harbour waters', rushing through the corn with 'one rending howl, like a dog in pain'.[13]

Crosthwaite continued, 'The shot was unlikely to miss by more than three or four feet. One knew that the next corrected shot was not more than ten seconds away. One fired smoke, but it could not build up in time. One zigzagged to provide a 45-degree surface which the enemy shot might bounce off. If one's gun happened to be in the right direction the gunner would have seen it and would fire madly. The German 88mm crew were probably as frightened as oneself.'

Yet another Grenadier, the then Capt A.G. Heywood, bravely ignored the awesome handicap of taking on an 88mm Tiger with a 75mm Sherman at a dangerous range. Lt Sir Howard Frank's 4 Troop was lined up behind a hedge near Le Prieuré farm when the troop Firefly saw and opened fire on a Tiger, appearing over a ridge at 900 yards. Sgt White, the Firefly commander, could not see the fall of his shot because the muzzle flash from the 17pdr gun was so large and blinding. A 17pdr shot had to travel more than 1,000 yards before the commander's visibility was restored. Tony Heywood therefore moved up alongside White to act as the Firefly's eyes. The Tiger fired, the Firefly was hit and White and his crew bailed out.

Heywood ordered, 'Driver, reverse!', in order to seek different cover. Nothing happened. He repeated the order urgently. Something was amiss with the intercom. Bassett, the gunner, asked, 'Shall I open fire, sir?' This would betray the location of the Sherman with its weaker gun, but his commander replied, 'Yes, open fire!'

The gunner fired armour-piercing shot. The 75mm flash was less than that of the 17pdr and Heywood could see the shot impact on the Tiger, with no effect. Too small the shot, too thick the enemy armour. Bassett shot off all the AP rounds handy in the turret. More hits. No effect. 'Try HE', ordered Heywood. Now the explosions on the hide of the Tiger were clearly visible although the tiny shards of shrapnel from the high explosive would do no harm to that armour plating. But surprisingly the Tiger, like a scared beast, began to reverse back over the ridge, superficially unharmed.

Heywood, claiming moral victory, assumed that the Tiger crew must have been deafened and unnerved by the rapid succession of bangs and crashes on their vehicle. A good Sherman turret crew could reload and fire three or four shots by the time the first one had struck.[14]

So the Grenadiers led the way and other units followed on. At 1015 the Guards' leading tanks were reported in front of Cagny. At 1230 2 Irish Guards were attempting to bypass Cagny. By 1630 1 Coldstream were in Le Poirier. At 1900 the Irish were pushing towards Vimont. 2000 and Cagny had been cleared. Good progress by Normandy standards before 18 July. Yet gradually falling behind the virtually impossible schedule ordained.

Irish Guards troop leader Robert Boscawen had reached the eerie wide open spaces around the railway line from Caen to Troarn. 'I felt uncomfortable crossing that line, as anything could fire straight down it from a long way off.' Now the traffic blocks locked in again. 'We stopped. The Grenadiers in front had been held up somewhere, no one knew quite what was happening'. The chaos grew worse. Panthers were reported on the left. 'Vehicles of all kinds were crowding up behind . . . half-tracks and some carriers of heavy machine-gunners, the Northumberland Fusiliers. Mixed up too were a few odd tanks of the 2nd Recce, Welsh Guards.'[15]

Boscawen was soon to become only too aware of what had been happening up front:

> The remains of Cagny . . . appeared empty with a few burning tanks. But beyond the railway the horizon was covered with burning tanks. I could count twenty, a whole squadron, burning in one field alone. More were hidden behind the black smoke of others brewing up, while yet others were still being hit and bursting into flames . . . a number of men were crawling towards us through the corn. The Commander decided then 'we must not add to this disaster' so must move under cover of the railway embankment round Cagny.

With hindsight Boscawen comments, 'Certainly those of us who saw the dreadful sight of the 11th Armoured Division's tanks, just ahead of us, being hit one after the other and bursting into flames, and found their wounded crews scrambling back in the corn through us, could not forget it. I have always thought it spoke volumes for the stolid character of our soldiers, how little they seemed to be affected by the sight of our petrol-driven Shermans being such an easy prey to the 88mms of the German Panzers on our first day in action.'[16]

An epic act of bravery was now carried out by another troop leader of the Irish Guards, John Gorman, who won the Military Cross, with his driver, Cpl James Baron, who was awarded the Military Medal. It is important to know what was in Gorman's mind as his moment of destiny struck. They had been told, on landing in Normandy, that the Germans had a supertank. They had the Panthers, which were fast and very good tanks; they had the Tigers, which had immensely heavy armour; and they had a new tank called the Royal Tiger, a gigantic vehicle, which had been seen on the Eastern Front and it was believed they were going to use on the Western Front. 'None of us had seen one, so all we could do was hope we wouldn't come across one, because its armour was impenetrable to our ordinary gun.'[17]

Gorman described his reactions as he ordered his tank to advance carefully around a corner:

You're looking at the amateurishness of this . . . I hadn't got out of my tank and looked around the corner [he had no infantry with him to do this], that was not my mood. So we turned the corner and there was the Royal Tiger, the only one, actually, seen in Normandy. There was a bit of good luck: it was at right angles to us, with its gun ninety degrees away from us. I had already discussed with Cpl Baron what would we actually do? Ours was a paper-thin tank with a gun that couldn't possible penetrate it. And we had decided – sounds mad, I know – we decided on the naval tactic of ramming.

I ordered, 'RAM!'

Gunfire couldn't do much good but my gunner, Gdsm Scholes, managed to get one shot off. Then he put HE in the breech as I wanted to hit the Royal Tiger while we were going at it, for three hundred yards, I suppose, but very fast, I mean Cpl Baron went as fast as he could, because, behind the Royal Tiger, and to our right now, were three ordinary Tigers supporting the great beast. Our tank HIT the Royal

Tiger on the left rear, very hard. Bert Scholes put a shot – a very explosive shot into the back of the Royal Tiger which would create an awful lot of noise and worry to the people inside the tank.

The German gun had swung and hit the Sherman turret with a tremendous 'clang!' The two tanks were jammed fast, like two elephants (one much larger than the other) with tusks locked together. The Guards baled out and found themselves mixed up with the German crew also bailing out, all partially dazed. Another Sherman commanded by Sgt Harbinson hove in view, firing at the German tanks. The 88s replied and Harbinson's tank disappeared within a huge sheet of flame. Gorman shouted 'Run!' Like a not-so-funny comic opera the Guards jumped up and ran one way, while the well-disciplined Panzer men jumped up and ran the other way.

Comedy quickly merged into tragedy as Gorman went to find his Firefly tank which could contend on equal terms with the 88. That tank was commanded by Sgt Workman. Gorman was horrified to find that 'the Royal Tiger had fired at Workman, had shot a bit high, and had taken his head off. So he was lying in the tank, over the gun, with no head, and the turret was absolutely full of blood. The gunner was covered with blood, the loader in the same state. They were totally disorientated. So we got the poor body out of the tank, cleaned up the gun sights as best we could. The tank itself was OK'.

Gorman spotted a tall hedge near the Tigers. He was able to move along the hedge, fire his 17pdr at the Tigers and then withdraw, certain that they would not follow. Passing near Harbinson's tank and believing the crew to be dead inside the inferno, he was delighted to see 'three scarecrows in a ditch – men on fire, totally on fire'. Gorman's crew put out the smouldering fire on the men's overalls, lifted them on to the back of Gorman's tank and then raced back to the aid post. Harbinson, the worst burned, was rushed to England that same night but, with more than 50 per cent burns, succumbed to pneumonia. Gorman paid tribute to Harbinson whose deliberate sacrificial intervention saved Gorman and his crew.

There was much urgent activity on the German side, although the word 'frantic' might not be entirely apt. The pause at Cagny had allowed a new unit from 12th SS Panzer Hitlerjugend to move up. These young but already very experienced and highly trained soldiers were able to start infiltrating among the attacking tanks. At the same time, because the British attackers were lacking in numbers of infantry to seal off gaps in the advance, the clumsy, huge, enemy self-propelled guns were able to use woods and hedgerows to withdraw and locate themselves afresh on even more commanding ground. Von Luck, von Rosen and Becker were busy marshalling these moves.

Next out of the milling Goodwood traffic congestion came the Shermans of 1st Coldstream Guards. Conditions meant that the mad charge of the morning had sobered down, so that following units would be able to avoid some of the worst excesses of self-imposed catastrophe. But the enemy still dominated the lower levels of the good tank country.

George Teal was with the Coldstreams, on a tank named Codrington. As he saw flaming Shermans ahead he was very conscious of 'the 150 gallons of petrol in our petrol tank'. He commented, 'The 18 July shocked the armoured divisions to the core. [After it] they didn't want to get up and go. They knew bloody well what was waiting for them.'

He described the Coldstreams' advance: 'Going along like the bloody clappers, y'know; turrets in front of us blowing up and tanks zigzagging – the turret weighed 5 tons and hit by an 88mm it was just blown to pieces and all black smoke and God knows what. Just seemed like – we'd never been in action before, y'know – seemed like . . . like Hell on earth. Our commander said, "This is madness. Fire smoke!"'[18]

There were some British infantrymen, though too few, up front, the men of the 1st Grenadier Guards, a motorized unit. In all the massed confusion of Goodwood some infantrymen would encounter the silence and loneliness which can occur in battle. Lt Geoffrey Picot, a mortar officer, referred to this strange fact. 'Those who get their picture of a battle from films where seemingly hundreds of rival soldiers are packed into a few hundred square yards, may have difficulty in imagining a real battlefield. You and a couple of pals can be hundred of yards away from anybody else; you may not have much idea where friend and foe are. You fire from a concealed position on to a hidden target.'[19]

This Goodwood contradiction was also brought home to Guards infantry officer Maj A.R. Thurdley-Wickes. He was leading his company forward furtively in the dark near Cagny, using a compass as a guide. Then his wireless failed and he was out of touch with battalion HQ. Runners were unreliable and likely to be shot in the constant crossfire. So, handing over command, the major himself crawled back, keeping head well down, along intersecting ditches and gullies. He found HQ, only to be ordered to withdraw his company. There followed another lonely crawl forward along the same ditches, and a third imitation of a worm's progress with his entire company back to the start line.

In the motor battalion, Grenadier G. Marsden heard the radio message, 'Watch for snipers and Germans in the cornfields.' He observed that 'the whole area was on fire, and the earth shuddering from the bombing and shelling. Moving towards Cagny our captives were mere boys, running towards our lines with hands on head. But they still retaliated with shellfire and the dread Moaning Minnies. To be caught in their fire was certain disaster.'

His company reached Cagny at last and the order was given to dig in. Marsden thought the area looked just like a typical English village. 'I had to dig my trench in a potato field. The ground was hard and stony. By now it was growing dark. I saw some dead comrades being buried nearby already, about seven graves. Now I knew why the white crosses had been issued before the battle.'[20] The burial of the dead was a necessary task in the high summer heat. To bury one's own dead was sad beyond recounting. To bury the enemy dead was often obnoxious.

Laurie Lacey learned that three of his mates had died. He was about to unfasten a shovel clipped to the side of the tank when his Capt Webster asked him what he was intending to do. 'Upon telling him I thought he would require a burial party, he said he considered it more appropriate if someone who did not know the casualties carried out that duty.' Such sensitivity was not always possible in battle.

As the Guards struggled to move ahead, the Desert Rats behind them still found that 'the road was too full of chaps'. Roberts of the 11th was later to give his opinion that the fighting in the desert had had the effect of making the Desert Rats 'a little wary – a little less eager to go round the corner . . . their view of Operation Goodwood was a bit less enthusiastic than ours.'[21] He may have been right, but the Desert Rats may have been justified when they saw the disastrous carnage ahead of them. Pat Dyas, who had just become adjutant of 4th County of London Yeomanry (CLY), was one officer who had reason to be cautious. A short while previously he had come within 20 yards of a Tiger, had fired his own 6pdr gun and had seen two of his shots bounce off the Tiger harmlessly. At 20 yards in the same short street. The Tiger then took one leisurely and derisory shot to brew up Pat's tank.[22]

The 7th had 4 CLY plus 1st and 5th RTR as their armoured regiments up front. However, unlike the 11th and the Guards, the 7th had the lighter, if faster, Cromwell as their main tank. They did have a limited number of Sherman Firefly tanks to strengthen their firing capability. By 1530 on 18 July they were still reporting lack of progress due to 'congestion of troops on the ground'. Only by 1745 was it possible to direct leading tanks of 5 RTR towards Soliers 'and recce towards La Hogue'. At 1805 approaching Soliers it looked as though the village might be undefended. But within the hour 5 RTR had to report Panthers inflicting casualties. Brig Hinde looked for a way of outflanking the Panthers, but there was no room to move outside 5 RTR's own lanes as it would entail 'crushing up on people on left or right'.

In these circumstances accidents happened, with the freak occurrence of 'friendly fire'. The Irish Guards' MO had been astonished to find bullets coming from behind him. One Sherman commander saw an unfamiliar tank heading from the direction of the enemy lines near Demouville. He ordered his gunner to open fire. The two tanks then engaged in a duel to the death. Both tanks brewed up. The Sherman commander was killed and the entire crew of the unknown vehicle perished. It was some time later that it was established that the unknown was a new type of British self-propelled gun which had got lost and was finding its way back to safety.[23] It happened to the Germans too. Von Rosen lost two Tigers, presumably to British guns although none were observed. Later it proved that German SPs had shot mistakenly at the too far advanced Tigers wreathed in battle 'smog'.[24]

In fact there was no safe place in the Normandy bridgehead and the vagaries of war were impossible to foresee. Irish Guards medical orderly,

Gdsm Hill, was slightly wounded and in no danger, but the hospital ship conveying him to England was sunk and he was drowned. He was succeeded by another Hill, no relation, who had his skull fractured during a whiplash accident when his half-track crashed.[25] Three of Laurie Lacey's troop were killed when a mortar bomb exploded between them when they were eating a meal behind the lines. Another was mortally hit behind the ear by a pea-size fragment of shrapnel while washing. Ian Hammerton and two friends of XXII Dragoons obtained permission to go to the beach on a rest day. Ian did not want to swim. His two friends did, and swam off happily in the waves. A stray shell killed them as they swam.[26] The MO of 23 Hussars reported a mini-epidemic of enteritis cases, some serious, as a result of millions of flies breeding on corpses around Demouville.

Although the heavy bombers had departed after the massed morning raids, there was still much air activity. Lighter bombers and Typhoon rocket planes supported the ground troops where feasible in the throng of vehicles. There were also fast Spitfires and Mustangs carrying out photographic duties even during the battle. One French courting couple under a convenient hedgerow, unaware of the wider war, were astonished when a Spitfire crashed into the field beside them, having been shot down by anti-aircraft fire as it aimed to photograph a V launch site near the Emieville château. The plane would become a salvage project fifty-seven years later, headed by a little boy who also witnessed the incident.[27]

The planning of Allied operations would have been much more difficult had it not been for the dedicated work of RAF 83 Group's recce planes taking photographs in situations of great danger: an obvious requirement was to fly straight patterns back and forth several times over a well-protected target. In three months from D-Day the group flew 1,240 sorties and took 143,000 photos, from which one and a half million prints were distributed, 'often down to platoon level, providing the ground forces with up-to-date information on enemy dispositions'.[28]

The Luftwaffe, in perhaps even more detrimental circumstances and in spite of jokes both German and Allied, managed to make some appearances. The ERY saw that 'several ME 109s and other German aircraft flew over the regimental area on Butte de la Hogue and were engaged by as many of the Regiment as possible . . . the day before we had one success, shooting down an ME 109.' Ian Hammerton with XXII Dragoons also reported, 'It was a boiling hot day and we were sweltering in or on the tanks. Suddenly a flight of Messerschmitt 109s appeared screaming low over the hedges. They were gone before we could get a shot at them as we spotted the black crosses on their wings'.

Some of the specialist British anti-aircraft guns were more successful. The Guards light anti-aircraft regiment, the 94th, downed three enemy aircraft and claimed another six badly damaged, some probably destroyed on 18 and 19 July. Their Royal Artillery colleagues of 21 Anti-Tank Regiment were also on target. Q Battery under Capt E.D.G. Smith knocked out three Panthers at Le Prieuré. One single gun of Y Battery boldly took on two Tigers at close range and destroyed them, earning for Lt F.A. Hook the MC and for Sgt F. Holford the MM.

Away beyond where the British tanks hoped to reach, objectives like Bras and Hubert-Folie, the Canadians had been ordered to try to rehabilitate the southern crossings of the Orne, leading out from around Caen railway station, and so secure the outer suburbs of the city. Free French guides were very effective in this Operation Atlantic, the Canadian element of Goodwood. The Canadians probed south from Caen racecourse, a real horse racing venue, not a code word.

Guy Merle, a French lad, guided Lt Buzz Keating's 18 Platoon of the Regina Rifles as they placed planks across yawning gaps on a partially demolished bridge, dangling above water 8 feet deep. They scrambled over and then charged into the railways sidings:

> A German m-g opens fire . . . our m-gs fire, sweeping under the abandoned goods wagons . . . slowly we progress! . . . an order – four men detach to the right, go throwing smoke bombs into the immense warehouse. This moment, like from an anthill, 'Fritzes' flood out. We profit and take a leap towards the waiting room. After a serious cleansing of cellars we round up sixty-nine prisoners. The station is totally occupied.[29]

Already on 14 July the Reginas' scout officer, Lt Bergeron, had taken a midnight patrol across what was left of the Epron railway bridge near the station. Now he and French guide Pierre Chatelain, with fifteen men, painfully crawled over the broken and warped girders to set up a tiny bridgehead under constant m-g and mortar fire at close range. Their support group, carrying the wireless pack, was unable to cross as five fast-firing Spandau m-gs set up an unceasing weave of bullets, clearly visible by their tracer. Chatelain crawled alone over the bridge to carry messages to the Reginas' HQ. The battalion was struggling to bring mortars and heavy machine-guns up through the ruins of Caen as Bergeron and his men tried to construct a link across the bridge.

Chatelain tried to cross the bridge for the fifth time and was killed by the m-g bullets. After two hours the battalion had assembled enough fire power on the near bank to drive away the Germans hanging on around Bergeron's little group on the far bank. The way was open for infantrymen followed by engineers rushing to make a crossing stable enough for vehicles.

As the fateful day of 18 July drew to a close VIII Corps calculated the damage, declaring '118 of our tanks k.o'd but only 85 were Z casualties' (destroyed beyond repair). Objectives had not been reached, but in his haste to put the best gloss on affairs Montgomery initiated a new war, a war of words, which still continues. The issues were: what did Montgomery really say after Goodwood? What did he really mean? What did he really intend as the outcome of the operation?

There should be no doubt about what he said. His report to his British chief, Alanbrooke, is on record:

Operations this morning a complete success. . . . Present situation as follows.

11th Armd Div reached Tilly 0760 [map reference for Tilly-la-Campagne] – Bras 0663. 7th Armd Div passed area Demouville 1067 and moving on La Hogue 0960. Guards Armd Div passed Cagny and now in Vimont. . . . Have ordered the armd car regts of each div . . . to reconnoitre towards and secure the crossings over the Dives between Mézidon and Falaise.

. . . It is difficult to see what the enemy can do just at present. Few enemy tanks met so far and no (repeat no) mines.[30]

This was a considerable fabrication. Tilly, Bras and Vimont had not been occupied, or even 'reached'. It could be said that comparatively 'few enemy tanks' appeared but what havoc they had wreaked! Mines had been encountered, in addition to the bottleneck caused by the narrow gaps in the British minefield. And there was no way an armoured car was going to advance even 100 yards in the direction of distant Mézidon or Falaise when the largest British tanks were being annihilated at 2,000 yards range.

But perhaps Montgomery was too far away from the scene to know what was really happening? Not so! At 1800 that evening Montgomery visited Dempsey at his HQ. Dempsey was fully briefed about the situation having been liaising with VIII Corps all day. More than one historian has pondered, 'Why Montgomery elected to send such a wildly over-optimistic evaluation is a mystery, but it was the first of several blunders he committed during Goodwood that were to damage his credibility. . . . It was bad enough for him to have misled Brooke but he foolishly compounded the mistake by reading a communiqué for the BBC implying similar gains.'[31]

Certainly the British press had been given the impression that 'this was IT': the long-awaited break THROUGH! More than one headline trumpeted to the British public 'BREAK-THROUGH EAST OF THE ORNE'.[32] On 19 July a highly respected war correspondent, Christopher Buckley, interviewed Montgomery and reported:

'We did well yesterday [18 July]', Gen Montgomery said today, at his Normandy HQ, speaking about the current battle. 'We achieved tactical surprise. We have got strong armoured and mobile forces in a bridgehead south and south-east of Caen. In doing this we have written off a great deal of enemy material while our own casualties in men and equipment have been very light – in fact, almost negligible.'[33]

One hundred and eighteen of our tanks knocked out (even if only eighty-five were Z casualties): negligible?!

CHAPTER SEVEN

CRESTFALLEN AT THE CREST

The 'morning after the night before' feeling seemed to be afflicting much of VIII Corps in the early hours of 19 July. In the words of one unit, 'Motor Coys remained in position but the Brigade virtually sat tight.' The tactic which the Germans had most feared during the night had not been used – a massed attack in the dark by infantry towards Bourguebus, although two British infantry brigades were available.[1]

Of course a number of tank units had been badly battered. Terry Boyne had stood on the top of his turret when returning to the 2 F&F leager to get an overview of the regiment. 'I counted 9 Shermans – that view in the morning would have been 55 Shermans. The C Sqdn lane was empty.'

Among the burned-out skeletons of the previous day's Shermans along the slopes some wrecks seemed still to be writhing in their death throes. Charles Pearce of 4 CLY remembers, 'some tanks still burning and at least one had the engine running which had run all that night'.[2] Lt Langdon, Bill Close's 1 troop leader, found his knocked-out tank of yesterday still smouldering. Bill Mosely has vivid recall of hearing 'high pitched screaming' and tracing it to a tank which had been disabled without brewing. After a long period of smouldering the slow fire had penetrated the engine:

We watched fascinated as the turret spun round and round, wailing like a demented banshee – the oil in the power-traverse system must have overheated, driving the turret round and round. Then with a series of explosions the ammunition went up, sheets of flame shooting through the turret hatches, blowing smoke rings high into the night sky.[3]

1 Bob Levine, who lost a leg in the battle, ascends Mont-Castre years later to trace his platoon's battle route. *(Elson)*

2 The *bocage*: the author surveys a typical hedgerow, fourteen feet high, on top of a 2-ft bank, correspondingly thick. *(Jai Tout)*

3 Jim Flowers (*left*), at peace with Fritz Uhlig of 5th SS Parachute Div., who fought against him on Hill 122. *(Elson)*

4 Sid Jones, now in his 80s, on his BMW, has been a long-term marshal of the TT races in the Isle of Man. *(Island Photographics)*

5 Sgt Sid Jones *(centre)* with his fitters of B Sqdn, 2 NY, who were trained to mend vehicles and found themselves tending men. *(Jones)*

6 One of the fateful railway arches between Soliers and Bras. Sid Jones buried Niblock on the embankment to the left. *(Tout)*

7 The ruins of Caen after the air raid made it impossible to pass large numbers of heavy vehicles through the streets. *(Tank Museum)*

8 Col Hans von Luck, who fought Goodwood in full dress and reinforced orders with a drawn pistol. *(Bundesarchiv)*

9 Authors of Goodwood, happy enough before it began. Left to right: O'Connor, Dempsey and Montgomery. *(Imperial War Museum B7407)*

10 Single file over one of the Goodwood bridges. Little room for tank driver errors. *(Imperial War Museum B7652)*

11 The air bombardment photographed by one of the attacking aircraft. *(Imperial War Museum HU52367)*

12 Sherman tanks in open country. A sight for sore eyes as far as German 88mm gunners were concerned. *(Tank Museum)*

13 Maj Gen G.P.B. 'Pip' Roberts, DSO, led 11th Armoured Division for Goodwood, an onerous induction at that level of command. *(Imperial War Museum B9183)*

14 Irish Guards Sherman Firefly 'Ballymena' (AD 2002), reconstructed from rusted relics by André Lechipey who, as a boy, saw the original tank advance down his village street. *(Lechipey)*

15 The fate of this Sherman crew at the moment when its 5-ton turret was blown off is not recorded. *(Tank Museum)*

16 The slavery of infantry life, constantly digging in. The fertile Norman soil was often surprisingly stony. *(Imperial War Museum B7773)*

17 Civilians saved poor-quality wartime film to 'snap' their liberators: Cpl Reg Spittles *(centre)* with Tpr Wells, Barnet, Baggeley and Garrett. *(Spittles)*

19 Jean Goubert, civilian, shot dead for aiding US paratroopers to escape near Lessay. *(Pinel)*

18 John Cloudsley-Thompson commanded the CLY tank troop which reached the high-tide mark of Goodwood. *(Cloudsley-Thompson)*

20 21-year-old *Obersturmführer* Werner Wolff, commander of the formidable 7th Panzer Company, of 1st SS LAH, which counter-attacked at Bourguebus Ridge, Mortain and Chambois. Killed in action in Hungary, March 1945. *(Stiller)*

21 GIs occupy Hebecrevon, first Cobra village towards Marigny, as signaller connects phone cables. *(US Army Military History Institute)*

22 Shermans stuck in the mud during the rains that halted Goodwood and delayed the start of Cobra. *(Tank Museum)*

23 US engineers clearing nests of mines, Lessay town square. *(US National Archives)*

24 Sherman with Rhino teeth at front and close supporting infantry, Cobra. *(Tank Museum)*

25 Horror pending! Thousands of stray animals were killed as they wandered onto the fields of battle. *(Tank Museum)*

26 Incongruous but welcome, this Sherman, camouflaged for the hedgerows, liberates an inhabited village in Brittany. *(Tank Museum)*

27 Maj Gen, later Lt Gen, Marcus Rose, brilliant tactician, sadly killed in action in last days of the war. (*Tank Museum*)

28 Gen Bayerlein saw his elite Panzer Lehr Div wiped out and was himself in mortal danger. (*Bundesarchiv*)

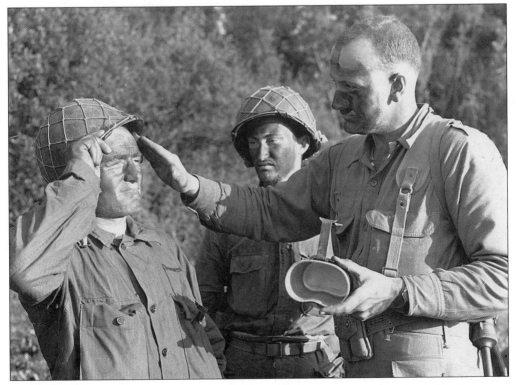

29 Louis Aubert, French Resistance guide (*left*) daubed with camouflage by Lt W. Shreve, as Pfc G. Peterson translates (*US Army/Dava Still*)

30 The public image. Left to right: Bradley, Patton and Div Cdr 'Bulldog' Walker, uniforms well creased for the camera. *(Patton Museum)*

31 The hidden reality: a haggard Patton and a thoughtful Bradley returning from a visit to the 'sharp end' in Brittany. *(Patton Museum)*

32 Von Kluge (*left*), with staff, in (for them) happier days of rapid blitzkrieg advances. (*Imperial War Museum GER 1270*)

33 Polish tank men in a Firefly with its avenging 17pdr gun, closing the Falaise pocket. Someone had thrown them flowers. (*Tank Museum*)

34 US military police and tanks escort German prisoners after Normandy battles. The Shermans have amphibian engine chutes. *(Tank Museum)*

35 The crucial factor: assembly lines produced Shermans faster than the enemy could knock them out. *(Tank Museum)*

'Sending up smoke rings at intervals, rising slowly in the still air, like dying gasps', according to Terry Boyne.

It might have been a morning of static reorganization for most of VIII Corps, but the Germans appeared to be able to reorganize on the move. SS Panzer-Grenadiers from Four advanced at 0700 and recaptured le Poirier. On the crest of the ridge the Germans had now assembled a group of soldiers who might have claimed to be among the most skilled, experienced and well equipped of any army anywhere any time. It was like a gathering of minor gods of war on Mount Olympus. Their names had long been celebrated in Germany – Teddy Wisch, Panzermeyer, Jochen Peiper, Werner Wolff, not to mention von Luck, von Rosen, Becker, and, sitting comfortably on his Tiger behind them, the greatest individual tank ace of all, Michael Wittmann. The formidable battle groups of Waldmuller and Wunsch were also drawing nigh.

Brigadier Roscoe Harvey's 29th AB, yesterday's shattered spearhead, was combining squadrons, two instead of three to a regiment. Knocked-out crews were returning with replacement tanks. Mercilessly, bruised Maj Bill Close was ordered to return to the place of previous sorrows and observe movement around Hubert-Folie and Bras. Filtering between the smoking hulks of the previous day, Lt Langdon was immediately targeted by the big guns on the ridge. He had hardly passed his tank of the previous day when his replacement tank was hit. Fortunately the crew managed to escape into high corn, where they gained some kind of revenge by collecting twenty prisoners of the Hermann Goering regiment.

In a similar repeat action, Bill Close, seeing other tanks going up in flames, jumped out of his tank to help the wounded from other crews. His own tank was then hit. The gunner and operator were killed. He again had to commandeer another tank in order to resume giving orders to the remainder of the squadron. There was neither a way forward nor a safe way of reconnoitring close up to the enemy.[4] Away to the right 2 NY were probing towards Cormelles, but this was not a major coordinated attack. No plans would be made for a concerted advance until midday.

2 F&F's Lt Col Scott found that, with replacements, he had only twenty-five tanks available to fight. He allocated twelve to A Sqdn under Maj J.H.C. Powell and eleven to C Sqdn commanded by Capt J.E.F. Miller, who

had been knocked out the previous day. The remaining two tanks constituted the regiment's HQ. As Maj Powell began to walk back to his tank from the O group the threatening sinister siren noise of Nebelwerfer bombs was heard. Through his periscope Terry Boyne saw Powell begin to run, ducking lower and lower. The clutch of bombs descended, exploded. Powell disappeared from Terry's periscope view. At that moment a wireless message came through for the major. His operator's voice responded, 'He is unable to answer.' He would never be able to answer.[5]

A conference of higher commanders now attempted to revitalize the entire operation. 3rd Inf Div on the left was ordered to attack Emieville. Four times they attacked. Four times they were rolled back by superior enemy fire power. The Guards again assaulted Cagny and Four. The Desert Rats now had enough people forward to advance towards Soliers and Bourguebus, the latter village already known to the frustrated attackers as Buggers' Bus and similar variants.

The motor coys of 8 RB were once more allocated to the armoured regiments. Bill Close's long suffering squadron heard that 2 NY were to capture Bras before 3 RTR had another 'go' at the crest around Hubert-Folie. Although the 'open, level plain' was a constant chorus theme of the Goodwood operation, it was not all level just as it was not all open. The area through which 3 RTR had probed was *Les Fossettes*, the Dimples, represented on the map by a swirl of close contours. The fateful iron ore railway ran on top of a 20-ft-high embankment outside Soliers, but within 300 yards it descended to ground level and then plunged into a 20-ft-deep cutting by Hubert-Folie, so irregular was the ground. In reality the railway did not 'descend' at all but simply failed to keep up with the sharp incline of the land. This dimple effect did give some room for manoeuvre if it was possible to escape the prying eyes of the German gunners.

2 NY were officially designated as the armoured reconnaissance regiment of the 11th. They were equipped with the lighter Cromwell tanks. They had no Sherman Firefly. The new lengthened, strengthened and upgunned Cromwell variant called the Challenger had not yet been delivered to them. Now Bill Close warned the 2 NY colonel of the enemy 88s lying in wait at Ifs and elsewhere on the ridge. Undergunned and with frail armour plate, 2 NY were ordered to take Bras.

Keith Jones was a rear link officer in 2 NY. The tank's wireless set had three networks. There was intercom on which the entire crew could speak. There was 'A' set which carried the voices of the commanders of all fighting tanks, on which the individual crews could eavesdrop. Then there was 'B' set or rear link, a restricted circuit on which the rear link officer could talk more securely to the colonel commanding the regiment. The problem with this system was that when Keith's squadron leader Maj McGillycuddy, 'Big Mac', was giving orders urgently on A set, Keith had difficulty in transmitting the colonel's even more urgent orders to Big Mac. More than once Keith had to descend from his own tank, climb on to Big Mac's and thump him on the shoulder to deliver the message orally. It did not help that Big Mac had been hit behind the ear by shrapnel, was bleeding profusely and almost deafened.[6] (Other regiments ignored the B set and the colonels took the risk of talking to their squadron leaders over the open A set.)[7]

Watching the squadron tanks move towards Bras Keith felt that the enemy gun and mortar fire was even heavier and more accurate on the 19th than on the 18th. It was also clear to him that the advance was slower than the mad charge of the 18th. He saw 'Panzer-Grenadiers digging in at exemplary speed on a slope between Cormelles and Bras. They disappeared below ground with the despatch of crabs into sand. Their camouflage was remarkable.' 2 NY's orders sent them out of the woods near Cormelles and out of sight of Bras, but 'the whole operation out in the open would be under observation from enemy artillery-spotters on higher ground further south along the ridge, as well as initially from places along the river valley to the west where the Canadians had not yet reached like Ifs.'

The right-hand squadron moved into the gap between Ifs and Bras and the forebodings of Bill Close and Keith Jones proved correct. Here again it was a 'duck shoot' or a 'skittle alley' as the 88s blasted into action against Cromwells whose guns could not reach the hideouts of their tormentors. The squadron disintegrated and its Maj Peck was killed. Keith's own group of tanks crested a slight rise and there just in front of them was the desirable village of Bras. At that moment the 'B' set came to life, again sending Keith over to Big Mac's tank with the message, 'Orders! You will

NOT close to the objective. Halt well clear of the perimeter. Make feint attack by maintaining fire into area until ordered to stop. Real attack will be made from other side by friends on left [3 RTR]. Acknowledge. Over.'

Both 2 F&F and 3 RTR had been advised that 2 NY would be making the main attack on Bras. Somebody told the 2 NY colonel something different. Whatever the truth, Lt Col Silvertop of 3 RTR picked up the torch and sent his remaining tanks with infantry of 8 RB into and through the defiant village. The 8 RB report identified the enemy as 1SS Panzer, 'the Adolf Hitler Div, which has, if any Div has, the right to be called the crack Div of the German Army'. The report continued that 'the speed of the attack and the mopping up was such that almost the whole garrison was killed or taken prisoner and their 3rd Bn was considered largely written off.'

As 8 RB's G Coy joined up with 2 F&F to occupy Hubert-Folie (known to 8 RB as Hubert's Folly), there was a moment of frustration and inter-regimental anger:

> They were held up for while by what seemed to be Bren [Browning] fire from a Sherman, and they said some hard things about 2 F&F Yeo: but it turned out to be a Hun who had got into one of our Shermans knocked out the day before and once discovered he was soon liquidated. The clearing of the village took a short time; it appeared to contain only a few stragglers from Bras.

In Bill Close's squadron at the end of the battle only his and Sgt Kite's tanks survived. The flank squadron of 2 NY had been virtually eliminated. Similarly other units had again lost tanks in situations such as that described by Keith Jones: 'The whole area was becoming a Hades of flame and smoke, tree splinters and other debris. I had seen nothing human there . . . and yet it was illusory because the enemy *was* there, making the best of available cover.' Keith himself was invoking the colonel's authority to evict the bleeding, deafened, cursing Big Mac from his turret and evacuate him.

Big Mac was only one in what seemed an unending procession of burned and wounded, being carried or guided back for treatment, with the MO of the 3rd SS P-g battalion, now a prisoner, lending professional aid. Generally front-line soldiers commiserated with the enemy wounded. Keith Jones's crew spotted what appeared to be several dead Germans in a large crater. When one of the corpses moved Keith jumped down to have a closer look. The Germans were all alive but badly wounded. Keith's crew agreed that, although their own drinking water supply was almost exhausted in the heat-wave weather, the wounded needed water more than the unscathed. Someone found an old tin hat with a bullet hole through it, carefully poured water into it and lowered it to the most active of the Germans. John Finnis, age 23, took command of the squadron.

Among the often unsung heroes of the battlefield were the stretcher bearers, frequently denied the opportunity to duck and dive when everybody else was taking cover. Sgt George Cooper of the Regina Rifles witnessed one act which engraved itself on his memory:

Noted a stretcher bearer calmly going into the open field while shrapnel was still scattering all around, to attend to a bleeding soldier, staying in the open to apply a tourniquet and then remaining crouched over the wounded soldier until the shelling moved on. Only then did he come back to get a volunteer to help carry the wounded one back to where we sheltered in our slit trenches. No time to write a citation![8]

Regiments had been careful to assure their men that there would be quick and efficient attention for the wounded. The padre of 24th Lancers had even written an article entitled 'R.I.P. at the R.A.P.' describing procedure. First it would be a nearby aid post 'where the MO will be tying you up, no big stuff'. Then a couple of miles to a Casualty Clearing Point, 'more elaborate treatment but not lengthy. Here the very-nearly-dead are raised to life by blood transfusions.' Then to an Advance Dressing Station or a Casualty Clearing Station, 'complete with operating theatre, dental surgeon and "real nurses" . . . then shipped back to England.' And so you would not need the services of the padre![9]

In reality there were always problems. The MO of 23rd Hussars confessed that 'my own medical crews were three short and we had to replace them with untrained men from reserve tank crews'.[10] Then, of course, on 18 and 19 July there was an 'epidemic' of critical burns cases to an extent (in total cases and in percentage burns to bodies) never before encountered. Those burning petrol Shermans were responsible.

Maj Gordon Brown of the Regina Rifles had been admitted to a British 'field hospital' for removal of a piece of shrapnel which had struck a vertebra, and was shocked at what he saw:

> While I was in the hospital there were more than 300 British tank soldiers arrived. All wounded and in many cases burned very badly. I went with one of the Medical Officers to see the wounded men. It was one of the most sad experiences that I ever had. . . . I had great admiration for our tank crews who lived very much on the edge, and who suffered so terribly when their tanks burst into flame.[11]

Nobody had demonstrated to tank crews before D-Day how suddenly and viciously Shermans could flame. Nor had the good padres explained that at that time nothing much could be done for burns cases in the first few miles of evacuation. The standing regulation at that time was that 'no major burn case should receive any local treatment at the first-aid station apart from covering the exposed burn areas with clean cloths or *tulle gras*'. (*Tulle gras* was a dressing made from wide mesh curtain netting to allow discharges to seep through, and then impregnated with vaseline and Balsam of Peru.)[12] Also, very relevant to areas where decaying corpses lay long unburied, was the warning about the danger to raw burn wounds from flies, described as 'streptococcus-disseminating villains', against whom, failing a 'flit gun', the main weapon would be the simple 'swotter'.

The humblest soldier was aware of the need to bury the dead, both as a hygiene precaution and as a mark of respect for those who had their 'names on a bullet'. Laurie Lacey was relieved of that duty by his considerate captain, but the troop of Geoff Hayward, 2 F&F, surrounded by dead bodies, was asked for volunteers to bury some of the dead. Geoff did not relish the task of removing corpses from burned-out tanks, often requiring ropes to lift the charred bodies, which then disintegrated back into the turret. Only one volunteer emerged from Geoff's troop – a man who had been a grave-digger in civilian life.[13]

As the swelling procession of wounded and enemy prisoners continued to move to the rear, a much larger procession continued to urge its way forward. One heroic gunner, watching the tremendous toil of his men in manually unloading tons of ammunition, gave a thought also to those who brought the loads forward. The supply trucks came loaded with huge cargoes of live ammunition. An enemy shot into one of those 'soft-skinned' vehicles could cause a conflagration compared with which a brewing Sherman might be a mere flicker of a nightlight. The gunner admired the bravery of the sometimes derided 'tail' of the army:[14]

You ponder the lot of drivers who must toil night and day, moving up supplies of all kinds for the fighting troops, carrying on in obscurity, without the attention of war correspondents forever preoccupied with infantry and tank units with proud names and regional associations. Churchill said it so well before the turn of the century in his book *The River War*: 'Victory is the bright-coloured flower. Transport is the stem without which it could never have blossomed.'

As the tank formations opened out, infantry battalions moved through to clear the obstinate enemy resistance in villages with their solid stone-built farms and cottages. Reg Robbins with the Herefords looked around him and saw that 'in this area the enemy had plenty of 88s and quite a few tanks and Moaning Minnies. There were snipers in farmhouses. It seemed that we were getting hit from three sides. In the daytime we had to keep our head down from 88s. And we had to be on our best guard when prowling around on patrol at night.'[15]

Canadian footsloggers directly south of Caen had been successful in clearing difficult villages and suburbs, including Louvigny, Cormelles and later Ifs. The elite German SS defenders now launched a massive and merciless counter-attack against the threatening Canadian spearheads, causing bloodshed equal to any in Canadian history. Units like the South Saskatchewans and Essex Scottish could do little in the face of the massed Panzers. One company trying to advance ran into m-g nests in manure piles, haystacks and the tall wheat. Enemy rocket planes flew down at the few Canadian tanks. The churning tracks of huge Panzers crashed over partially dug slit trenches, crushing bodies of men lying exposed in a pea field or crouching in the wheat. More Panzers appeared on the flanks, pouring a continuous fire of high explosive and m-g tracer bullets into the infantry platoons, whose clumsy PIAT anti-tank tubes were smashed one by one.[16] An Essex Scots corporal was left commanding the remains of his company.

The Guards and 7th armoured divisions had been allocated tasks to try to maintain movement towards the original objectives, once so near, now seeming so far away. The 5th Guards armoured brigade had been given the objective of capturing Vimont but found an impassible screen of hidden, well-dug-in 88s across its path. Its orders were reduced to an injunction that it was important to 'HOLD' Cagny. In the 7th Armoured Div it was 5 RTR which was given the task of finally subduing the vital ridge village of Bourguebus. Frustrated by the 'crush of people' on 18 July, 5 RTR set out for Soliers and by 1120 on the 19th had entered that village, the enemy drawing back judiciously. But an advance by 5 RTR towards Bourguebus at 1740 found the enemy not yet disposed to yield that strong point, and at 1855 it was agreed that Bourguebus could not be taken that evening. It seemed almost as though the Germans were dictating the speed of the British advance. However, 5 RTR persisted and on 20 July occupied the village with its incredible views right across the entire 'open plain' of Goodwood.

Another Desert Rats regiment, 4 CLY, which had suffered direly at the hands of Michael Wittmann some time previously, now had an opportunity to redeem its reputation. This time it could be said that 4 CLY did too well! They went where no Allied soldier had been, and where none would stand upright again for quite a while, high on the Verrières segment of the ridges.

4 CLY had followed 3 RTR and 2 F&F in the area of Bras. John Cloudsley-Thompson was 3 troop leader among his regiment's lead tanks as they breasted the skyline (18 July) and tucked in behind a hedgerow. 'Cornfields sloped gently for nearly a mile up to the hedge, giving absolutely no cover and in front seven burning Cromwells [of 2 NY] indicated that an earlier attack had failed.' John's regiment were also 'horsed' on the vulnerable Cromwells, although with support from a small number of Firefly Shermans.

They had clear evidence of what German guns could do to Cromwells venturing into empty space. They were ordered to stay there all night.

'We were all rather frightened and two men from my Troop Corporal's tank came up and said they would rather face a Court Martial than go on.' It is easy to criticize such an attitude. But these men had been forced to sit and stare at the simmering incineration ovens that had been the Cromwell tanks; tanks just like their own; tanks committed to obedience of orders just like their own; tanks containing the blackened corpses of men just like themselves: in a prolonged preview of their own imminent cremation.

The troop survived the night and then, with Lt Alan Bailey's 1 troop alongside them, they moved into that menacing empty space, ringed with woods and farms where enemy guns could lurk, 2,000 yards away, invisible, yet fully able to brew up Cromwells. 'German infantry were hiding in the corn all round us [no doubt armed with the very effective hand-held, tank-destroying rocket launcher, the Panzerfaust]: we fired at them with machine-guns and high explosive. Took many prisoners. . . . The blast from our gun set fire to a haystack . . . a sergeant tank commander captured a small ridge firing a Sten gun from the turret of his tank when both his machine-gun and 75mm had jammed . . . we were shelled and mortared all the time.'

They crossed the main Caen–Falaise road, drove up the slope and captured a small wood in the area of Troteval Farm. German tanks were reported as approaching. The two troops disposed themselves in the wood, facing outwards in all directions. They did not know that this was the high-water mark of Goodwood. To them it was just another defensive position where to await the rest of the army. Nobody else arrived!

At this point, John recalls, 'The shelling continued and several tanks were hit. [Not being solid shot the shells did not knock out any tanks]. The explosions were deafeningly close and although the air reeked of cordite and petrol we thought it wiser to close the turret flaps in case a shell should fall inside. [Moaning Minnies fell vertically.] The sun shone warmly and I could barely keep awake.'

They were relieved, if a little disappointed, when the wireless crackled and ordered them to withdraw. They had been sitting on a prime target for a Canadian artillery barrage of hundreds of guns, preparatory to a massed infantry attack towards Troteval. It would have been very difficult to amend the barrage. Much easier to move a few tanks a mile or two back.

The men of the two troops felt added relief as numbers of more powerful German tanks began to appear on the skyline. The Cromwells, possibly the fastest tanks of their size, turned tail and bolted for the hedgerow where their Firefly tanks had lined up. The Germans began to fire and to follow. The 4 CLY men in the Cromwells were astonished to see Bob Moore's Firefly shoot at the enemy while the range was still a vast 2,300 yards. Amazingly the shot hit home 'bang' on target, and the enemy tank burst into flames. 'Cheers for the Firefly', they all shouted over the intercom, 'that'll teach the buggers.' Even a Tiger would have difficulty in essaying such a range.[17]

The Canadian infantry who followed up the barrage made good progress at first but then typically were subjected to ferocious counter-attacks by overwhelming concentrations of first-line SS Panzers. The French-speaking Le Régiment Maisonneuve (the Maisies) lost 200 out of a total strength of 300 riflemen. Les Fusiliers Mont-Royal had most of two companies destroyed, and for their final attack on the ridges, drew remnants from all companies to make up an under-strength attacking company.[18]

The Canadians fought on undeterred. Lt Gilles Gamache of the Fusiliers led his platoon towards Beauvoir Farm. Most of his men were killed or wounded en route. He himself was badly wounded. Reaching the entrance to the farm he seized a Bren gun and went in shooting. He then formed a defence and beat off counter-attacks from front and rear until he collapsed from loss of blood. He was one of very few lieutenants to be awarded the Distinguished Service Order. In spite of such gallantry the area where 4 CLY tanks had stood briefly was still being disputed fourteen days later.

4 CLY with the remainder of the division were then loaned to the Canadians for a period in a mainly defensive role on the Verrières slopes. Charles Pearce would never forget that they were 'continually bombed and shelled for the next ten days'. The Desert Rats' own report described those days as probably their worst experience in four years of warfare.[19]

Luftwaffe planes were as active as any time in north-west Europe. VIII Corps reported 159 brigade HQ hit by ME (Messerschmitt) 109s. 23 Hussars were attacked by thirty FW (Focke-Wulf) 190s. Eighteen ME 109s circled twice over the Monmouthshires near Bras, machine-gunning and rocketing them. twenty FWs strafed 7th Black Watch. All this was at a time when the British press was reporting that, with the Allied command of the air so total, the RAF was now able to release trained personnel for duties in other arms of the services.[20]

Identification of the enemy on the ground was still a major problem for pilots. The Regina Rifles expressed 'sudden amazement' when a Spitfire 'flew by and then came round from our rear and with its guns blazing strafed our column . . . with our yellow smoke and us waving yellow scarves he flew by dipping his wings as if to say "I'm sorry for the mistake". A few minutes later this lone US Thunderbolt at our rear released its bomb', killing men in the ammo column. Three young French lads, Michel Guillot, Roger Othon and André Quesnel, evacuated by the Germans from Bourguebus, were riding on their bicycles, mistaken by an RAF plane for enemy soldiers, strafed and killed.[21]

Ground troops, both Canadian and British, had no doubts about the morale effect on the enemy of the fast Typhoon rocket planes, which were originally credited with destroying many enemy tanks. However, later research suggested that indeed the most important impact of the Typhoons was on morale rather than on materiel. Scientists of No. 2 Operational Research Section combed the battlefields. They examined some hundreds of destroyed enemy armoured vehicles. Their report suggested that these tanks' 'demise was most often due to ground fire, mechanical defect, destruction by crew or lack of fuel', and relatively few from air-borne rockets. From the same research it was caculated that 'the cannon and machine-gun of the Spitfire [and Mustang] proved the most effective in ground attack, in other words strafing.'[22]

The dual depredations of air and ground fire, Allied and enemy, left the French countryside devastated and villages uninhabitable. The evacuated residents of Bourguebus, returning home in September, found their houses flattened and dozens of knocked-out vehicles fouling the fertile earth, in some places rendering it infertile for over half a century. Only the bakery (still in existence today) and one farm remained standing. In Soliers one house was habitable. In Hubert-Folie none. It would be three months before all streets were cleared of obstructions, two years before prefabricated huts began to arrive from Sweden to replace the temporary shelters amid ruins, and eight years before basic services were fully restored.[23]

For military reasons the Germans had evacuated all inhabitants from the villages which were to be converted into strongpoints. Some French people did hide away to escape evacuation, as did Jean Cardon at Bourguebus, only to be shot. One exception was made. The mother of André Lechipey had just given birth to daughter Mado. It had been a very difficult confinement and Madame Lechipey was critically ill. A German MO certified that she could not be moved. So with her sister and 11-year-old André and one other daughter she was allowed to stay in their small farm on the outskirts of Frenouville, then only a few houses in the countryside. Other relatives and friends heard about the exemption of the Lechipey farm. Furtively they found their way into barns and cellars there until a total of nineteen people were sheltering on the property, fourteen of them illegally.[24]

As the uproar of battle became louder and closer, with bombs and shells beginning to fall on all sides, André came in from herding the animals to safety. He held his mother's hand, trying to be the 'big man' around the house. But the big man was badly scared when a German soldier burst into the house, armed with a sub-machine-gun, and charged up the stairs into a bedroom. From behind a curtain the man watched for British infantry approaching over the fields.

Three times little André heard and saw British soldiers advancing along the street beyond the house. Three times he saw them withdraw as German bullets combed the open space, smashing windows and thudding into stone walls. From upstairs came the rattle of the uninvited guest's gun as he fired down into the street. At the third rush of British guardsmen there was a scream from the bedroom. The German tumbled down the stairs and into the main room where the family were cowering. He was bleeding profusely. André's aunt ripped open his tunic. She made bandages from strips of old shirts. She cleaned the man's wound. Having no other salve she poured neat Calvados on to the wound. The man screamed again. The aunt bound the wound as best she could. She gave the German a push and he ran into the street and away before the guardsmen made their fourth and successful advance among the houses.

An impressionable 11-year-old, André saw Irish Guards advancing and their 30-ton Sherman Firefly tank come down the street, with the name Ballymena painted on it. 'Ballymena' meant nothing to the boy at the time, but the sight registered indelibly on his memory. Nearly half a century later he would purchase the wreckage of a wartime tank and recreate Ballymena in all its glory, complete with the painted Guards' emblem of the watching eye, in his own industrial workshops at St-Malo as a tribute to the liberators. He would also motivate like-minded people around Cagny to unearth the Spitfire which had been shot down when taking photographs.

After all considerations of upgunning and undergunning, the outcome of a battle often depended on morale. Andrew Horne, a driver who had to bale out of three Cromwells, 'was frightened many a time' but got through by 'thinking that my Maker was looking after me'. He repeated what numbers of soldiers said, 'There were no atheists before going into battle.' Also Andrew thought that humour sustained them at the sharp end. When his regiment, 1 RTR, were so close to the enemy they joked that they were 'doing Orderly Sergeant for the Jerries'.[25]

Humour often derived from shared experiences of soldiers thrown together at random. The 'Micks' laughed about Sir John's bath. Major Sir John Reynolds had a collapsible bath, and when he was away his servant, or batman, Charles Parker, obtained permission to use it. The Regimental Sergeant-Major then appeared and insisted on having a bath himself. Others queued up. Suddenly, unexpectedly the shadow of Sir John himself fell across the sun-warmed bath. He then chastised the trembling Parker: 'I don't mind you using my bath; I don't mind the RSM using my bath; but I don't want the whole bloody regiment using my bath.'[26]

The German were not as humourless as sometimes portrayed. Maligning the Luftwaffe as usual, they said of aeroplanes, 'If it's white, it's American; if it's black it's British; if you can't see it, it's the Luftwaffe.'[27] German morale was not always totally resolute, especially in the case of conscripted non-German nationals. One little boy herding goats near Emieville saw a section of German infantry crossing a field, led by an officer. As they approached the officer shouted an order and then he himself dashed behind a bush. The men marched on and disappeared. The little goatherd began to wonder about the state of the officer's bowels. But, after a while, the officer emerged from the bushes, now dressed in the civilian clothes of a French farm labourer, and walked off in the opposite direction.[28]

Generally, during Goodwood, the German soldiers felt that the 11th Armoured had 'had the air taken out of it'. They were confident that 'the loss of a position did not mean a breakthrough would follow'.[29] It must be remembered, points out SS tank commander Gerhard Stiller, that while for many British tank men in Goodwood it was the first and perhaps the major event of their soldiering, for the 1st SS men it was 'just a quick memory' a 'single episode between numerous battles east and west'.[30] Philip Brookshaw of 3 RTR was not alone in observing that 'the SS divisions particularly didn't know what the words "give up" meant. They were red hot . . . and Goodwood was the nastiest operation of the lot.'[31]

7 Panzer Coy of 1st SS felt very confident in their principles of defence, which insisted on:

1. perfect camouflage along the hedgerows;
2. maintain absolute radio silence, communication only by messenger and flare signals for an enemy attack;
3. no opening fire without express orders from a company leader.

The Charging Bull history points out that the Germans were even prepared to shell Bras while their own defenders were still in the village, on the assumption that more attackers than defenders would be hit. A ruthless 'percentage game'.

Most reports of the fighting, involving two of the SS divisions most accused of infamous conduct, suggest that Goodwood was carried on strictly according to the accepted rules of warfare. Exceptions were noted. An army MO awaiting the start of Goodwood wrote, 'I attended here my first civilian patient, a little girl suffering from a grenade wound in the head and a revolver wound in the shoulder, both of which were caused by SS soldiers who had also raped her mother and killed her father. Where the SS had been, the French were markedly pro-British!'[32]

The German Army certainly needed to maintain its morale at this time for the most remarkable casualty of Goodwood, at some distance from the field, was the most famous Nazi general of them all, Erwin Rommel, the commander on the spot. He had been, perhaps, too much 'on the spot' as his car hurried in daylight along Normandy roads noted for the danger of RAF and USAAF attacks. Rommel was only severely wounded when his car was hit and crashed. It was Hitler himself who ended the general's life. He compelled Rommel to take poison after the failure of the plot to assassinate the Führer at the time of Goodwood, in which Rommel was implicated. As to the bomb plot against him, Hitler's own original 1920s and 1930s bodyguard, now 1st SS 'Life Guard Adolf Hitler' were far distant from the scene of the attempted assassination. They would only comment that 'the men were too involved in [Goodwood] combat to give it much thought'.

As the earthbound mortals slugged away in the increasing impasse of Goodwood a greater power sought again to intervene, as more than once in Normandy – the weather god. John Cloudsley-Thompson, sweating in his Cromwell in the heat of 20 July did not, as he might have done in peacetime, think 'there's a storm on the way'. Smoke obscured the thunderclouds and gun flashes feinted for the lightning. Artillery drummed out the rolls of approaching thunder. 'Quite suddenly the sun went in,' John noted 'and it started to pour with rain.'

With the greatest bang of all, the weather god had again called, 'Halt!' For many Goodwood soldiers their actual battle memories are hardly more remarkable than their sufferings from two extraneous factors, the Demouville mosquitoes or flies, and the Great Storm. At 1500, 20 July, the Canadian Camerons reported 'raining very heavily'.

The Scottish Seaforths echoed, 'The Thunderstorm burst upon us and by evening the whole place was a shambles. Nothing that human ingenuity could devise would keep the tide at bay. We bailed. We made roofs with capes. We piled compo boxes into the mud and lay on them, only to be awakened as the water lapped over the top. By the morning our trenches had three feet of water in them.'[34] 7th Black Watch were still at the infamous Demouville when 'the deluge started. It was amazing how quickly everything turned into a morass; there was no real shelter for anyone as the village had been flattened; slit trenches deep in muddy water . . . a very brief taste of 1914–18 conditions . . . the Guards tanks were completely bogged down in the quagmire.'[35] A gunner in his dug-out found 'muddy water, pouring steadily down the earthen steps, has risen almost up to your crotch'.[36]

On the Canadian sector, steep as it was, 'the flooding had the effect of returning the surrounding sewage, faeces from live humans and worse from dead bodies into the tiny slit trench'. More importantly, 'heat-wave dust settling on guns, then heavy rain which turned dust to clogging mud' made 'keeping weapons in working order impossible', even though men tore up their shirts for cleaning rags.[37] Tanks sank deeper and deeper as their desperately churning tracks dug into the slush. In all this, Sid Jones and fitters like him worked continuously for three days and nights under shelling, retrieving wrecked tanks, cannibalizing some to repair others, and still removing the fetid bodies of crew members.

Among the prime human movers, Field Marshal von Kluge, uncertain as to whether or not he should become party to the assassination attempt on Hitler, lost his initial enthusiasm for the defence of Normandy. On 22 July he wrote to Hitler, 'In face of the enemy's complete command of the air, there is no possibility of our finding a strategy which will counterbalance its truly annihilating effect, unless we give up the field of battle. . . . The moment has drawn near when this front, already so heavily strained, will break.'[38]

Montgomery was continuing his policy of obfuscation and obstruction. His head of operations and planning believed that in Goodwood 'he succeeded in his purpose'.[39] Others thought that Goodwood had fallen far short of his expectations. There is evidence that Dempsey, O'Connor and Roberts all had much higher expectations.[40] Whatever the expectations the storm had terminated Goodwood, so it was said, and has been frequently repeated. 'But this was rubbish; it had been stopped two days before'[41] by the Germans' immediate, devastating and demoralizing reaction.

British losses in numbers of tanks knocked out were astronomic. But the actual numbers killed in action were, as one historian puts it, 'curiously few' because so few infantry were involved. Brewing tanks are horrific but statistically less significant than would have been the case in any infantry attack. Progress was made. A recent American study calculates that Goodwood gained 34 square miles of territory and netted 2,000 enemy prisoners, for 4,000 casualties and one-third of the British armoured force in Normandy.[42]

A salient factor is the comparative permanence of 'writing down' of the enemy, which was one of Montgomery's proclaimed objectives. On the British side replacement of men and equipment was almost immediate. On 17 July 2 NY started with seventy-two fit armoured vehicles. By evening 18 July this had fallen to forty-six fit and on 19 July to thirty-five fit. But during the night of 19 July the regiment was restored to 73 per cent strength and by 21 July to 100 per cent, men and vehicles.[43] By contrast in the four weeks to 1 August 1st SS Panzer Div had lost 1,413 men, but had received only eight reinforcements and five returned from hospital. They could assemble only 101 out of 182 Mark IV and V tanks, with hardly a replacement in view.[44]

An interesting fact is pointed out by the man who would command the remains of Britain's Yeomanry after the Wilsons, Thatchers and Blairs had depleted Britain's armoured resources to an extent that Hitler never achieved. The number of tanks knocked out during Goodwood, about 400, exceeds the total tank strength of the present British Army at the turn of the Millennium.[45]

Some have questioned British soldiers' determination to fight. When 'Big Mac', Maj McGillycuddy, was finally expelled from his tank, bleeding and cursing profusely in equal measures, he was sedated and ferried back to a British hospital. Waking up at night and finding himself in a hospital bed, he got up and, locating his uniform in a cupboard, dressed quietly and escaped from the hospital. Outside he hitched a lift to the nearest docks. There he hitched another lift on a supply ship. Just as another officer was being given command of his squadron he reappeared like an inflated ghost, declaring, with many extra-curricular words, 'Oh, no! It's MY squadron.'[46]

CHAPTER EIGHT

COBRA UNDER THE CARPET

'Anything you can do, I can do better' was a contemporary song that some GIs might have wanted to sing when American Operation Cobra succeeded British Operation Goodwood in July 1944.

As in Goodwood, there were massed armored divisions waiting to pounce. As in Goodwood, there were a thousand or more bombers sitting on UK runways, bombed-up, ready to go. As in Goodwood, there would be an urgent quest for wide open tank country. As in Goodwood, there would be the tactical snag of a great wheel to the right. But, while in Goodwood there was a river to cross, in Cobra it was a road that intervened.

And what a road – white, wide, open, straight, clear, empty and menacing. St-Lo to Perriers and Lessay. Along that road an enemy 88 could fire with impunity at anything within 2,000 yard range. Along that road eyes would be watching through thick hedges, noting any attempt to advance and bringing down the massed fire of Nebelwerfers, with their howling vertically falling bombs, and Spandau m-gs, with their calico-ripping rasp of rapid firing. Beyond that road waited the elite Panzer Lehr, in theory a teaching division but in reality a fusion of highly skilled instructors culled from training regiments and well-trained graduates from those regiments. And some GIs were already almost too tired and shattered to cross the width of that road, even at a pedestrian crossing.

Montgomery had forecast that once Bradley's First Army 'can get a footing on that road, it will be able to deliver a real blitz attack'.[1] But Montgomery had not spent the previous seven weeks slogging through the notorious *bocage*, which, on the American sector, extended far more to the south than on the British sector. In their drive to reach St-Lo, the Americans had 'eaten the guts out of the German defence . . . the whole battle is one tremendous bloodbath, such as I have never seen in eleven years of war', said German 84 Corps commander, von Choltitz, a First World War veteran.[2]

The *bocage* had taken many Americans, farmers included, by surprise. Tank driver Martin Goldstein summed it up, 'Surprisingly our Intelligence, I don't know why, they did not brief us about the hedgerows. We had to learn the hard way. I never visualized a hedge to be so high, 2 or 3 ft maybe, but these were 8, 10 or 12 ft high.'[3] With their 'corned beef tin thin' bottom armour the Shermans presented a luscious target to German defenders as the tanks tilted up to climb over the high banks on which the hedges were planted. So it became largely a frightening and wasting infantry affair of silently slithering, suddenly striking human snakes. Or as one soldier described it, 'living like moles in deep, mud-filled holes'.[4]

A German lieutenant climbed out of his slit, over a *bocage* hedge and jumped down into an American slit the other side – the two 'front lines'. Fortunately for the German, Walter Padberg, the astonished GI fired harmlessly between Padberg's legs, and the latter, like a man shot from a gun, vaulted back the way he came. Another GI slit was invaded by a real snake. One man picked it up with a forked stick and tossed it into the nearest German trench. So near! Yet another observer, Ernie Pyle, saw the 'hedgerow business' as 'thousands and thousands of little skirmishes, no single one of them very big' . . . but added up . . . 'you've got a man-sized war with thousands on both sides being killed'.[5]

The casualties before the commencement of Cobra had indeed been enormous and immensely discouraging to the men who crawled forward, hedge by hedge, ditch by ditch, yard by yard, with no visible objective or notion of final triumph. In one fifteen-day period before St-Lo, rifle platoons in the US 30th Inf Div were estimated to have suffered 90 per cent casualties.[6] From 4 to 16 July American infantry advanced 10 kilometres nearer St-Lo at a cost of 10,000 men (one per metre). 90th Div needed 150 per cent officer replacements and 100 per cent other ranks.[7] An officer of 314th Regiment likened the list of his unit's casualties to a list from a telephone book.[8]

Tank men, unable to see over the high hedges, found the *bocage* equally horrifying and frustrating. A tank captain recalled an incident which he was aware of but heartily glad not to have been directly involved in:

The American tank company had pulled into a small field to spend the night. The tanks were dispersed around the hedgerow boundaries. In the middle of the night another column of tanks came down the road and pulled into the same field. As you know, Normandy nights are as black as any I have ever seen. There was a man on guard duty in the turret of each of the first arrivals, waiting to find out more about this new group, but of course assuming they were Americans.

Gradually the motors of the new arrivals were shut off. A momentary silence followed. Then a voice shouted something in German. Another man replied in German. There was laughter and sound of people getting out of the tanks, preparing to eat and settle in for the night. Everyone was wide awake by this time but no one knew what to do. Suddenly someone opened up on the Germans with a tommy gun and that set it off. Guns blazed from every side of the encampment, some of the bullets obviously hitting their own tanks on the other side of the field. The Germans, of course, were overpowered and helpless, with a few taken captive.[9]

The incident may seem somewhat hilarious but aptly illustrates the problems of fighting in the very poorly charted fields. The incident was also tragic for the American tank captain, an artist and book illustrator in peacetime, who had fingers torn off his painting hand.

A major contribution to offsetting the bulwarks of the hedgerows was made by a humble group of tank men discussing the problem, literally at ground level. There already existed Sherman tanks fitted with bulldozer blades, and these could dig through hedges. But they were too few to make a major impact on the battle. Jack Broadhurst was a tank driver who had to swim ashore on D-Day. A strut holding up the canvas gunwales of his amphibious tank had broken and Jack was ordered overboard to hold on to the strut as the tank struggled ashore. The crew then transferred to a dozer tank. But Jack found that the dozer was used for a multiplicity of tasks, smashing through hedges, scooping up mines, pushing knocked out vehicles off the roads, clearing ruined buildings and so on.[10] More hedgerow-clearing equipment was urgently needed.

A recce sergeant named Roberts, who had an agricultural background, suggested fitting ploughshares to the front of a Sherman and 'ploughing' through the hedges. The idea was viable, but a French comment points out that the Contentin area was basically stock-breeding farmland, so that spare ploughshares would be hard to find.[11] It was Roberts's colleague, Sgt Curtis Culin (with the unlikely background of a cab driver from Chicago but now of 102 Recce Battalion) who gained lasting fame with a brilliant variation of Roberts's idea. Culin said, in effect, 'If we can't get enough ready-made ploughshares, surely there's enough scrap metal on the beaches, the remains of the D-Day defences, to provide "tusks"?'

On 22 July Lt Belton Cooper was summoned to an impressive meeting of top brass in a field with the Divisional Commander, Maj Gen Watson, and none other than General Patton present. They were to watch a demonstration by a tank fitted with Culin's tusks, four heavy prongs mounted on a bar down at the front of the tank. The spikes embedded themselves in the hedge bank, cut the hedge roots and then the weight of the tank was sufficient to shovel the entire mass forward, thus scooping out a gaping hole in the obstacle.

Watson expected that his division would have to attack the next day, and it was calculated that fifty-seven of the new devices would be necessary. His engineer, Col Cowhey, immediately stated that he would have fifty-seven ready and welded on to tanks by 0700 next morning. Cowhey then called Cooper and other practical engineers and said, in appropriate terms, 'Do it!' Warrant Officer Douglas, a peacetime welder, effectively took charge, other welders were assembled, and the job was done on time – because bad weather fortunately delayed the attack. Some of the welders worked so long without rest that they became temporarily blinded by the welding arc.[12] Culin saw the motions of the adapted tanks as similar to the burrowing antics of the rhinoceros, and so 'Rhino tanks' they became for posterity.[13]

The invention of the Rhino, while only partially solving one of several combat problems, was most opportune in the framework of action proposed by Supreme Commander Eisenhower. He was expecting the feint attack in the Noyers/Evrecy area to be followed by Goodwood on 18 July and Cobra on 19 July. He then anticipated either a land dash to grab the Brittany ports or a combined amphibious/airborne assault on the same ports.[14] The feint attack and the Goodwood strike got off on schedule, but the start of Cobra was delayed until 24 July and then 25 July for three main reasons.

Firstly, after the harrowing bloodletting in the *bocage*, it was only on 18 July that Maj Gen Corlett's XIX Corps eventually smashed through into St-Lo, the pivotal city for Cobra's start. VII Corps on the right cleared the area north of the vital road from St-Lo through to Lessay. Secondly, Gen Bradley considered that some American units needed more time for training and reorganization before being launched into 'the Big One'. Thirdly, the gods of weather, having successfully intervened in Goodwood, switched their legions of thunder, lightning, rain and mist to Cobra.

Eisenhower's own words reported the storms 'turning the low-lying country into a sea of mud which afforded an effective check to further tank operations. . . . The men of the First Army were compelled to huddle in their foxholes under the dripping hedgerows in conditions of extreme discomfort.' A somewhat more farcical delay was noted by the British Chief of the Imperial General Staff (CIGS), Viscount Alanbrooke. Mr Stimson, the US Secretary for War, was visiting the UK and Normandy. 'Stimson had visited Bradley's HQ and had remained with him so long that orders for an attack could not go out, and the attack had to be postponed for 24 hours.'[15]

The grand plan for Cobra relied on a massive air bombardment as its first phase. An area, one mile deep beyond the main road and for five miles along the road itself, would be saturation bombed by 'the greatest air show of the war'.[16] The infantry (4, 9 and 30 Divs) would then surge across the road and walk through the carpet-bombed fields. Once the infantry had opened up a gap, the 'heavy Armored Divisions', 2nd and 3rd, would dash through. However, beyond the 'carpet' area the main roads ran diagonally across the direction of the initial attack, so the armored divisions would have to wheel right in order to follow the outline of the terrain. The spearheads had three main concerns: first, to occupy the dominating features of ground; second, to bypass enemy strongpoints; and thirdly to keep roads clear for essential battle traffic.[17]

Commanders sought to encourage the already weary infantry by forecasting that the carpet bombing would totally eliminate all opposition in the rectangle of countryside beyond the main road. Some soldiers were so convinced that they almost expected to have a summer afternoon's stroll, trailing rifles, to their objectives. Others were not so naïve. One veteran remembered the colonel coming to brief each company as to the simplicity of the job before them, stating that 'it would be "just Remington rifles against bows and arrows". When the Colonel had gone the Captain growled "Y'all heard what the man said, but remember, arrows can kill". One GI near me snorted "Yeah, and remember Custer!"'[18]

What encouraged most GIs more than such extravagant forecasts was the knowledge that the control of the main attack would be in the capable hands of 'Lightning Joe' Collins. Described as 'looking far younger than his forty-eight years he was known as "the GI's General". He drove his commanders and his men hard . . . his policy to hit hard and keep the enemy on the run . . . but he was no "smash-and-grab" commander. Thorough in planning and flexible in direction, he was most adept at subtlety and surprise.'[19]

But before Lightning Joe could smash his steel gauntlet through the enemy defences there was to be an internecine warfare of ideas between soldiers and airmen. Gen Bradley wanted the air fleet to fly in longways, parallel to the main road and across the carpet area. He felt that this would prevent 'friendly' bombs dropping on massed US troops on the other side of the road. The airmen refused, saying that it would be impossible to identify targets and that the forward soldiers must withdraw some 3,000 yards from the road. Flying parallel and south of the road would expose them unduly to enemy anti-aircraft fire. They wanted to fly in over their own troops' heads. Bradley insisted on the parallel approach, allowing him to keep his troops close to the road, ready to leap across. He thought that his method had been agreed. He was in for a massive shock. The air chiefs did it their way.[20]

The glib forecasts of some commanders, together with subsequent jibes that 'the Yanks had an easy ride', ignore the reality of what could have awaited the Americans on 24 July. One estimate suggests that Panzer Lehr had forty-seven tanks available, 17 SS Panzer-Grenadiers had fifteen SP guns and 2 SS Pz had another sixty tanks.[21] When it is remembered what only four SPs did in the initial stages of Goodwood, the Cobra defence prior to the air attack has to be seen as formidable.

The Americans had no Firefly, their largest 76mm tank gun being little better than the normal Sherman 75mm. Eisenhower had written to his American chief, Marshall, on 5 July, 'I have just returned from a visit to the First Army where I found them deeply concerned over the inability of our present tank guns and anti-tank weapons to cope successfully with the German Panther and Tiger tanks. . . . Even from the flanks our present weapons and ammunition are not adequately effective.'[22] The German infantry, if weak in numbers, did not panic when overrun. 'Men isolated continued to fight on to the end in woods, orchards and standing corn; in thick country their snipers hung on . . . often using telescopic sights. The art of fighting in woods had been a feature of their training at Paderborn and Luneberg Heide.'[23]

In one way the delays caused by the gods of weather were 'a blessing in disguise' for the Americans. Responding to Goodwood and assuming that the Goodwood attack would be resumed immediately, the enemy command had moved 2nd SS Panzers from the St-Lo area towards Caen so that it was not available to bear the brunt of Cobra on 24 and 25 July. It was rushed back belatedly during 26 July.[24]

Early on 24 July the bad weather was still persisting but better was forecast. The Air Commander, British Leigh Mallory, had a problem. He had ordered the main air attack to start at 1000. At 1100 heavy cloud still hung over the carpet area. Leigh Mallory ordered 'Postpone until 1200.' Then at 1120, with little change in the cloud, he imposed an indefinite postponement. The vanguard of the vast air fleet had needed to take off and head for the St-Lo/Periers area well before bombing time. Things started to go wrong.

Not all the planes were in direct radio communication. Some carried on and bombed. Visibility was poor. One bomb aimer accidentally flipped his toggle switch and bombed a friendly airfield, destroying two P47s. Others seemed to have aimed by the 'informed guess' method. Under the American system, when a bomb leader released his bombs, his entire flight followed suit, so that a wrong decision by the leader caused all his planes to drop their bombs in a close pattern.

Three hundred and seventeen planes had carried on, dropping 10,124 HE and 1,822 fragmentation bombs, most of them on US troops. They had been flying in the way Bradley had prohibited. Twenty-five men of 30 Div were killed and 131 wounded.[25] US infantry who had moved back 3,000 yards from the bombing area now found that the Germans had immediately moved forward and taken over the positions north of the road. The foot men had to reconquer their own positions. The 39th Regt had to sustain a pitched battle for seven hours to regain the road trenches. Their 54-year-old colonel, Harry 'Paddy' Flint, grabbed three guns, went up front and inspired his tiring men. Enemy fire ripped through his clothes and then a sniper's bullet drilled into his skull. His dying words, however incorrect, were, 'You can't kill an Irishman. You can only make him mad.'[26]

While Bradley fulminated against the airmen, the episode of apparently grave bungling had a fortunate by-product. Fog in the air linked to fog in the mind allowed some German commanders to deduce that they had decisively repulsed a major attack – the cobra's head had been crushed. Bayerlein, commanding the Panzer Lehr, 'ignorant of the fact that Allied plans had gone awry . . . congratulated himself on the achievement of his troops. They had apparently repelled a major American effort and prevented the troops from crossing the Periers–St-Lo highway.'[27] Higher up the command structure, Gen von Bock was also of the same opinion.

Von Kluge was puzzled and indecisive. Then, at 0700 on 25 July, 901 Pz Regt phoned Div HQ to say that the Americans opposite were abandoning their trenches and retreating everywhere. If the Germans were puzzled so were some GIs at the bottom of the military heap. Yesterday they had been ordered to withdraw and then ordered to recapture their old trenches. Today they were being ordered to withdraw again.

In the early hours of the morning of 25 July a solitary plane flew peacefully over the Cobra region. It took no offensive action and was a *pianissimo* prelude to the *fortissimo* symphony about to begin. Its internal machines clicked over quietly and it damaged no one. It was, in fact, a meteorological plane sent out to try to frustrate the gods of weather with their freakish interventions. The forecast: fine weather.

Tank Capt Jim Cary aptly depicted what happened next. 'It had been only a whisper in the wind. . . . There it was again. . . . Some of the soldiers waiting nearby looked up. One pointed at some faraway specks suspended motionless just under the broken clouds. "They're coming", he said. Now the whisper in the sky was like the buzzing of a swarm of bees. Soon there were more specks and the buzzing turned into the distant throb of many powerful motors.'[28]

Americans and Germans alike looked up, 100,000 pairs of eyes watching, minds suspended in disbelief, amazed at the endless pageant of hundreds of specks growing into flies, into black birds, into huge lumbering machines, their size dimming the visual impact of their high speed, some of the mightiest aeroplanes ever constructed, the Flying Fortresses (each one a true fortress of protruding machine-guns) and Liberators; and for ever behind them more specks appearing and growing in what was yet still only 'the greatest air show of the war', as their brutal tuba and drumming fanfare rolled ahead of them, swelling up to disturb the clouds and shame God's own thunder, and then slamming down like an invisible millstone of unbearable noise on human spectators still too hypnotized to plunge into the trembling earth for shelter.

'White, upturned faces . . . and moments later the first long string of bombs, tumbling like tiny sticks in the air, spewed down out of the belly of a leading plane. More strings followed and the tiny sticks turned into hailstorms of screaming death', visible, audible, comprehensible, inevitable.

'There was a moment of tense expectation, then suddenly the earth heaved and the first shattering explosions smashed against the Germans' eardrums. In the sweep of a few seconds Nazi soldiers were hurled from the calm stickiness of a summer morning in France into a fiery hell of earsplitting explosions, screaming men and roaring planes'[29] as human-generated earthquake wrestled with earthquake, volcano lashed at volcano, tempest battered at tempest, as the earth was disembowelled and mortal minds reduced to madness.

Tom Raney of 30 Div, with a tank destroyer unit, no more than a quarter of a mile from the nearest bombs, struggled to stay upright as his woollen trousers flapped against his legs in the hot gales of blast. He saw

88mm anti-aircraft bursts in the midst of the bombers and three planes began to smoke and fall. But hundreds and hundreds more continued to advance.[30]

Walter Klein, a German medical orderly in the middle of it all, was almost physically restrained in a dug-out by the force of the continual blasts and could not move to render aid. Later he could recall:

> What happened was terrific . . . 2,000 planes had produced a rain of bombs . . . the effect was devastating; all our anti-aircraft guns and artillery were destroyed. Tanks which tried to get away were destroyed by pursuit planes. When a wave of planes had passed, one could hear the crying of the wounded and shouting for help of medical personnel. I had just the time to carry one of my comrades, who was badly wounded in the thigh, into the dug-out, when a second wave started bombing . . . many of my young comrades went mad.[31]

The entire air operation was so monstrous that nobody had time or desire to count the marauding planes. One sober, recent study summed it up thus. 'At 0940, 350 fighter-bombers hit . . . the strip of land. . . . The mission was immediately followed by 1,887 heavy and medium bombers and 559 fighter-bombers, dropping more than 4,000 tons of explosives on the target.'[32]

The 'strip of land' was south of the road, but as, in defiance of Bradley, the heavies flew down across their own front-line troops, there was little to cheer about. The same sober study continued: 'Again human error caused some bombs to fall short of the target area. Two lead bombers released bomb loads without positive identification of their aiming points. The lead pilot of the third formation prematurely ordered bombs away, and all planes in his unit prematurely released bomb loads. Fragmentation bombs and high explosives again dropped within the American lines. The 30th Infantry Division again took the blunt of this massive fratricide. The losses were staggering: 61 killed, 374 wounded and 164 others cases of shell shock. These casualties exceeded those of any other single day in combat in the history of the 30th Inf Div. In all 111 men from the US VII Corps were killed.'

A British operator of a pinpoint aiming system code-named OBOE explained one of the difficulties of USAAF pilots. While the new Mark II OBOE system was available to the bomb-aimer in each RAF plane, making him responsible for the aim of the individual plane, the USAAF did not yet have it in each plane. Additionally the bombs themselves were erratic and not aerodynamic. They 'lacked any pretension to streamlining. When you dropped one of them it seemed to stop, wobble, look around, and then go on its own way.'[33]

The OBOE operator continues, 'The Americans were in a much less favourable position. Except on a few rare occasions they did not have the OBOE. . . . Their navigation to the target was by a Lead Navigator; and their bomb-aiming controlled by a Lead Bombardier. When he bombed, the other Bombardiers dropped their loads as soon as they saw the leader's bombs leave his aircraft. . . . I think the Fortress and Liberator crews were the bravest of brave men. The odds against them were so great.'

Other minor factors contributed to the 'fratricidal' massacre. One was that 'neither the British nor the American troops seemed to have been adequately warned of these risks, for, with touching faith in the infallibility of their airmen, they always stayed out in the open excitedly watching these kinds of attacks.'[34] GIs on the ground responded in the regulation manner to aerial errors. 'Orange smoke pots were lighted across the front to mark their positions but the prepared colour signal was quickly swallowed up in the billowing clouds of dust.'[35]

As to the reason why there was misunderstanding about the direction in which the bombing was carried out, a recent study confesses, 'Confusion persists. . . . There appear to be no joint army-air force records of the precise coordination agreed. Either someone lied or . . . misperception on both parts may be the answer . . . the confluence of mismatched personalities, the convoluted relationship between air and ground commanders, and the lack of a sound doctrine . . .'[36] It is, however, of interest that Quesada, himself an air general, sided with Bradley and complained emphatically to the commander of the heavy bombers about their choice of approach.

Little wonder then, that without inside knowledge of the problems in the air, harassed ground troops began to sing a bitter little ditty:

Into the air, junior birdmen,
Into the air upside down.
Drop your bombs, junior birdmen,
On your own troops on the ground.[37]

The statistics for US casualties during the air raid were one too few. They omitted the death of one who, in theory, was not there and, for the time being, was never there. In order to deceive the Germans into expecting a second D-Day on the short Channel crossing route around Calais and Dieppe, a fictitious Allied army had been invented. Gen Patton, so feared by the Germans, was held back in the UK in command of non-existent troops. Many kinds of deception were practised. A very senior general, Lesley J. McNair, was announced as the commander of the 'second invasion'.

McNair had been invited to Normandy to watch the Cobra launch. Observing from close to the target area he was killed by a stray bomb. Although a distinguished soldier, his death was kept secret. He was silently buried on the spot in a funeral attended only by a handful of those in the know, like Bradley, Patton and Quesada. Another suitably senior man would be rushed over from the States to replace McNair and maintain the very successful 'second invasion' deception.

While medical knowledge had progressed since the First World War the dangers of 'blast lung' were still not fully understood. It is likely that a number of those caught in the air raid blasts would have suffered more seriously than at first thought. The reaction of soldiers is that, if they can walk and swing an arm, they can get up and fire a rifle. 'Subpleural or intra-pulmonary haemorrhages' from blast would be noted only under X-ray, not immediately available close to the battlefield. In the meantime a general anaesthetic could be dangerous. Blood transfusion could also be fatal.[38] And only later post-mortem studies revealed that the widespread practice of applying sulphanilamide (then a wonderful life-saver, the chemotherapy of 1944) could cause liver lesions in 'blast lung' cases. twenty-five per cent of those succumbing died within forty-eight hours and another 30 per cent within 120 hours.[39]

The experience of the Americans suffering from the 'friendly fire' was tragic and horrifying, but in statistical and tactical terms it was trifling compared with its impact, as extremely unfriendly fire, on the enemy. In captivity the distressed Panzer Lehr Commander Bayerlein was able to give a dramatic account of what happened on the German side, where he himself was lucky to escape with his life. He described the scene:

> The front after the air bombardment . . . looking like a *mondlandschaft* [a landscape on the moon] 'all craters and death'. At least 70 per cent of personnel were out of action, either dead, wounded, crazed or stupified; the thirty or forty tanks in the front line were all knocked out. In one farm [I] found the whole command post of 902nd Panzer-Grenadier Regiment completely destroyed in the very centre of a bomb carpet.[40]

Eisenhower's own report on the stupefaction factor revealed that 'the bewilderment of the enemy was such that some men unwittingly ran towards our lines and four uninjured tanks put up white flags before any ground attack was launched'.

The Bayerlein catalogue of losses continued: 'The front line had been annihilated by the air raid. The infantry trenches had been useless for they were incapable of protection against the bombs. Individual slits were crushed and their men buried and the survivors were incapable of rescuing them. The long duration of the attack, without any possibility of opposing it, created depression, a sense of powerlessness, feebleness and inferiority. The morale of the men fell to such an extent, given this sense of uselessness that they either gave themselves up to the enemy or fled – anything to survive.'

Shock caused as much damage as physical wounding and death. Some went mad. Others became prostrate, incapable of doing whatever was necessary. Bayerlein confessed that although he had spent the entire war in the most exposed places, this was the worst experience he had ever undergone. Even many soldiers in deep shelters were sealed in, killed and buried at once. The set positions of infantry and artillery were blown away. The region had become transformed into a field of craters in which only the odd human being remained alive. Guns and vehicles were destroyed or overturned without possibility of repair because the roads were blocked.[41]

In another account, Bayerlein described that 'all signal communications had been cut and no command was possible. Several of the men went mad and rushed dementedly around in the open until they were cut down by [bomb] splinters. Simultaneous with the storm from the air, innumerable guns of the US artillery poured drumfire into our field positions.'[42]

Bayerlein was one of the superior breed of German commanders who would not wish their troops to go where they feared to go. The fortunes of war found him right at the epicentre of the air-fuelled earthquake. The same changing fortunes delivered him relatively unharmed to record his experiences for posterity. He had himself been directing affairs at a regimental command post near La Chapelle-en-Juger, in the central target area of the bombing. The post was in an ancient Norman château, its 10-ft-thick walls giving relatively good protection from the blast. Time after time the clouds of bombs descended and swept across the fields, often peppering the château walls. The ground shook so much that it was difficult to walk. In any case the blast and shattering bomb cases filled the land with splinters and the dust of destroyed houses. During the morning it was impossible to emerge from the shelter of the great walls without being hit. It was well into the afternoon before Bayerlein emerged, one of the first, into the foul air, only to find the roads totally blocked and the village turned into a mound of ruins.

Walter Klein was there or thereabouts and saw that when the heavy bombing stopped there was no respite. 'Over the sector of my company were approximately eighteen to twenty-five Lightnings, which were firing systematically on every hedge.' Although there were constant cries for help, 'it was impossible to give any help as long as the air raid lasted. Several companies of the 5th Para Division that had tried to withdraw to the north were entirely destroyed by Lightnings, pursuit planes and bombers. On that day my company lost one officer, thirty-four non-commissioned officers and enlisted men [out of fewer than 100].'[43]

Although Klein was a medic he was speaking for all the fighting men of his front-line company. 'At 1950 I brought the last wounded to the dressing station. The general opinion of my comrades and even of the officers was, that, if the enemy made another attack, it would be our end.

We had no more heavy weapons. Only one small weapon was left, but only six rounds of ammunition. Of our trench mortars only two were left. Worse than the losses of weapons was the effect that the attack had made on our morale.'

Even the toughest and most war-tempered of soldiers wilted under the barrage of bombs. 'A corporal, who was decorated with the *Deutsche Kreuz* in gold, for having destroyed five tanks by anti-tank mines on the Eastern Front, said to me, "I tell you one thing, Sani, this is no more war here in Normandy. We are simply sent to death with insufficient arms. Our Highest Command doesn't do anything to help us. No aeroplanes, no sufficient ammunition for our artillery. Well, for me the war is over."'

Tom Raney, following up in his tank destroyer, found that at least some Germans were better off than 'the hapless Americans. Some had shelters deep enough to withstand the uniformly heavy concentrations of American bombardment. When the assault troops approached they found many of the enemy still doing business the same way at the same stand in the same old merchandise – dug-in tanks and infantry. Enemy artillery was still splattering the main routes of approach.'[44]

A number of forward US units were in disarray, and one or two were now incapable of advancing due to the 'friendly fire'. Only the colonel survived out of the entire command group of 3 Bn, 47th Infantry. A lesser general might have held back the infantry attack to reorganize and advance more neatly. It soon became evident that some sections of the German's foremost defences were still functioning. Collins had to weigh the odds and make a 'Lightning Joe' decision. He decided that it had to be 'now or never'. So, the 119th Regiment of 30th Div passed its start line at 1114, just fourteen minutes after the appointed H hour. The 120th were off the mark at 1130. German gunners came up out of the deep shelters, cocked their guns and began to fight back.[45]

Of Panzer Lehr's 3,600 fighting men, about 1,000 had been killed by the bombing and as many again badly wounded or stupefied. The German field telephone system was almost completely out of order. 'But the bombing was patchy. The damage was worse in the centre of the bomb zone where the heavy bombers had struck, while some defence positions closer to American lines – including about half the tanks – had gone unscathed.'[46] The German 5th Parachute Division was quickly able to organize a stern defence of its sector.

It was at this point that the major difference between Goodwood and Cobra was most marked. Whereas on 18 July, as the air circus turned away, it was the three armoured divisions which made the mad charge to open a gap in the enemy's defences, on 25 July, as the sound of the bombs was still echoing, it was the infantry who walked forward to widen and link up the gaps made by air power. At 1100 on 25 July, 2nd and 3rd ADs were doing their last engine checks, their last gunsight adjustments, their last gun barrel pull-throughs, but they were not yet called to charge. There were tanks and tank destroyers supporting the infantry but the heavy divisions waited and chewed their gum in impatience.

Bradley knew what they were calling on the infantry to do, but considered that the first phase could better be handled by walking men than by riding crews. Bradley himself described the infantryman's lot:

The rifleman trudges into battle knowing that statistics are stacked against his survival. He fights without either reward or relief. Behind every river, there's another hill, and behind that hill, another river. After weeks or months in the line only a wound can offer him the comfort of safety, shelter and a bed. Those who are left to fight, fight on, evading death but knowing that with each day of evasion they have exhausted one more chance for survival.[47]

Another general, also a Second World War company and battalion commander, carried on the theme:

Life day to day was about survival. . . . An infantryman's world, German or Allied, became a deep, cold muddy trench. He ate and slept and cowered there like some four-legged creature, as shells crashed around him without let-up. The most terrifying times came when he was ordered to emerge from his slimy haven and charge, gun at ready, into a solid curtain of fire. He might exchange a word with a buddy one moment and then witness the man's unspeakable mutilation the next.[48]

25 July would not be a cold day. There would still be mud remaining from the storms. Thirst would be a bigger enemy than filth. But some GIs found it loathsome and debasing to have become lousy. This was something from a previous war which should not happen in the current conditions. Many of those afflicted blamed the Germans. In reality the GIs had for weeks been moving forward into trenches previously occupied by the enemy, where discarded clothing, rotting body parts, and unspeakable slime greeted them as they stayed an hour, a day, rarely much longer, accumulating lice and other objectionable matter on the way.

All this was forgotten or put aside for the moment as the infantry pushed forward into yet another lottery of battle. Which American unit would find its path blasted clear and which American unit would be scythed down by the guns which the bombs had missed?

With the towns of St-Gilles and Marigny as their main targets the infantry encountered vastly differing reactions. In 4th Division one battalion virtually walked across country to a point near Chapelle-en-Juger. Their partner battalion hit firm German defence and needed to organize two set battles with tank support in order to get through and link up at Chapelle-en-Juger. Towards St-Gilles men of 30th Div were astounded to be strafed once more by their own planes. It was suggested that anger at their own planes drove them on to 'take it out of' the enemy. Gen Eddy of 9th Div applied classic principles in slowing down faster advances to link with slower advances. That had not been the principle of Cobra, which was to break through anywhere and bypass resistance.[49]

The reports filtering back were obviously extremely varied and gave rise to some confusion as to how well the attack was going. Collins was required to make another lightning decision – to continue with the slow attrition of sporadic resistance by his infantry or to make the big throw of the dice and unleash the armored division through what gaps existed. By 1745 hours on 25 July he had decided on two courses of action: infantry to continue widening gaps during the night; 2nd and 3rd armored to dash through on 26 July.

On the flanks of Collins's VII Corps, there was supporting movement by other US forces along the line of the main road. VIII Corps was commanded by Maj Gen Troy Middleton, an infantryman with little confidence in armor. He had been allocated the 'Super Sixth' AD but was reluctant to use it.[50] At this vital juncture there appeared at Middleton's HQ 'a big six-foot general, wearing gleaming pearl-handled revolvers and a helmet shining with three bright silver stars'. None other than George Patton, who, as far as the Germans were concerned, should have been in England poring over maps of Dieppe and Le Havre.

About to take command of a newly constituted US Third Army, he was given, for a day or two, the rather incongruous title of 'Deputy First Army Commander' in order to assist, cajole or bully Troy Middleton. He asked, 'Where are your tanks?' Middleton pointed back on the map to the assembly areas of 4th and 6th Armored. 'Let's get them up front, in front of the infantry', Patton suggested without fear of rebuttal. The cobra was stirring from under the carpet.[51]

The Germans were rushing up reinforcements, without much hope of staunching the flow. Two columns were heading for the central Chapelle-en-Juger point. One was a regiment from 353rd Div and the other a regiment from 275th Div. Now occurred one of those extempore quirks which can decide battles. US fighter-bombers located the 275th unit and pounced. Like buzzards attracting other buzzards, more and more fighter-bombers swarmed in. The destruction of the column was total, their vehicles becoming one concentrated flaming funeral pyre. So total was the elimination of the unit, and so confused the systems of communication, that the German command continued to plan on the assumption that the regiment was still in being, fighting to reach its ordained goal. That assumption left a gaping hole where the only obstruction to the Americans was the mass of burning wreckage.

While staff officers in the battle area fretted over inconclusive reports, the Bletchley Park listening station in England picked up a vital message which Ultra translated and transmitted to Bradley and Collins. It was from von Kluge to his Supreme HQ and stated starkly, 'As from this moment the front has burst.'[52] Bayerlein was equally emphatic, stating, 'Not a single man is leaving his post. They are lying silent in their foxholes for they are dead. You may report to the Field Marshal that the Panzer Lehr Division is annihilated.'[53]

However, the most emphatic message received at the front that day from German Supreme HQ was that, consequent upon the failed plot to assassinate Hitler a few days before, the normal German army salute had been abolished and the Nazi salute would now be used by all ranks.[54]

The battle raged the length of the St-Lo–Havre de Lessay road. Wounded soldiers were quickly evacuated to the beaches. A few, a very few, were made prisoners when fanatical German counter-attacks surrounded small units. And some GI prisoners contrived to escape. One such escape resulted in a French civilian making the 'supreme sacrifice'.

Jean Goubert was aged forty-four in 1944. A schoolmaster, local councillor and freemason, he had been forced to resign all his posts when the new Vichy government of Petain outlawed freemasonry. He joined the Resistance. He subsisted on what he could grow on his property. He helped fugitives to hide and escape. On D-Day his unit was ordered to cut enemy communications into St-Lo. They were driven back by a massive Allied bombardment of the city which did the job for them.

The Germans were using an empty farmhouse near the harbour of Lessay to temporarily keep prisoners of war. Goubert helped four American paratroopers to escape and hid them in an old bakehouse near his property, awaiting the arrival of the liberating American troops. Unfortunately a massive German reinforcement convoy arrived and entered every building to find overnight billets. They discovered the four paratroopers. An observant officer noticed that the bakehouse door had been locked and secured from outside. He smelled French Resistance.

Among the few civilians remaining in the area Goubert was quickly identified as the guilty person and arrested. He denied guilt but anticipated further rough questioning and torture to reveal accomplices. Death at dawn was likely. Suddenly he kicked off his heavy wooden clogs and ran. He could run much faster than the heavily equipped Germans. There was a building ahead and a narrow path into the woods and safety. As he was two yards from that haven, a German pulled out a pistol and, at long pistol range, hit Goubert twice, killing him instantly. Goubert was posthumously awarded the *Croix de Guerre* (1945).[55] The four paras later contrived to escape again.

CHAPTER NINE

COBRA STRIKES AT LAST

'Hell on Wheels'! Here they come, the heavy armored divisions. It could have been Goodwood. It could have been anywhere that tank met tank in deadly anger. It was, in fact, Cobra. A 2nd AD report stated:

H Company, 66th Armor, encountered three German Panther tanks which delayed their advance for about three hours. The Americans tried sneaking some tanks forward through a smoke screen. Finally Sgt Joe Young maneuvered his tank to a protected position only about 200 yards from the Germans. Even at that close range, the first three armor-piercing rounds bounced off the side of the Panther. The first round from the German tank penetrated their turret, killing one tanker and wounding Sgt Young.

Platoon leader Lt E.V. Helms had orders to take the position at any cost. In a final desperation move, he and a skeleton crew charged the enemy, alternately firing smoke and armor-piercing shot at the Germans. Other tanks followed the lieutenant, with orders to continue the attack if he were knocked out. The Germans apparently lost their nerve and withdrew without firing.

The 3rd Battalion, already reduced in number, lost an additional fourteen tanks, reducing their strength to ten. But by mid-afternoon they had taken the high ground near la Poemelière and sent a patrol of two tanks into town, only to have them destroyed.

Collins had gambled. Enduring 'the agony of generals in decision',[1] he ordered his armored divisions to thrust into a situation which was still fluid and obscure. Bradley said of Collins that he had 'unerring tactical judgement with just enough bravado to make every advance a triumph'.[2] Now he calculated that the Germans would rush reinforcements into the contested zone. It could even be that the enemy had purposely withdrawn their front-line troops at first sight of the bombing raid (as they did in Caen city) and would now be rolling forward again. So he unleashed the 2nd 'Hell on Wheels' Armored Div under Maj Gen Edward H. Brooks towards St-Gilles. The 1st Infantry, together with part of 3rd 'The Spearhead' Armored Div, under Maj Gen Clarence A. Huebner, would strike simultaneously at Marigny.

Combat Group A (CCA) of the 2nd was commanded by Brig Gen Marcus Rose, the son of an immigrant Russian Rabbi. It was said of Rose that he had as much tactical experience with tanks as any officer in the US Army. He had gained a Purple Heart when wounded in action on 13 September 1918. Now at 0200 hours on 26 July he gathered his subordinate commanders and gave his orders for the attack with infantry riding on the tanks. At 0945 the first 'Hell on Wheels' tanks crossed the start line. By 1035 they had broken through the thin 'front line' hastily assembled by the defenders, and were counting and interrogating their first prisoners.

The 2nd and 3rd Armored Divs were larger than the average, either American or British. Between them they put into the field about as many tanks (nearly 800) as the three British, Guards, 7th and 11th did at Goodwood. Once again, prior to H hour there was the amazing sight of entire divisions massed in confined space. One participant was a little concerned about it:

The entire division concentrated in an extremely small area in the Bois du Hommet. We had tanks, half-tracks, artillery pieces and wheeled vehicles jammed bumper to bumper, some 4,400 vehicles in an area approximately one mile square. This was completely contrary to our training. The fact that the German Luftwaffe showed little strength during daylight, and the fact that we had to concentrate like this for the attack to come off rapidly enough, made the risk worthwhile.[3]

2nd Armored worked on the calculation that they needed 12 miles of ordinary road space for just one of their battalions.

The heavy bomber attack, delivered by 8th USAAF, was devastating. The lighter, faster attacks by 9th USAAF, brilliantly coordinated over the heads of the tanks, were equally effective. Gen Quesada, who commanded this air cover, had learned very quickly from the British Goodwood experience and also developed his own ideas. He created 'Air Supporting Parties'. These consisted of a patrol of four planes permanently flying over the lead tanks of a column and able to intervene at any moment, as well as calling up air reserves as necessary.

Among the leading tanks of each column there travelled a 'Visual Control Post', an air pilot installed in a tank with a VHF radio in direct contact with the pilots overhead. The procedure was for the VCP to alert the flying pilots to any target, while higher air command monitored these conversations and moved reserve flights accordingly. An infantry sergeant saw how this worked:

We were riding on the rear deck of a Sherman, flat and plenty of space. We had a good system going. As soon as an enemy tank was located, or as soon as we noticed some hedgerow or barn where the Panzers – they were marvellously camouflaged, y'know, disappeared under a bundle of leafy tree branches, you could not see them from more than twenty yards – Panzers or what might be hiding, our Sherman halted. Switched off engines. The Fritzes always left their motors running ready to do an immediate scram. So we listened. Could not see them but could hear them good. Two or three of us then hunted forward on our bellies, found where and what it was and got back. We had a young air 'loot' on the tank and he spoke into his radio. Suddenly our fighter-bombers were streaking down like lost souls trying to escape from Hades, and hit the Panzer 'Blam!' or whatever. And we laughed at thoughts of the Fritzes caught with their trousers down, retreating like crazy and asking 'how the *donner und blitzen* did they do that?'[4]

Before Cobra, and with tank requests for air support directed via HQ controls, Quesada had reported an average delay of eighty-eight minutes from the time of request to the time of the first bomb dropping on the target. In order to test his idea for the new system Quesada had requested the loan of a tank and found himself in the midst of utter farce. The first tank was delivered to 9th Armored because the officer concerned thought that the invoice to 9th TAC (air force tactical HQ) was a typographical error. When the tank was eventually delivered it was 'returned to sender' by the duty air officer, who replied in terms like, 'What in hell does the air force need a tank for?'[5]

The distribution of Ultra information, derived from Allied breaking of German codes, was strictly limited as it was necessary to prevent the Germans from realizing that the Allies were breaking their codes and using their messages. However, Gen Quesada was one of those on the restricted list. He was 'tickled to death with Ultra, especially the movement orders which gave him ready-made targets without having to search for them, and woe betide any German tank or transport which put its nose out from under a hedge or wood in daylight.'[6] On the other side of the fence, Gen Heinz Eberbach was quite clear in his mind about the value of Quesada's force: 'Our daily losses in men and material from close support planes and fighter bombers were high in good weather. Their effect on the morale of our soldiers was considerable. On the other hand, the enemy suffered practically no losses from our planes.'[7]

It was well that the Quesada system worked efficiently because the American tank crews in their Shermans (with 75mm or 76mm guns) and their light Stuarts were even more out-gunned than the British had been during Goodwood. The latter could at least call up a Firefly to deal with a Panther or Tiger. At first, having trained on lesser tanks, American tank crews were quite impressed by the Sherman. Martin Goldstein, a driver, was intrigued by the Sherman's size and 'thought it, yes, was going to be able to do the job very well against the enemy'.[8] John Seemes, tank commander, liked the turret system with its advanced Westinghouse electrics. 'Our traversing was beautiful – much faster than theirs.'[9] The Sherman is often quoted as 'fairly fast' with a speed of 24 or 25 mph. Most crews would agree that 30 mph was more accurate, with 35 mph attainable if the governor (device to restrict the motor revolutions) was removed.[10] An excellent device, which only came into its own in Cobra, was a phone installed in a box in the tank's hull through which the infantry could communicate with the tank crew.[11]

Staff Sgt Arden Gatzke did not like tanks – period! He described the vehicle, from experience, as 'a stinky, noisy, crowded, overheated (or freezing cold), bone-shaking, iron coffin'.[12] Lt J. Hammell's main problem was with motion sickness and tiredness after long periods of confinement.[13] Staff Sgt Arte Krenn, who lost four Shermans in battle, thought 'we had better tanks could go a lot longer without repairs, gasoline mileage was not that great ½ mile to a gallon, but the gun, the 75mm was a big joke, Hell, it was left over from WW1.'[14] In battle the previously optimistic Martin Goldstein found 'our armor was only about half the thickness of theirs. Their guns, the rounds they fired, could cut right through [the Sherman] like butter.'

One German, however, defended the American tanks: 'The German tanks were too large to be used in Normandy. When they were driving along the sunken road, they had no sight, nor could they operate between the hedges. In comparison with them the "Sherman" tanks, with their high and narrow construction, had all the advantages. The hedges, however, permitted our tank destroyer troops to approach the enemy tanks without being seen.'[15]

On the American side there was much discussion about the merits of a larger tank, the M26, and also about the usefulness of the 'tank destroyers', anti-tank guns either towed or self-propelled. Marcus Rose opposed Patton, arguing that a larger tank with a larger gun was urgently needed. Patton, probably wrong on this occasion, disagreed, and being the great American prophet of tank warfare, won that debate. This was unfortunate as the Sherman fitted with a 76mm gun was little more effective than the normal version with the 75mm. The 76 had a much higher muzzle velocity but too small a propellant and inferior shaping of its shot.[16] Eisenhower was heard to say, 'You mean our 76 won't knock these Panthers out? Why, I thought it was going to be the wonder weapon of the war. . . . Now I find you can't knock a damn thing out with it.'[17]

In the other debate, about tank destroyers (TDs), Patton lost the debate. He had argued that they were not needed and that tanks should take their place. Nevertheless eleven battalions of towed and eleven battalions of SP

TDs were landed in Normandy. Tom Raney was in a towed TD battalion in Normandy and thought it 'one of the US Army's stupidest organizations: ten men riding in an open half-track with a gun weighing almost 6,000 lb, very difficult to manhandle as opposed to an M-10 [SP] with only five men'. As the TD recce platoon leader, Raney himself had two armored cars and five jeeps.[18]

The thing that wireless operator Joseph Fetch most remembered was what happened frequently enough on 26 July. 'The message "0.0.0.", meaning "everybody else get the hell off the air!" When you heard a message in the Army in World War II and it started "0.0.0." everybody that hasn't got immediate business gets off and listens.' It would be a message of such urgency and importance that everybody else must stop sending messages.[19]

The '0.0.0.' messages had certainly gone out from Marcus Rose on 26 July. Heading for St-Gilles he had 'hurled his columns against the village proper and by mid-afternoon rolled past the last shattered German gun emplacement protecting the town'. The writer of the record (a tank company commander) continues describing the action:

> German artillery came screaming down on his accelerating tanks as they came spewing out of the other side of St-Gilles. Clusters of exploding mortars tore at the ground around them, but the tanks spread out, laid down a withering fire, and continued to advance. Mines exploded, sending geysers of dirt into the air and spinning tanks around and halting them in strangely tilted positions. But other tanks surged on by, at times picking their way in twisting paths across ground badly cratered by the heavy aerial bombing. Then . . . General Rose felt a sudden give in the strength of the defenders. The armored spearheads picked up speed. Resistance was melting away. The roar of tank motors echoed triumphantly across the countryside. . . .'[20]

Triumphant or not, such advances were not achieved without cost. The battalion commander of 2nd Bn, 66th AR, had his tank destroyed by enemy fire. He mounted a coy cdr's tank and continued to command the battalion from there. Standing behind the turret he was shot in the side.

In great pain he refused to be evacuated and carried on until the objective was reached. He had the satisfaction of totalling the number of enemy accounted for, over 300 including prisoners.[21]

The policy of bypassing strong points and pressing on, while finally successful, caused some problems as lines were blurred and the two armies became intermingled. Sgt Frederick Morse was given the job of getting prisoners back to the cages being constructed. His own vehicle having been blown up, he found and commandeered an enemy Volkswagen pickup truck. Part of his twisting route was infiltrated by enemy m-gs. As he made his trips he began to realize that, while he was fired on going back to the cages with a full human cargo, the enemy did not fire as he returned empty to the leading tanks. He could only assume that the machine-gunners thought he was a German trying to escape from the closing trap.[22]

Tom Raney, way ahead of his TDs and the tanks, decided to do a quick walking patrol towards a nearby building. It proved to be an abandoned café. Entering carefully they found about twenty Germans sitting as though waiting to be served. 'In my very best phrase book German, I ordered them out with hands up. Fortunately they had been looking for a chance to surrender. We marched them back to a POW collecting point.' They had been demoralized by the air bombing and the fast American advance.[23]

Elsewhere life was tougher for troops trying to advance in the more westerly area of Periers and Lessay. The 79th and 81st Infantry Divs of Middelton's VIII Corps were probing outside the air bombing carpet and found fierce resistance on 26 July as they crossed intervening streams in portable boats and encountered thick minefields. They managed to obtain a foothold in Lessay but the Germans were firmly dug into the ruins in the streets. During the day the corps lost 1,150 men and collected only 100 prisoners, before calling an overnight halt.[24]

It has been noted that there was some difference between the US heavy armored divisions and the British units which fought in Goodwood, so some explanation may be appropriate about the 'heavy' title as well as Combat Commands A and B (CCA and CCB). When the Germans launched their blitzkreig into Poland in 1939, followed by the invasion of

France in 1940, the USA had no suitable main battle tank and no properly organized armored formation in the way that tank warfare had then developed. It will be remembered that Britain also was unable to supply a full armored division in 1939. It was as late as 25 May 1940 when a group of American tank experts met and planned the setting up of an armored division capable of fighting in a 1940s war. Two divisions were quickly set up but with no adequate equipment.

The huge American industrial potential was switched to war production. A new tank was planned, first the General Grant, with a 37mm in its turret and a 75mm in the hull, and then a development of the Grant, the General Sherman with a 75mm in the turret. The latter became the basic tank of the Allied armies. K.T. Keller, President of Chrysler Motors, responded to a direct challenge from President Roosevelt and built an entire tank production factory in one month. 48,000 Shermans were produced in total, double the number of all the tanks produced in Germany.

Meanwhile, under the influence of Patton, who had commanded the US tank attacks in 1918, the 2nd and 3rd Divs were constituted with two regiments (British = brigades) of tanks to one of infantry, instead of the one to one more common in 1944. 2nd and 3rd retained this 'heavy' formation after service by 2nd in North Africa, Sicily and into Normandy.

However, for general tactical purposes the divisions were divided into regular Combat Commands, CCA, CCB and CC Reserve. For Cobra, Rose's 'Hell on Wheels', CCA consisted of 66th Armored Regiment, 22nd Infantry Regiment, 702nd TD Bn, 14th Armored Field Artillery Battalion, plus detachments of engineers, anti-aircraft, medical and maintenance arms. It was a cohesive formation, capable of independent action and reinforcement. It had a similar function to the German battle groups, although the latter tended to be much more of a temporary nature depending on requirements. The CCs system applied similarly in 3rd, 'The Spearhead'.

Morale was high in these highly trained and motivated units with their provocative titles and symbols. At the ground level some troops were not significantly aware of tactical issues. Joe Solarz confesses that he often did not know the names of the battles or even the villages. It was just one goddamn objective after another with Berlin nowhere in sight.[25] Tank commander John Semmes put great emphasis on the family unity of the crew. 'We had great camaraderie – the five members of the crew learned to rely absolutely on each other.' 2nd AD boasted a Bn Sgt-Maj Victor Prawdzik who walked up and down in the open behind his line of defenders with his well-known slogan, 'God dammit, trooper, get a move on: get a move on, trooper'. It was said that the men feared Prawdzik more than they feared the enemy.

On the German side there was much ambivalence. Artillery officer Gunter Materne stated that 'we were trained to believe that final victory would be ours . . . but during the fighting many of us came to have a certain scepticism. But of course we had to be very careful about saying this: one could be court-martialled for being a defeatist. . . . The worst part was seeing comrades, whom I had been with for a long time, suddenly dying from some enemy action. I said, "Man, is it worth this costly price in human life to go on?" But one could not say this out loud.'[26]

Non-nationals conscripted from occupied countries into the German Army were the least dependable and the quickest to surrender after harsh aerial or artillery chastisement. Lt Col Jesse Hawkins, the G2 of 2nd AD, set up a public address system which broadcast to the German lines. He had Polish, German and Russian speakers call messages emphasizing the good treatment, and plentiful food, afforded to POWs by the Americans. The Polish and Russian national anthems were played and then the announcer ordered, 'Go to your foxholes.' Immediately a sample artillery barrage was put down on the enemy lines. On the first day three prisoners surrendered. Next day they were given the microphone to tell of their kind reception from the GIs. More non-nationals surrendered. A variation of the microphone theme was played by Lt Col 'Rosie' King of 1st Bn, 33 AR who had a speech impediment which made his orders hard to follow and too prolonged. So he used WO John Vickers-Smith as his known 'radio voice' and successfully commanded his unit in that way.[27]

German nationals were much tougher and harder to convince. And perhaps the toughest Nazi division of all had arrived opposite Collins's corps. 2nd SS Panzer Das Reich, although numbered '2', was the first SS division to be prepared as a front-line fighting force. 1st SS LAH had in the 1930s been carrying out its original duties as Hitler's praetorian guard. It also became a front line unit at a later date. Das Reich had been stationed in the south of France, but after D-Day was ordered to Normandy. On its way it was impeded again and again by the French Resistance. In revenge, and quoting international rules forbidding the use of civilian fighters, the SS men had carried out cruel reprisals in Toulouse and Oradour, later cited as war crimes. The notoriety of the Oradour massacre sometimes tends to obscure the fact that Das Reich was a highly skilled and experienced fighting division from the Eastern Front. Fortunately for the Allies, it did not function as a complete division in Normandy. Its units were dispersed to plug holes and reinforce sagging defences.

While some American tank gunners were firing, or still waiting to fire, their first shots in action, the Panzers had produced tank aces who were idolized in the Fatherland as were the air aces of the previous war. Some of them were already household names in Germany, men like Ernst Barkmann, Emil Seibold and Michael Wittmann. Propaganda Minister Goebbels maintained an industry of media glorification, and some historians feel that the reputations of such aces were over-dramatized. There is no doubt that they were formidable opponents, and Barkmann certainly made his presence felt in the Cobra area. One instance of his gunning accuracy will suffice.

He had positioned himself under a large oak and was camouflaged to merge into its shadows. Two Shermans approached to within 200 yards. Barkmann let them come and then with two shots set them blazing. A number of supply vehicles behind them halted in confusion. Barkmann took his time to add those to the inferno blocking the road. Two more Shermans took up the fight. Barkmann knocked out one. The second American scored two hits on the Panther but the shots failed to have any effect on the thick armor plate. With the confidence of many such encounters Barkmann turned his attention to the surviving Sherman and it blew up. A bomb from a fighter-bomber damaged the track of the Panther but Barkmann was credited with two more Shermans before he retreated. Unfortunately at least one exaggerated version of the story has Barkmann's tank retreating to HQ when in a condition which would have immobilized it totally.[28]

Speed was the Americans' best resource. The ordinary German soldier found this confusing. A medical orderly taking some wounded to the dressing station found American tanks already driving past him. From an observation post in a tall tree it was possible to discern large concentrations of American tanks ready to advance. But when the outnumbered German detachments tried to withdraw they found other Shermans already behind them. When an order to withdraw was eventually received it was only possible to move at night.[29]

One success enjoyed by the Germans was when they captured the sergeant commanding a knocked-out Sherman complete with his well-marked map showing the American intentions. The confusion was too great to allow them to take much advantage of the information. An irritation to the advancing troops was the profusion of accurate snipers. As Sgt Arte Krenn so aptly put it, 'German snipers loved tanks' because most Sherman commanders fought with their heads out of the turret. Records of Das Reich claim that one unit of the division repelled thirteen separate attacks during 26 July before orders and counter-orders, based on Higher Command's ignorance of the local situation, broke up the cohesion of the defence and led to a chaotic withdrawal. The few remnants of Panzer Lehr also fought on.

As the continuous German front cracked and disintegrated, their defence relied on a relatively few top-grade units able to move from one crisis to another. 'We were known as the fire brigades. Anywhere something was happening – a breakthrough or whatever – we were sent there to repel it as much as possible', remembered Pz Cpl Friedrich Bertenrath. 'Then it was off to the next place. . . . The tiny dirt roads and the large hedges everywhere provided good cover from air attacks.' German infantry, with mainly horse-drawn transport, often marched or cycled up to 30 miles during the hours of darkness.[30]

Brave as American tank men were, there must have been some deterrent factor in the sight of Shermans blazing. Commanders must have been inhibited to some degree by the knowledge that, as at Goodwood, an attacking tank company could be wiped out in five minutes, and a battalion disabled in half an hour. Rarely mentioned in histories, but added to the apprehension, were the factors of the decreasing 'attention curve' in weather reaching over 90 °F (32 °C), and the continuous blinding sun shining from the enemy's quarter, making the use of commanders' binoculars dangerous as they reflected back to the enemy. The deep shades produced by the midsummer sun wrapped themselves protectively around the enemy while leaving the attackers spotlight clear as targets.[31]

Cobra crews were now joining the elect communion of those, like the Goodwood crews, who have endured the sight of mass cremation by Sherman. In the closer *bocage* Shermans had blown up, but often this event was closed off from general view by the baffle-board hedgerows. Even the demise of Jim Flowers' platoon (Chapter One) was not immediately witnessed by other crews. The havoc wrought by Barkmann was instantly visible to all the troops pushing past in more open ground.

Tank crews like Jack Hammell and Arte Krenn had no illusions. The latter says, 'Just think how many tank men died in battle, after all with five in a tank, some never made it out of the blazing tank, others only on fire themselves. I never saw any tank (on fire) where they all got out. I know because one of my jobs was to help the CO write to the folks back home about how they died.' A more formal study found that 'the Sherman was dangerously vulnerable to all calibres of German anti-tank guns. The statistics were stunning. Sixty per cent of Allied tank losses were the result of a <u>single</u> shot from an enemy 75mm or 88mm. Two-thirds of all tanks "brewed up" when hit.' In sixty-five cases studied, only three enemy shots hit a Sherman and failed to penetrate. None of the failures was from an 88mm.[32]

Lt Francis Fuller had to write to Hubert Wolfe of 310 US Inf, 'I don't know if you have ever seen one of our tanks burn? But when 180 gallons of gas start burning, and ammunition starts to explode, the best thing to do is keep away. Your brother's tank continued to burn all night, but in the morning we were able to go out and investigate. We determined that your brother had been killed instantly, as the shell had hit right above his seat. There was nothing visible but a few remnants of bones that were so badly burned that, if they had been touched, they would have turned to ashes. As for personal effects, you could not recognize anything because the intense heat and the exploding ammunition had fused most of the metal parts together.'[33]

Fuller wrote to Wolfe in those terms because Wolfe was himself experienced in battle. Normally the 'letter to folks at home' would probably have said simply that it was a clean bullet through the brain about which the deceased knew nothing. American artillery Col Roberts, a hero a day or two earlier, was a brewed tank victim whose body was reduced to ash. He was identified solely by the serial number of his partially melted pistol. Yet another witness was most graphic:

The flames are explosively fierce and yet are tightly contained in the hollow steel shell. From the turret black smoke alternating with intense flame thunders forth in a monstrous jet. From time to time the smoke is forced into huge expelled puffs by the exploding shells within. The perfect black ring shooting up from a burning tank suggested some grotesque devil's game, a derisory joke of the fiends, over dying men. A burning tank looked like a monster, a dying dragon, vomiting up the life within it in black gouts. A red and white glow would roll in the eyes of the dead monster, the hatch holes, through which the crew had entered, never to emerge again.[34]

Medical officers themselves were often horrified by tank wounds even while exercising professional judgement on their treatment. 'The pain suffered by these patients is often indescribable. This seems to stamp an impression on the patient's mind and many, even of the most stoical, suffer from tragic psychological collapse. Some remain "nervous wrecks", others become chronic alcoholics.'[35] Another surgeon found 'tank wounds horrible things to treat. They are always accompanied by more or less severe burns and are multiple in nature. . . . One digs out pieces of armour plate and large lumps of hard rubber and nuts and bolts.'[36]

Fortunately, in many cases, shock blocked off the worst pangs of pain until sedatives could be applied. Staff Sgt Arden Gatzke 'watched an American soldier get up from the ground after an enemy shell exploded next to him. He slung his rifle over his shoulder and walked back to my tank saying, "The dirty S.O.Bs just shot off my arm. Where are the medics?" I pointed to the rear and he kept on walking, holding on to the stub of his arm.'[37]

Another MO was astonished by the actions of a man who had both legs shot off. 'All the time I am treating him he keeps struggling up, saying "for God's sake, Sir, I must have a shit". I turn him over, pack a lot of cotton wool between his legs and tell him to go ahead. He does and then says he feels OK and can he get up? He thinks he can walk away!'[38]

Suffering might have been far worse but for the general sympathy which existed on both sides for the seriously wounded who could fight no longer. The German medic stopping during the stealthy midnight patrol to dress Jim Flowers' burns was typical. After a particularly bloody fight at Seves Island the US chaplain negotiated a three-hours truce to attend to the wounded. Walter Klein's battalion was content to leave seventy-eight severely wounded soldiers in a German dressing station, with an MO, a surgeon and a stock of medical equipment for the approaching GIs to take over. Klein stated that during a terrific fire fight, 'I made field dressings for the wounded, while nobody fired at me . . . all men who were wearing the Red Cross could help their wounded without being fired on.'

There were times when the confusion of battle caused normal conventions to become impossible to observe. Lt Eddinger's infantry had trapped some Germans in a wood and the Germans began to indicate that they wanted to surrender. As a US non-com went forward to accept the surrender he was shot and a colleague was hit by a grenade. It was not clear who was shooting. The Americans were forced to return concentrated fire during which the Germans preparing to surrender were also shot.[39]

During their transit from the south, Das Reich had been brutal in their treatment of French Resistance fighters wearing civilian clothes. During Cobra, French Resistance men were given American uniforms and rendered excellent service as guides. Louis Aubert was thirty when the war broke out. He was conscripted and sent to the Cherbourg garrison. Very soon the Germans arrived and took him prisoner. However, it was not possible to imprison the entire French Army, and civilian workers were needed under the German occupation. After a few weeks behind barbed wire Louis Aubert was detailed to work on the trains in Normandy. He found this more dangerous than soldiering in the Cherbourg garrison, for the Allied air forces constantly attacked the railway system.

He hid when his village was liberated just after D-Day. Soon a French captain with the American Army, Capt Quetary, came looking for volunteers to act as guides to the troops through the *marais* and *bocage*. For Louis Aubert this was his opportunity for long-awaited revenge. It was with great delight that he put on uniform to serve with the US 79th Inf Div. With face blackened at times he went crawling along ditches and well-known farm paths on night patrols. At other times he perched on the lead tank negotiating the tortuous bends of the Lessay byways during Cobra. He guided his GI friends through to Coutances and Le Mans before returning home a satisfied man.[40]

As the night of 26 July drew on, advances had been made but no real breakthrough could yet be claimed. Collins had stated that until a breakthrough had been achieved tanks could not advance any faster than infantry. So the spearheads were ordered to keep going through the night in search of the elusive hole in the defences. Although not yet evident, such a gap was opening up between Pz Lehr and 352 Div around Canissy. This was due to the destruction of so much of the Panzer unit, a fact of which higher command was not yet fully aware. One road allocated to Pz Lehr was now virtually undefended.

On the morning of 27 July rain and mist replaced the sunshine: this was a problem for tank crews needing to view the land through misted periscopes. The pressure was to keep moving fast in spite of all hazards. Speaking of periscopes, Sgt Robert Lotz, of 2nd AD's infantry regiment, distinguished himself by shooting out the periscope of a menacing 88mm SP and then shooting the commander. Early in the morning Cpl William Giblin's tank was brewed up and he was badly burned. He saw that his captain, whose tank was also knocked out, was being made a prisoner by the enemy. Giblin charged single-handed at the enemy, firing his tommy-gun. Three Germans surrendered and the captain was saved. In the mayhem, with the two opposing forces again intermingled, MO Capt Mario de Felice coolly moved around the contested area, finding and treating the wounded. He remained with them until the area could be cleared and the men evacuated. This deed won him the Distinguished Service Cross.

Lt Col Richard Nelson had temporarily 'mislaid' the vanguard of his 1st Bn, 67th AR, and had driven forward in his tank looking for them. Going round a bend into a village he saw about forty Germans coming out of a church, assuredly not from a religious service. Reacting quickly he turned his guns on the group and either killed or forced the entire group to surrender. An artillery group, moving to an advanced site, found German infantry defending it. In a hurry, artillery Col Thomas Roberts called for fifty artillerymen to volunteer for infantry duty. They attacked, tanks arrived to help and 175 prisoners were taken, together with a supply dump which the Germans had been defending.

As the heavy armored divisions continued to roll forward, swinging right to follow the trend of the valleys, the 4th and 'Super Sixth' ADs also began to force their way through widening gaps. The front was becoming so congested that the 6th had only a single paved road along which to advance. Inevitably some confusion ensued. Hit by shots from an unexpected angle, the 'Hell on Wheels' local commander calculated that he was being fired at by 4th AD. When he radioed to the 4th, the local commander of the latter assumed that it was a German speaking fluent English and trying to mislead him. The firing continued. It was only when, interlaced with appropriate obscenities, the 2nd threatened to report him to their 'P' that the 'friendly fire' colleague desisted. 'P', short for Professor, was the nickname for Div Commander, Maj Gen Woods, a nickname that the Germans would not be likely to know.

With massed armored formations driving down every available road and track, as well as across more open country, the Germans were finding it impossible to bring in adequate reinforcements. Walter Klein's regiment was 'promised to get an artillery detachment and a pioneer company with heavy weapons as reinforcement. The whole reinforcement, however, consisted of sixteen dismounted gunners and twelve men of the pioneer company without their flame-throwers. . . . Approximately 10 per cent were left of our combat strength. . . . The proportion of strength was about twenty to one, without mentioning the fact that our only heavy weapons were two trench mortars against fifty to sixty enemy tanks here against the sector of my company (we were thirty-six men including the company commander, when the attack started).'[41]

German reinforcements of any size could only be moved at night. Lt Gunther Materne recalled the horror of night moves. 'The worst part was sometimes the aerial observers would drop Christmas trees – clusters of lights – which would light up the area. They photographed us, our march direction, how many vehicles, and of what type. Then they were prepared for the next day's bombing attack.'[42] German attention was also drawn away to the Bourguebus–Verrières ridge, where the Canadians continued to attack, with numerous casualties, long after Goodwood had ended, in a new offensive termed Operation Spring.

On 25 July the Canadians had lost more casualties than on any other day except the Dieppe raid. The Canadian Black Watch had advanced with about 320 men into a veritable Balaclava, 'guns on all sides', trap. Only sixteen survived being killed, taken prisoner or badly wounded. The total Canadian casualties for Spring were 450 killed and 1,100 wounded as the farms which John Cloudsley-Thompson had briefly conquered during Goodwood were occupied again. The Canadian commanders were well aware that their main mission was not to liberate relatively insignificant villages, but to hold the enemy troops opposite them, and keep them away from the Cobra sector, by the threat of a post-Goodwood break-out attempt.[43] On the German side the 116th GAF (Luftwaffe) Div had been virtually eliminated and the 21st Pz Div reduced to battalion strength, losing 109 tanks.[44]

So the German command was beset by confusion and competing priorities. Das Reich commanders complained about being ordered to withdraw into positions already firmly held by their enemy. Often the GIs were also attacking blind. Speeding American tanks roared through a tiny village, smashing walls, windows and doors with HE and riddling interiors with m-g bullets, unaware that Gen Bayerlein and his staff were within one of the houses. After dark Bayerlein and his officers moved like darker shadows through the obscure recesses of high hedgerows and were lucky enough to find a way out through the Cobra spearheads. Bayerlein's sad task was then to report that his fine division had virtually ceased to exist.

That night the eager Ultra listeners at Bletchley picked up a signal from von Kluge, countermanding an order from Seventh Army Commander, Hausser, ordering surrounded German units to break out to the southeast. The signal revealed not only that the German Army was completely off balance but that von Kluge had no real knowledge of what was happening. Details contained in the message were despatched express to Quesada, whose fighter-bombers homed in on the mass of trapped enemy and their equipment. Few of those troops managed to escape.[45] The largest and most crucial gap was opening up down the Germans' left flank, towards the Atlantic coast, where 4th and 6th ADs were impatient to be on their way.

The Cobra troops had indeed, in Montgomery's unfortunate words, 'hit them for six'. When Montgomery had addressed American GIs before D-Day he had chosen to inspire them with the old cricket slogan, 'Hit them for Six!' The bemused GIs, baseball fans almost without exception, had been unimpressed and enquired, 'Six what?'

Americans training in England had become used to the strange vernacular. Trying to make phone calls by the operator system, they waited patiently and then heard the operator's voice at last say, 'You're through!' The frustrated Americans then put the phone down. It had to be explained to them that 'you're through' in English telephonese meant simply 'you have a connection' and not, as in the States 'you're finished'.

On the night of 27 July there might have been some echoes of 'you're through' along the Cobra roads: 'you're through' in the sense of having broken through the main enemy defences, but not 'you're through' in the sense of 'you're finished'. The next days would still see fanatical German resistance, sporadic and outnumbered perhaps, but always requiring very determined generalship and many more bold deeds from the troopers at the sharp end. There total numbers of troops engaged meant little to the individual Sherman commander faced by one invisible enemy anti-tank gun.

CHAPTER TEN

COBRA HYDRAHEADED

Cometh the hour, cometh the man, with the tanks.

Citation: **Sgt Hulon B. Whittington, Medal of Honor.**

For conspicuous gallantry and intrepidity at the risk of life above and beyond the call of duty. On the night of 29 July 1944, near Grimesnil, France, during an enemy armored attack, Sergeant Whittington, a squad leader, assumed command of his platoon when the platoon leader and the platoon sergeant became missing in action. He reorganized the defense and, under fire, courageously crawled between gun positions to check the actions of his men. When the advancing enemy tried to penetrate a road block, Sergeant Whittington, completely disregarding intense enemy action, mounted a tank and by shouting through the turret, directed it into position to fire pointblank at the leading Mark V German Tank. The destruction of this vehicle blocked all movement of the enemy column, consisting of over 100 vehicles of a Panzer unit. The blocked vehicles were then destroyed by hand grenades, bazookas, tank and artillery fire, and large numbers of enemy personnel were wiped out by a bold and resolute bayonet charge inspired by Sergeant Whittington. When the medical aid man became a casualty, Sergeant Whittington personally administered first aid to his wounded men. The dynamic leadership, the inspiring example, and the dauntless courage of Sergeant Whittington above and beyond the call of duty, are in keeping with the highest traditions of the military service.

By the end of July the German Army opposite the Cobra columns was merely 'wet henning', in military terms plugging gaps in a disintegrating structure.[1] (cf. German *wetten* = to gamble!) By 28 July the smell of victory was in the air. But Sgt Whittington and others were to find that the 'wet hen' plugs were usually elite troops of Das Reich and remnants of Panzer Lehr, who tended to fight the more furiously the more disastrous the situation that surrounded them. The records of the 'Hell on Wheels' regiments seem to indicate more need for heroics as Cobra progressed. A glance through those records, at random incidents from 28 July onwards, will bear this out.

The division, under Maj Gen Edward H. Brooks, was advancing in its binary formation, CCA under Marcus Rose and CCB under Isaac D. White, probing for more gaps in the enemy defences. CCA had worked out a unique method for probing forward. There would be five lead tanks in a box formation. Two Shermans would forage along wide on either side of the road, trying to flush out any German tanks or anti-tank guns. About a hundred yards behind, alone in the centre of the road, would be a fast Stuart, serving as bait to persuade hidden enemy guns to betray themselves. At a discreet distance further back, two tank destroyers would be ready to pounce on the guns which took the bait. This went well. However, while providing a normal defensive screen the Germans also relied on sudden concentrated counter-attacks against American units, often at night. As all American units were moving as fast as possible, without establishing deep continuous defence systems, such counter-attacks could often find temporary gaps and cause great confusion to both sides.

The counter-attack which caused Sgt Whittington to resist so courageously, as well as Whittington's own delaying action, resulted in hard-hitting German groups scouring the countryside for loopholes. One group of about 600 infantry with tanks crashed into the command area of 2nd Bn 41st AR, where Lt Col Wilson D. Coleman was quietly going about the task of setting up and checking outposts at midnight. Suddenly he became a single-handed outpost as Panzers roared towards him. Grabbing a bazooka from his jeep he calmly fired and knocked out the first enemy tank. Given a moment of breathing space he jumped into the jeep and accelerated back to warn his own men. The overwhelming impact of the concentrated enemy force crushed the outposts, and as Coleman rallied his main force he was killed in the fire of massed guns. The defensive action enabled divisional reserves to hurry forward and do their own version of 'wet henning'.[2]

Night attacks often caused so much confusion that neither side held a total advantage. On the German side it was again to *wetten*. One observer recorded striking impressions:

> . . . enemy groups wandering lost in darkness between American groups. GI road guides staying in their lonely crossroads posts to guide in lost vehicles. In HQ Coy column [41 armored engineers] isolated personnel from wreckers, ambulances, tanks and vehicles of other units were gathered up into our vehicles from hiding places in the deep ditches along the side of the road.
>
> The confusion and uncertainty of the situation in dense darkness was further heightened by the constant stream of bullets overhead, the rumble of friendly and unfriendly tanks, intermittent flares of all types and descriptions, and by the ominous coughing of enemy burp guns from all directions.

As the confusion continued the attackers 'were repulsed in savage hand-to-hand, grenade and bayonet fighting', although massed bayonet fighting was rare in Normandy. An infantry commander, Capt W.C. Johnson, called over the radio for artillery support and heard the order 'B Battery fire direct'. This meant that a barrage would come down on his own position on the assumption that, if the defenders kept their heads down in their slits, the exposed attackers would suffer far more. The artillery of 62nd and 78th Armored fired from map readings, correcting by sound and sight of flash, a very approximate way of shooting but one which proved extremely effective.

Tanks came up to thwart a final German attack through a pathless swamp. 'In the morning almost 300 bodies were found in the swamp . . . the scene rivaled Dante's *Inferno*. Almost 600 dead including three women soldiers[3] and a major general. Maj Jerome Smith called the scene "the most godless sight I ever witnessed on any battlefield". Capt James R. McCartney, a veteran of French Morocco, Tunisia and Sicily, said, "I had not seen such horrible carnage in all my battle experience". Bulldozers had to be used to clear the roads' of bodies. The Yanks were not having an easy ride.

Confusion also bred friendly fire. Lt Col Amzi R. Quillan, commanding a cavalry group, went forward to direct the fighting personally as the opposing troops again became intermingled, with Germans counter-attacking the fast-advancing Americans. Out on his own, Quillan was mistaken for a fleeing enemy commander and was shot up by one of his own squadrons. He died shortly afterwards.

More than one GI unit had to retake an objective after being forced back by overwhelming enemy counter-attacks (mounted by the Germans at the cost of denuding the defences in other areas). In one fight 702nd TD Bn had already destroyed 11 Panzers and eliminated over 300 infantry, but found that they could not get their high-profile vehicles forward of protecting hedgerows without being brewed up by the larger enemy guns. Tech Sgt Arnold O. Pederson became impatient with the impasse. He got out of his tank and borrowed a bazooka from the infantry. He then led a squad of infantrymen, also carrying bazookas, cautiously forward on foot. Within a very short time they were able to locate the defenders and destroy or drive them away. The TDs could then move into the open.

Tom Raney also found that a bazooka was more manageable than those awful, huge towed TD guns. They had carefully passed by a burning enemy Mark IV tank and stopped to listen. They heard the starting motor of another Mark IV close at hand. Lt Tom and Sgt Hannah equipped themselves with a bazooka each and approached the sounds of the motor. They were surprised to come on the German crew coolly trying to repair a tank track which had apparently been damaged by one of the enemy's own land mines. Obtusely, Raney fired the bazooka at the track and spoiled the crew's attempts to repair it. Hannah at the same time hit the tank turret. The lieutenant tried another shot but the bazooka rocket was a dud. In the silence that followed the surviving Germans raised *Kamerad* hands high above the ditch where they had taken instantaneous refuge.[4]

There were many minor skirmishes involving a single tank and a clutch of infantry on each side. Cpl William D. Yockey's tank on point duty was attacked by such a team. Rather than retreat into shelter he took on the enemy and eliminated them all. His own tank was hit and he was killed in the moment of victory. The Sherman blazed in the usual manner. T4 Floyd Allan helped three wounded crew to escape with their clothing on fire. He then procured a fire extinguisher, returned to the Sherman, doused the blaze and drove the tank back into a hide.

The Germans excelled at concentrating defence on sites of utmost importance. Seeking to obtain a river crossing, one Sherman tank company of nineteen tanks lined up behind a hedge, ready to carry out 'do or die' orders to reach the objective at any cost. German gunners, observing the movement, knocked out ten of the Shermans before they could crash through the hedge. Four Shermans with Rhino fittings ploughed their way through the hedge but were knocked out as they did so. Five Shermans survived to fight another day. Reconnaissance in the darkness then found that the marshy banks of the river at that place were too soft to sustain the weight of tanks.

It was at another river crossing that Marcus Rose, by then a major-general, demonstrated that leadership which enabled him to manage CCA through battles of the utmost bitterness. An armoured column had halted because a bridge had been mined. Several mines had been removed but it was not clear whether the bridge was yet safe. Rose solved the problem simply by himself driving across the bridge and then driving back again. The bridge was safe, although Rose might not have been. Rose was killed towards the end of the war, again riding well up front in an armored column. As often happened, the German anti-tank guns allowed the first platoon of tanks to pass unscathed and then destroyed the command group in its lighter vehicles. Rose was in one of those.

With their Cobra missions successfully achieved, the CCs of the 2nd were beginning to receive orders to disengage and move back to rear areas in order to rest, reinforce and reorganize. Even the most pugnacious soldiers were glad of the promised respite, feeling that they had achieved great things. They considered that they had clearly proved they were 'Hell on Wheels'. What they did not know was that at that precise moment

Churchill was contacting Eisenhower with news. The Ultra listening post had picked up Hitler's instructions to von Kluge. The Field Marshal was to gather all his remaining elite forces, including those facing Caen, and strike at the neck of the precipitate American advance around Mortain. The maps had suggested to Hitler that a counter-attack towards Avranches would cut off all the spearhead American armored forces now spreading out into a hydra headed threat to the German rear areas. There would be no respite for the American armored divisions as yet.

Von Kluge and many of his commanders were not enthusiastic about Hitler's idea, for they were straining every nerve, scraping the barrel until the barrel staves were coming apart, in order to stem the continual onrush of the Allied armies. The three British armoured divisions from Goodwood had now been reinforced, and the powerful fresh Canadian and Polish tank divisions were also advancing. There were in addition several independent British armoured brigades which, with infantry collaboration, were proving virtually as effective as the specialist divisions. But Hitler in his bunker was still moving pieces around the map as though units like Panzer Lehr and Hitlerjugend were still at fully effective battle strength.

The formidable Das Reich, its life blood being drained away in a dozen different places in a score of hopeless stop-gap actions, was ill fated in its high command. Already on 24 July *Brigadeführer* Lammerding, its widely feared chief, had been wounded. *Obersturmbannführer* Tychsen took over, pending the appointment of a new general. On 28 July Tychsen himself was killed and army commander Hausser escaped after being fired at point blank by a GI gun. Baum of 17th SS *Goetz von Berlichingen*, took over, amalgamating his division with Das Reich in order to form a regiment-sized total group, a third of the normal SS division size.[5]

2nd SS itself was talking of mustering 'fragments of remnants' to put into the firing line. A comb-out of echelon cooks, clerks and other normally non-combatant personnel produced an infantry platoon, which was issued with rifles and ordered to attack. Every SS man was a trained soldier and had sworn a special oath of loyalty. But 1940s oaths could not make up for lack of anti-tank weapons and mortars, to say nothing of tanks and SPs. Their 1st Bn of artillery had been totally wiped out.

When the 'Super Sixth' drove towards the River Sienne they found it guarded on their route by enemy troops composed only of Russians, Georgians and Poles, almost all unwilling conscripts.[6] Eisenhower's own report estimated that 'the 5th Parachute Division, Panzer Lehr Division, and 353rd Inf Div were almost completely accounted for by this time, although, in accordance with German practice, they were reconstituted at a later stage of the campaign'[7] – but not in Normandy. Again the Allies were counting their blessings that, due to joint Allied strategy, Das Reich never fought as an entire division in Normandy, this roaring lion of a formation reduced to wet henning.

The succession of hopeless missions was beginning to affect German morale. A comrade, helping Walter Klein to carry a wounded man, said, 'I don't care for anything. Two of my brothers were sacrificed in Stalingrad, and it was quite useless, and here we have the same movie.'[8] 2nd SS Lt Fritz Langangke was sent to a rendezvous with paratroop infantry to hold a vital location. No infantry arrived and only one other tank of his own company. They destroyed three advancing Shermans. Mist came down across the road. Like ghosts the expected paratroop infantrymen drifted along the road. At last! But then Langangke realized that they all had their hands up and were meekly surrendering to the Americans.

An infantry officer of 30th Div asked for tank support and was told that the Shermans did not have powerful enough guns to face the German tanks. He retorted that 'the tanks could have wooden guns for all he cared, for their mere appearance boosted American morale and deflated that of the enemy.'

Even conceding that German morale was deteriorating, 41st Armored Infantry were surprised first of all to see an entire German company marching out under a white flag of surrender. They were even more surprised to learn that the company commander had been captured by the Americans in the First World War. He had told his men of the kindness and liberality of the Americans towards prisoners and that he was going to surrender now in this war. The company could do what it wanted. The entire company agreed to go with him and sample American hospitality.[9]

Gen Hausser himself graphically described the condition of some of the survivors of devastated units:

The stragglers are for the most part in a very bad state. . . . Condition of clothing is appalling. Many men are without headgear or belts and their footwear is worn out. Many go barefoot. When they cannot obtain rations from supply depots, they live off the country, regardless of property rights, thus stirring up hatred among the population and intensifying terrorist activity. A not inconsiderable number of them disappear at the hands of terrorists. The paratroops are particularly unpopular with the local inhabitants. The morale of most of these stragglers is badly shaken.[10]

The desperation of the retreating army probably led to some infractions of the normal rules of battle behaviour. GIs guarding a bridge in Avranches saw a German convoy heading straight towards them. About to open fire they noticed that the wagons were all marked with the Red Cross. They held their fire. They allowed the wagons to pass, assuming that they were carrying wounded. At that point guns opened up from the convoy. The GIs then automatically fired back with everything they had available. Immediately several of the wagons blew up with massive explosions which revealed that they were carrying ammunition and not wounded men.[11]

In these circumstances Walter Klein observed that 'there was hardly anybody who was sorry for being wounded'. They yearned to know if the wound was serious enough for them to be sent home. Unfortunately for them, 'men who had lost a finger or were shot through their legs without breaking the bone, were sent back [to their units]. The young thought it better to be seriously wounded.' One of the seriously wounded, with shrapnel in his shoulder, said to Klein, 'This piece of iron that hit me, should have hit the Führer's head on 20 July [date of the failed assassination], and the war would be over already.'[12]

As the armored divisions fanned out the French Resistance became perhaps even more important than under German occupation. 'The French Forces of the Interior (FFI) had been formed into 'roving bands . . . guerilla type units formed, before the invasion began, by Frenchmen eager to help drive the Germans out of their homeland. The constant flow of information that these groups and the cavalrymen were able to give Patton was frequently the basis of his daring, onrushing tactics.'[13]

The long-suffering, ever retreating medic, Walter Klein, noticed the impact of the FFI. 'We avoided villages. In the evening we were fired on from a farm by some terrorists who escaped when our men were approaching. For five days we had nothing to eat but unripe fruit and the "iron rations" which we took from our dead comrades having no rations of our own left'. At that time the 'terrorists' could have been FFI in uniform and therefore legitimate fighters by German standards.

82nd Recon Bn learned to be a little wary of some FFI. Their small forward patrol into a village had been surrounded by large German forces. The patrol took to the woods, where they found the entire surviving male population of the village also hiding. All the Frenchmen claimed to be FFI. One of the uniformed FFI 'did an excellent job with A company's assault gun crew until Gen Brooks ordered *her* out of the company!' Another uniformed FFI 'did yeoman service until someone discovered that he was in fact a deserter from the German forces!'[14]

The Americans found light relief where they could. An initially disturbing local occurrence could develop into a good general joke. 3rd 'The Spearhead' men had a hearty laugh at their divisional HQ. This haughty assembly was roused by a 'carrier careening wildly' down the road, a sergeant standing up firing his carbine and shouting at the top of his voice 'GAS!' This caused disbelief, consternation, horror and panic in quick sequence. Very few high rankers knew where to find their gas masks. Personal belongings were flung everywhere as searches located the offending items and unfamiliar masks were dragged over command faces until all became anonymous.

It was, of course, a false alarm, although alarms had genuinely been activated. The chemical plaques placed for the purpose had responded automatically to a gas leak and had set off the correct alarms, sending the duty sergeant yelling war cries through the headquarters' compound. After investigation it was considered that smoke from a burning enemy ammunition dump had reacted with swatches of paint on some vehicles designed to react to poison gas.[15] The Germans never used gas in Normandy. At the Nuremberg trials Goering stated that this was because the majority of German transport was horse-drawn and there were no gas masks for the horses. A German gas attack would have wiped out their own transport. So he said.

HQ 67th Armor had been cheered up when liberated civilians provided them with a liberal meal of fried eggs, their first taste of fried eggs since leaving England. 305th Engineers combat unit were even more cheered when a Red Cross mobile overtook them bringing real coffee, fresh donuts and real American girls to serve them.

Where such physical means of encouragement were lacking, many GIs found religious consolation important in dealing with their fear. Arte Krenn found that, 'Fear was always with one and you had to respect it. And trust your Maker. Church was more packed after we lost our first Sherman to our first Tiger. Men got to know God better than in their whole life. I was no exception.'[16] For many tankers Patton shared the throne with God. They even had a Patton prayer:

> God, thank you, for letting me be
> In General Patton's armored infantry
> Fighting with brave 'armed company' men
> With pride and honor to the end.
> God keep an ever watchful eye
> Hoping our comrades will not die;
> And thank you, God, for letting me be
> In Pattons' armored infantry.[17]

Through all the ghastly carnage many GI s retained a streak of sentimentality and compassion. This was best evidenced in their horror about the battle sufferings of animals. Louis Gerrard, who shared the terrors of the Flowers' platoon battle, remembered, 'I used to see the cows eating grass, and the blood just pouring out of them like a faucet, just pouring out, and they're standing there eating.'[18] Another tank man was devastated to see 'shot horses, their intestines hanging like black bee swarms under their bellies, or standing on three legs like broken rocking horses, and still grazing, grazing the bloody grass.'

Joe Solarz and his crew made friends with a French farming family. The wife offered to make them a special meal of rabbit. 'She picked up the rabbit by the ears and approached me, handing me a knife to slit its throat. I turned away. I couldn't do it. None of us could do it. Funny, we could shoot at, kill and destroy Nazi Germans but none of us could tackle that rabbit.'[19]

John Cloudsley-Thompson and his crew on Verrières Ridge found their sleeping bags invaded by a frightened dog during a Canadian night barrage.[20] They did not have the heart to drive it away. MO William M. McConahey was dressing the shoulder of a wounded GI when a little mongrel dog appeared and jumped on to the soldier's abdomen. The dog had first 'joined the regiment' by jumping into the soldier's slit trench during a night battle. In the confusion the man became lost. He set off in what he thought was the right direction but was halted by the dog tugging at the bottom of his trousers. After some 'argument' with the dog the GI realized that the animal was trying to move him in the opposite direction. He followed the little mongrel and was both amazed and relieved when it led him directly to the American lines. They let the dog ride off on the man's stretcher.[21]

It is a moot point as to whether the dog would have been allowed a ride on a British or German stretcher. Differences existed between the the medical systems of the armies. In the British Army, Royal Army Medical Corps officers were attached to fighting units as MOs, but no RAMC other ranks were so attached. Regiments provided their medical orderlies from among the soldiers of the regiment, who retained their regimental status. The American Army Medical Corps, on the other hand, provided Medical Corps detachments, officers and other ranks, for all units down to platoon level. These were controlled by the Regimental Surgeon and did not become members of the fighting regiment.

'Collecting companies' of the divisional medical battalion conveyed wounded men to a clearing station with capacity for 134 patients. The stations were equipped with wooden camp beds as compared to the British steel ones, wooden beds being quicker to move although not so stable. The wounded could then be moved quickly to a field hospital if an urgent operation was required, or to evacuation hospitals of 400 or more beds near the beaches. Normally, as with other Allied troops, men destined for British hospitals could be off French soil within forty-eight hours.[22]

Fast evacuation was available in transport planes returning to Britain empty after unloading supplies. Personnel air services tended to be overshadowed by the incredible feats of the front-line bombers and fighters. And Cobra was a peak occasion for the innovative air tactics of Maj Gen Elwood 'Pete' Quesada. His 'IX TAC' planes seemed to be able to do anything to order. On one occasion a lone Sherman found itself surrounded by thirteen enemy Panzers. A frenzied call for help brought four Thunderbolts diving to the rescue. The air attack quickly caused the enemy tanks to disperse into cover and allowed the Sherman to escape the trap.

At the other end of the scale was the mass attack by Quesada's pilots on a German pocket at Roncey on 29 July. CCB of 2nd AD had swung behind a large enemy force being driven back by 3rd and 4th ADs. The Panzers tried to break through the ring during the night of 28 July, unsuccessfully. Next day a reconnaissance flight found the entire trapped enemy group stalled bumper to bumper and mudguard to mudguard, guns, tanks, vehicles of all kinds. A pilot reported up to 500 vehicles jammed together. Quesada alerted his entire command to fly a conveyor belt attack which lasted from 1510 to 2140 hours. It was truly a 'fighter-bomber's paradise'. Ground forces weighed in from all sides with direct anti-tank and tank fire as well as indirect artillery shoots.

The scene at Roncey was similar to the more discussed scenes of the final shambles in the 'Falaise pocket', gruesome and terrifying, if on a smaller scale. Even so ground investigators found over 100 tanks and 250 other vehicles destroyed or badly damaged as well as many more which had been abandoned by their escaping crews or drivers.[23] Attacking with bombs, rockets, napalm and machine-guns, the Quesada planes were able both to make direct attacks on targets and to drop delayed-action bombs for anticipated targets, as appropriate.

Some of the unenviable task of clearing a way through the Roncey debris fell to 3rd AD under Maj Gen Leroy H. Watson. The 3rd had been advancing parallel to the 2nd, with the right wheel to follow the general direction of main roads. They had been warned to ensure that the white identification markings on their vehicles were fresh and clear and to have their orange smoke ready so that Quesada's pilots could avoid inflicting friendly fire on them. Now the bulldozer tanks and Rhinos were summoned to clear the Roncey streets of overturned tanks, shattered remnants of unidentifiable vehicles, destroyed buildings and the piles of stiffening corpses. For some GIs it was a task worse than confronting Panthers.[24]

Unexpectedly CCA was attached to 1st Inf Div and CCB came under command of 4th Inf Div. The tankers were puzzled. They worked well with the infantry but not to be commanded by an infantry general. Slowly the story worked its way down. Maj Gen Watson, ordered to attack at dawn, had telephoned and wakened his boss, Collins, in the early hours to discuss the attack. Collins considered that a divisional commander should be capable of working out his own details. He took the 'Lightning Joe' decision, apparently unfair but justifiable in war, of relieving Watson of his command immediately and reducing him to the rank of colonel. The division was split until Marcus Rose, on promotion (7 August), could take over. The happy ending was that Watson continued to serve and was later restored to his general's rank, distinguishing himself in the Japanese war.

The CCB went dashing on, establishing bridgeheads over the Soulle, Sienne and See rivers towards their next big objective, Mortain, then just one more unremarkable town along the route to Berlin. In addition to the major confrontations like Roncey, divisional records refer to 'moderate enemy resistance' and 'scattered opposition' and also a 'brief field day' when 'The Spearhead's' own Sherman spearhead burst into an area of unguarded enemy service troops and supply convoys near the See. But, whatever the strength of opposition, the case for the men in the lead was always very similar.

Artilleryman Charles R. Corbin reported in detail on his reconnaissance adventures near Mortain. The section under Lt Patterson had a jeep, a half-track and nine men:

> Lt Patterson, Sgt Marik and I packed our jeep radio and went on foot with the infantry. We provided artillery fire and reached our objective after getting pinned down in a horse stable. When we arrived back we learned our jeep driver, Robert Horton, and Jean Parenteau had been killed by an artillery shell and put our jeep out of action.

At the same time tank gunner Tom Bell was sent from the command tank to find a code book in the Colonel's half-track. A German sniper put a bullet along the crotch seam of Bell's trousers as he bent over the vehicle, but without effecting a vasectomy. Bell himself described it as a 'close shave'! Lt Patterson and Corbin in their half-track were waiting for a Rhino to plough through an obstinate hedgerow:

Lt Cooper pulled up beside us in his tank and while waiting for another hole to be made he joking said, 'Wouldn't it be nice to get a million dollar wound and get the hell out of here?' His tank then passed by and was hit breaking out of the hedgerow. I could feel the heat of the next shell passing by as we backed up. I saw two tankers get out of the tank and pull Lt Cooper out and carry him past us. He didn't seem to be seriously wounded. I waved to him.

Another tank next to us went up in flames and a tanker was having trouble getting out. Another tanker jumped on the tank and tried to help but was hit by a bullet. Then a shell beheaded him. At this point we were hit and bailed out of our half-track. I was between two infantrymen and a shell landed behind us and seriously wounded the two of them although I thought at first they were both dead. All or most of our tanks had been hit and what men could get out retreated to the next hedgerow. A piece of shrapnel hit our driver, John Manual, in the arm and I helped him back.

All of our men were accounted for except Lt Patterson, who was kneeling over two infantrymen near our half-track. He waved to me to come to him. He had administered first aid to them and was giving them morphine shots. We loaded and strapped one man to the left fender and I held the other man on the right fender and the Loot got the damaged half-track started somehow and drove it back to safety. Fifteen of our seventeen tanks were knocked out and a corporal was left as the highest ranking man. It was one hell of a battle witnessed by this 19-year-old kid.

While the 2nd and 3rd had been continuing their twin advance, the 4th and 6th had been thrusting down the coast, ostensibly under Middleton's command but with Patton in the driving seat. As from 1 August Patton was to command the new Third Army. He commanded from the front. Col Thomas D. Gillis remembers Patton storming into the 4th HQ. 'I noticed that his boots, normally bright and shiny, were covered with mud. "Gillis! Where is P [Maj Gen Wood]?"'

As Patton embraced his old buddy Wood, the divisional commander reported, 'General, we're up against this unfordable river and drawing fire from the opposite shore.' Patton growled, 'That's strange. I just waded that damned stream myself.' He then demanded action, in words which might have scorched the paper they were written on if they had been taken down verbatim.[25] Wood himself was no slouch. He commanded much of the subsequent advance from a light plane flying above the leading columns. His nickname was 'Tiger Jack'.

A number of commanders made equal impressions on their men. Tanker Harry Feinberg remembers his remarkable colonel, Creighton W. Abrams, who later had a tank named after him. He commanded 37th Bn in the 4th. 'I lived with him for three and a half years. Never heard him raise his voice, was always up front with us in his own tank, 'Thunderbolt'. Treated everyone equally and fairly, stood in the chow line like everybody else with mess kit for meals, sat with his men, joked with us, but he was damn firm when he needed to be. Great man!'[26]

The twin drive of the 4th and 6th had resulted in Avranches being captured by 29 July. The river crossing in Avranches was a bottle-neck, and the city itself was 75 per cent ruins from an early bombardment just after D-Day. Beyond Avranches good roads opened out in all directions, allowing the hydraheads of Cobra to lash freely at the thinning enemy defences. One sad incident reported by the 6th was when the Frenchman ringing the victory bell was killed by a random shell exploding in his belfry.

In spite of the apparent heroics of the armored division, the men inside the tanks were continually wrestling with fear and often evil presentiment. Staff Sgt Joseph Solarz of 69th Tank Bn in the 6th tells a story which well illustrates this. After a heavy day's fighting they settled for the night in a forward location. Each man would take an hour's guard duty in the turret while the rest of the crew tried to grab some sleep. The loader, Willy Baron, had taken the second hour of watch. Trying to rest, Joe Solarz became aware that Willy was shaking and his teeth were chattering in the dark turret.

He asked Willy if he was cold. 'No, I'm scared!' the boy replied. 'We all have fear. Even the company commander', said Joe soothingly. Willy insisted, 'I've never killed anybody. I never pulled a trigger. I don't know why they want me in this man's army.' Joe ordered Willy to get down and rest while he himself again took guard.

Next morning they continued their advance, mopping up some docile infantry. A concealed anti-tank gun in some bushes fired suddenly. The shot hit the tank on the side where Willy sat. 'The shell came round behind me, ricocheted off the traversing wheel, penetrating the gunner's coat by his chest, and finally settled on his lap. All I saw was a huge red blast which knocked me and the gunner briefly unconscious.'

'Quickly the hot shell on the gunner's lap roused him and he shook me, bringing me too. "We're hit!" he shouted again and again, "We're hit!" I came wide awake, jumped up, out of the tank and rolled onto the ground. I realized then that I was wounded by shrapnel to my face and right arm. We got the medics for the gunner and me. But my loader and good buddy, Willy, was killed. Did he somehow know what was going to happen?'[27]

As the armored columns changed from jet to spray concentration, leaving Avranches for points east, south and west, the German High Command reports could not have been more pessimistic. 'Divisions which had been fighting continuously since the invasion began and had not rested or received any considerable reinforcement, i.e. the 77th, 91st, 243rd, 275th, . . . etc . . . , 5th Parachute, 2nd SS Pz and 17th SS Pz disintegrated into small groups. . . . Most of these groups were without officers or NCOs and roamed at random through the countryside.'

Some Allies scoffed at Patton's style with his pearl-handled revolvers to the fore like a latter-day Wild Bill Hickok. Well they might, at a distance! However, when Hitler joined in the scoffing he was taking a great risk. '"What does that cowboy general think he is doing", Hitler screamed angrily at his staff. It was high noon of 1 August 1944. Tanks were storming through the narrow corridor at Avranches in a torrent that split into columns driving east, south and west at breakneck speed.'[28]

That cowboy general was riding herd on a wild stampede of mighty longhorns which would roll over and crush all opposition across the open prairies of Brittany and Loire.

CHAPTER ELEVEN

SHAMBLES AT CHAMBOIS

'Now we get replacements who show no signs of training. We get clerks and mechanics and cooks who have suddenly become riflemen. In a group recently arrived – I asked for somebody to handle a machine-gun and not one of them spoke out. Nobody knew how! Nobody had ever handled the goddam things. Finally one of them said, "Hell, Sergeant, I'll fire the damn thing".'

Sgt Thomas Kirkman's frustrations at the lack of training of the new men in 119th Inf reflected the feelings of many old soldiers when ranks were thinned by death and wounding. As July merged into August, and the hard-slogging Cobra breakout merged into an often unopposed race for distant objectives, the wastage of the *bocage* weighed heavily. 'Tops' Kirkman further observed, 'The NCOs! – most of them are privates with stripes . . . leading replacements whose arches have fallen after the first 5-mile hike. . . . But the old man says "Jump!" And we jump.'[1]

On 30 July Montgomery had launched British 'Operation Bluecoat' towards Vire as flank guard for the American Army. British and American elements arrived in Vire almost simultaneously. Charles Pearce with 4 CLY remembers that there was a real fear that the Germans, always quick to counter-attack, might thrust down the dividing line between the two armies. He had strict orders to maintain close contact with the American troops on his right flank 'down the Tinchberry Road. Both US and British forces were actually on the road at all times. As OC recce I had to go to see the US unit commander to liaise. All these US troops were very competent and efficient.'[2]

On 2 August Hitler issued orders for a major counter-attack near Mortain in an effort to chop off the Cobra's head and a few of its multiplying coils. 'We must strike like lightning', he told a conference. 'When we reach the sea the American spearheads will be cut off.' His presence did not match his martial words. 'The Führer has become very bent, with cotton wool in his ears and frequently trembles uncontrollably; one must not shake his hand too violently', remarked Gen Werner Kreipe.[3]

In the meantime the armour rolled on, with many of its personnel unaware of the relative importance of one town over another, or, like Joe Solarz, not having known of a town called Mortain and the part it played in military history. The pattern continued, that the closer defeat appeared for the Germans, the more determined were they to resist. Lt George Greene had come up the line as a reinforcement and did not yet know the names of all his men in a TD platoon of four guns. He found that in thick fog 'attacker and defender groped for each other, fighting blindly, viciously, often trading blows and even bayonet thrusts – a rare occurrence in the Second World War'.[4]

Pte 'Tiny' Hurtado had sought the aid of his medics for a frozen shoulder. The doctor was about to prescribe a bottle of liniment when he thought to ask what Tiny had in the bulky sandbag he was carrying. It was full of hand grenades. The men were being issued with a sack each, or two if they could carry them. During the night German infantry had attacked, throwing five grenades around Tiny's slit. The next grenade bounced off his tin hat but did not explode. Incensed, Tiny threw all the grenades in his two sacks, then borrowed another four sacks and charged the enemy, showering them with grenades. The doctor observed, 'With good reason your shoulder has frozen', and handed Tiny the liniment, but did not order him to stop throwing grenades.[5]

All reserves were committed by the US units bearing the brunt of the first Mortain attacks (code named by the Germans Operation Liège). Capt Thomas H. Carothers, holding a thin defence line with nothing behind him, launched a furious grenade and bayonet attack and stemmed the local enemy onrush. He was recommended for the Distinguished Service Cross. Sadly, although it seemed happily at the time, Carothers and his men had captured a German paymaster and relieved him of his burden of cash, spending some of it on a company barbecue. (Front-line soldiers tended to distinguish between 'loot', civilian property, and 'booty', enemy property.) Higher authority learned of the pay acquisition and was not impressed. Carothers was cited for a court martial. His commanding officer protested, referring to the captain's outstanding bravery. Carothers was allowed to escape with a lesser reprimand, but his DSC recommendation was reduced to the award of a lesser medal.[6]

Charles R. Corbin, mentioned earlier, was still in the thick of it and was amazed by the reaction of some men. Sent with a message for his colonel, 'I started out when the shells were coming in. Again I hit the ground. I noticed Leo Zemitus walking around in among all the shit. Not ducking. He told me, "If you are going to get hit, it has your name on it" . . . I gave the message to Col Hogan and was halfway back when I saw a medic with Zemitus. A piece of shrapnel had passed through his arm. I saw another medic leading a man with his chin cut off and another with his arm hanging loose in his sleeve, and a sergeant who, although not wounded, was in a terrible shape of mental breakdown.'[7]

Nearby Capt George Stallings of 33rd AR had his tank set on fire by an enemy flame-thrower. Two of the crew were killed. True to his name, only Cpl Miracle emerged unscathed. Stallings bailed out on fire. He jumped into a wet ditch and rolled himself free of flames. As he lay there in a blackened uniform, his visible skin also scorched black, a German patrol came and, looking down upon him, decided that he was dead. With enemy guns firing all around him he decided that he could use his burned clothing as camouflage and crawled unobserved across the black tarmac road. He then boarded another tank and resumed duty. He was awarded the DSC.[8]

Battle danger often spurred men to superhuman efforts. Lt Henry A. Roberts was in a half-track hit by a mine and blown upside down. His driver, while not badly wounded, was trapped underneath. Roberts tried to lift the vehicle single-handed and failed. The driver's plaintive voice cried, 'Just six inches more, Lieutenant!' Roberts made a tremendous effort and lifted the half-track enough to allow the relieved driver to crawl out. Two days later Roberts came across his old vehicle still lying upside down. Out of sheer curiosity he went to it and tried to lift it. He could hardly lift it a couple of inches unaided.[9]

Infantryman Harold W. Vincent, with 36th AI, was setting up his mortar when he was blown over by a huge impact, like a giant's punch. Standing up gingerly and feeling himself all over, he found that a large object had penetrated under the skin of his shoulder. Patiently he waited for the medic to investigate. Probing carefully, the doctor found the live nose cone of a small German shell, still full of HE, jammed in between muscles and bones. It was recorded that everybody except 'Vinnie' dived for cover. Eventually a sheet of tank armour was procured and set up on the operating table. Surgeons operated, peering fearfully over the top of the shield. They succeeded in separating Vinnie from his unwanted bulge.[10]

On the German side Operation Liège was meant to be a surprise attack. The 'Deutschland' regiment had ordered a foot march up to the start line so that the sound of their vehicles would not alert the enemy. They could not know that Ultra had again picked up a vital signal, and so Bradley had a few hours in which to start switching reserves to meet Liège. Initial success soon ran into the inevitable storm of American air, artillery and tank fire. Many of the more experienced Germans, while continuing to fight tenaciously, had little belief in being able to cut through the massed enemy forces to any significant depth.

The desperate Mortain counter-attack barely slowed the post-Cobra impetus. In theory Cobra had achieved its objectives with the liberation of Avranches, but the opening routes ahead meant that the Cobra action continued ever faster and with ever more reinforcement. Patton was now commanding the new Third Army in those wide open spaces and driving his troops remorselessly.

Walter Klein, still retreating in a group of about 150 survivors, many of them wounded, was now surrounded by the flood of American armour:

We received a terrific fire from a brushwood which was occupied by Americans. I made field dressings for the wounded while nobody fired at me. I want to reiterate that the American infantry, tank and aviators fought in a fair way . . . all men wearing the Red Cross could help their wounded . . . I was made prisoner at 0700 hours. The American captain allowed us to recover our wounded, assisted by a surgeon and three medical officers of the American Army. I also helped to bring in the American wounded. Eighteen hours later the work was finished. . . .[11]

Much of the American advance was led by reconnaissance troops in the light Stuart tank. They were well aware that their main gun, a 37mm, was a relative pea-shooter. It is not necessary to be a mathematician to compare 37mm with 75mm or 88mm or 105mm guns used by the enemy waiting just around the next bend or behind the next hedge. Staff Sgt Max Lutcavish was 'a churchgoing man' who would only trust in God, but not the 37mm. Approaching a sinister-looking bend on 12 August, they came upon a German truck full of troops. The truck reversed back around the bend:

We pursued it and directed fire from the 37mm and co-axial guns . . . at a group of dismounted Germans by their truck. Then I heard a terrific explosion. I looked to the rear and the [Sherman] tank directly behind me was in flames. I caught a glimpse of a whirl of dust caused by a muzzle blast to my right under an apple tree about 125 yards away. I didn't know for sure what it was or whether it could be knocked out with my 37mm. But I knew I had to do something quick because it was already traversing its gun at me. There was no way back because of the burning tank behind me.

Again I heard an explosion and felt my tank lunge forward. A bazooka had hit me in the rear and set the rear end of the tank on fire. What a position for a church-going man to be in! There was nothing else to do but to dish it out!

That gunner of mine was plenty fast. In less time than it takes to tell he threw eight well-placed rounds of AP and had that thing on fire. Now we could definitely tell it was a tank, a huge one. . . . While we were wiping the cold sweat from our brow another enemy tank crossed the road about 400 yards ahead of us. We swung the turret in that direction but the tank disappeared in the brush. My tank was now burning badly, so I ordered the crew to abandon it . . . and we made our way back to the platoon, 'toot sweet', on foot.[12]

That was a most unusual result with a 37mm, requiring skill, luck and, no doubt divine intervention for the church-going man. But it was a trick which might merit a danger label, 'Don't try this at home!' Many church-going men did not survive such encounters as Patton's armies swung all ways, but most significantly left and northwards to meet the Canadians, Poles and British coming south from Caen.

After Operation Goodwood had staggered to a halt and the Canadian Operation Spring had been drowned in blood, 41-year-old Canadian Lt Gen Guy Granville Simonds was ordered to launch another attack down the main Caen–Falaise road. Reviewing earlier tragedies he resolved to employ novel tactics in order to cross the open ground so fatal to Shermans. In 'Totalize' he would attack at night, using armoured carriers for the infantry and bypassing the fortress villages on the way. On the night of 7 August he lined up seven columns of mixed tanks, infantry, engineers and artillery observers in low-lying areas near Cormelles. A massive RAF raid bombed parallel to the tank routes without hitting a single tank in the left-hand columns only about 800 yards away. By dawn all the columns were well behind the German lines and some had been on their objectives by 0300 hours.[13] By midday most of the bypassed villages had been reduced.

It was a unique stroke with minimal losses in tanks and in the infantry who were carried in the new carriers. Whereas O'Connor and Roberts had meekly requested such carriers, and had been rebuffed by culpable higher authority, Simonds simply went ahead, telling not asking. He borrowed some disused SPs from the US army, had the guns ripped out, the armour reinforced and infantry quickly trained to ride in relative safety. The Canadians had been reinforced by 51st Highland Div and British 33rd AB.

The German reaction was to counter-attack, and the famed Panzermeyer was there himself, watching and summing up the situation. Seeing the hundreds of Allied tanks approaching along the slopes, he quite instinctively ordered, 'Attack!' He had on hand the almost equally famous highest-scoring tank ace, Michael Wittmann, with his Tigers. What both men failed to take into account was that the classic Normandy situation had been reversed. 1st Northamptonshire Yeomanry at St Aignan and 144 RAC at Cramesnil, both with a total of about a dozen Firefly Shermans on call, had sidled up to the side of the main road and were hidden, awaiting just such an attack, the powerful Fireflys now defending.

The Tigers came down alongside the road, their guns bristling towards the west, where firing had been heard. They passed in front of the lone 1 NY Firefly guarding farthest forward supported by two 75mm Shermans. Capt Tom Boardman commanded Firefly gunner, Joe Ekins, to fire his 17pdr. Within minutes the Wittmann troop was wiped out by that one gun. Wittmann was proved not to have been immortal. At the same time, supporting counter-attacks by MK IV tanks and Panzer-Grenadiers were also repulsed by 1 NY and 1 Black Watch, with heavy infantry losses. So far, so good for Simonds.

Unfortunately at this point, and not entirely due to Panzermeyer's much glorified personal intervention, things began to go wrong. Montgomery had impatiently and unwisely insisted that Simonds should attack two or three days before the astute Canadian was ready. So one of the two fresh armoured units due to take up Phase 2 of Totalize, the Polish Div, was still coming ashore on the beaches and rushing up to the attack without proper preparation. The Poles had been waiting since 1939 to avenge themselves on their blitzkreig conquerors and charged enthusiastically across the fields beyond St-Aignan. Capt Tom Boardman, seeing their peril, tried to radio a warning, but not only was there a language difference, the Poles were also using different code signs. Time had not allowed for the type of difficult coordination which was needed.

Panzermeyer's battle group, repulsed a few minutes earlier, were now back in defensive positions and the roles reverted to the Goodwood scenario. The Poles became, like the Goodwood tankers, helpless targets in a 'duck shoot'. Trying to keep the advance moving that night, Simonds had to employ a new Canadian Div, equally enthusiastic but equally unprepared, in another night march. Where the more experienced tank men of the night before had found their landmarks in the total darkness, the new men lost direction. The battle group was wiped out. Simonds would have to try again.

This he did, a week later, with the code name 'Tractable'. Instead of nature's night he used smoke and dust to produce obscurity within which his tanks attacked. Unluckily the fog of aerial misunderstanding again closed down on the soldiers marching beneath the air fleets. The air bombing of 7 August, at least on the left flank, had been a masterly success, with Pathfinders marking their fleets onto targets within a safety margin which their commander could not believe. Tractable was to have been a repeat.

For Tractable the air crews were briefed to log onto the coast as they crossed it and then bomb at a very specific time calculated in minutes and seconds after crossing the coast. The master bombers were also to drop yellow target markers. Some of the air crews, forgetting to check their specially issued stop-watches, saw yellow flares and dropped their bombs: right on top of the assembled Allies waiting to advance! The Poles could only agonize again. They suffered 397 casualties (more than the total number of tank crew members in a full Polish regiment), with 150 killed. Canadians and Scottish Highlanders lost men as well.[14]

While smoke and haze contributed to the errors, the main problem was that the men on the ground, as was their custom when friendly planes seemed to be homing in on them, fired their yellow smoke, the recognized identity signal. A later inquiry blamed the Army for not advising the Air Force that yellow smoke would be used in this way, thus allowing the air commanders to plan to use yellow markers (in Totalize they used red and green). It requires an enormous elasticity of imagination to accept that, after two months in Normandy, with tank crews and infantry firing off yellow smoke (their only signal issue) in large numbers virtually every day, and with aeroplanes responding, waggling their wings and flying on to locate more legitimate prey, the air command could have been unaware of this standard yellow 'help!' signal and therefore needed to be specifically informed of it by the Army for the 14 August plan.

A more dangerous threat to the success of Tractable might have been when a major carrying the complete details of the plan got lost on the previous night, drove into the German lines and was killed. The enemy knew exactly what was going to happen and where. Another local problem was that Brigadier Leslie Booth, the skilled Canadian ground commander of the leading armour, was quickly killed and his entire tactical HQ wiped out, resulting in a bewildering gap in leadership at a critical moment. However, the Poles and Canadians, quickly inducted into the realities of war, were not to be denied, even by the total sacrifice of small groups of Hitlerjugend fighting to the end. Overnight on 15 August Falaise had fallen.

Much has been said about the superiority of the German soldier and much has been implied about the lack of skill and warlikeness of the Allies. It is therefore perhaps relevant to note that the Canadian force attacking Falaise, with most infantry battalions down to half strength at most, fell well below the accepted ratio of attackers over defenders (four or five to one) generally thought necessary.[15] It might also be noted that one US unit, 2 Bn, 66th AR in 'Hell on Wheels', served for eighteen consecutive days as an attacking spearhead without respite. It lost 51 per cent of its fighting personnel and 70 per cent of its tanks, but claimed enemy casualties 400 per cent of its own strength.[16] This is not in any way to disparage German skills and commitment, often superhuman.

Something like a detective mystery now enters the German chronicles. On 15 August their commander in Normandy, 'Clever Hans' von Kluge disappeared! Perhaps he had reason so to do. On 15 August Hitler was saying it was the worst day of his life, and was implying that the counter-attack at Mortain had failed because von Kluge had wanted it to fail. For twelve hours his radio was silent and nobody knew where he had gone. Late at night he arrived at the HQ of Gen Eberbach saying that he had been attacked by Allied fighter-bombers and had spent the day in a ditch.[17]

'Hitler however, strongly suspected that he had been trying to make contact with the enemy to arrange a capitulation.' He sent for Field Marshal Model to replace von Kluge. Suspected of being implicated in the failed plot to assassinate Hitler, von Kluge drove as far as his First World War exploits near Metz, spread a blanket on the ground and took a cyanide capsule. The strategic outcome was that Model, who was a much more loyal Nazi, was able to persuade Hitler to allow him to begin withdrawing troops out of the now narrowing 'Falaise pocket'.[18]

As well as conquering Brittany Patton had wheeled large forces towards Argentan where they might link up with Canadians from Falaise, thus encircling a large part of the German Army still contesting the Bluecoat advance in the deep bottom of the pocket. Patton had no confidence in Montgomery ('Monty does not want me as he feels I will steal the show, which I will'), and little more regard for his compatriots ('Bradley and Hodges are such nothings. Their one virtue is that they get along by doing nothing').[19] Now he was impatient to be allowed to close the gap. Versions differ as to why he was halted, whether by Montgomery's or Bradley's decision or both. In fact, when Patton started his tremendous advance a Falaise pocket was not a prime part of the general plan. The opportunity for trapping the German Army seemed almost to reveal itself in spite of what everyone else was expecting to do. If there was to be a trapping of large numbers of the enemy it was originally expected to be on a far wider encirclement extending up to a long stretch of the River Seine.

On 13 August Patton told his diary, 'This [XV] Corps could easily advance to Falaise and completely close the gap.' On 16 August he again confided in the diary, 'I had telephonic orders to halt . . . I believe the order emanated from 21st Army Group [Montgomery] and is either due to jealousy of the Americans, or to utter ignorance of the situation, or to a combination of the two.'[20] When the Falaise pocket was eventually closed and sealed off, the closure took place farther to the east, at Chambois.

Gerhard Stiller was a 1939 Panzer man who had seen all that war had to offer. He had camouflaged his tank at Tilly-la-Campagne, just above Bourguebus, and picked off numbers of Canadian tanks which had tried to improve on Goodwood. With 1st SS LAH he has dashed away to Mortain, recognizing it as one of the most hopeless missions he had ever undertaken. Now nearing Chambois, and his long-suffering Mk IV tank, No 711, having been finally destroyed, he joined his commander, Maj Gen 'Teddy' Wisch, in seeking ways of slipping through the closing Allied lines, to escape and fight again one day.[21]

All the superlatives uttered about the horrors of war so far were surpassed in the events around Chambois, as increasing numbers of Allied troops sought to weld tight the closure. Desperate, tired and battered German troops from inside the pocket attacked outwards, in organized units or small groups. Reserve formations from outside, still battleworthy, tried to burst through inwards as the welding process continued. The entire area became a slaughterhouse of men and animals as the majority of German transport was trapped. The fighting was so confused and intermingled that few accurate accounts of specific heroics survived, except to say that every encounter was heroic until such times as the exhausted Germans in the trap had no option but to lay down their arms.

Capt Gaskins in the American attack from the south-west said, 'It was the first time he ever had living proof of the old phrase "rivers of blood – blood was actually running in sizable streams in the gutters". Houses were burning, the stench of dead and burnt flesh was almost unbearable; there was an unbelievable clutter of dead Germans, horses and destroyed vehicles.'[22]

Among the Canadians first into the chaos was Major David Currie, who would be the first Canadian in Normandy to be awarded the rare Victoria Cross. Commanding a reconnaissance squadron of the South Albertas, his task was to deny the enemy an exit through the key village of St-Lambert as unnumbered hordes of enemy, some mad with fear, others fighting berserk, swarmed around Currie's tiny group. Within the narrow village Currie and his men had to deal with Tiger and Panther tanks by stalking them on foot. Lt Armour climbed onto one tank and was about to drop a grenade into the turret when the German commander emerged. The two men were so close that all they could do was wrestle until both of them fell to the ground. A private shot and wounded the German. Armour climbed back up with his grenade and disabled the tank.

The avenging Poles also formed a thin line, short on ammunition, water, food and medical supplies, and held a final hill top, Mount Ormel, to confound a climactic onrush of enemy. Lt Niewinowski remembered:

Hills thickly covered by trees and bushes were very difficult to patrol . . . the enemy directed their attacks with a fury of desperation . . . German tanks approached the very edge of Polish positions . . . the wrecks of Panthers and Shermans were soon standing face to face with each other, gun against gun, destroyed by point blank fire. Supplies by air drop proved a failure . . . soldiers exhausted by lack of sleep . . . the suffering of the wounded, the mortality rate quickly rising . . . prisoners began to outnumber the defenders.[23]

As the end drew near, 'A continuous rain of fire descended on the remaining Germans as they tried to escape over roads and fields littered with burning tanks and vehicles. . . . Dead cows and horses, their bodies bloated with gas, were everywhere. Maddened horses that had broken loose from their harnesses raced wildly across a landscape marked by pillars of flame from burning gasoline supplies. Capt Jack Galvin of 712th TDs was told by a prisoner that in a valley below . . . there were thousands of Germans who wanted to surrender. The captain walked down into the valley and led 1,100 prisoners to safety through the American lines above.'[24]

Most horrific, Lt Belton Cooper described 'the burned bodies of German tankers climbing out of their tanks looked like charcoal mannequins. . . . Many horses were killed because they could not escape the traces holding them to the burning caissons.'[25] Cooper saw that at Roncey. It was repeated at Chambois on a much greater scale. Surprisingly some sources described it all as a German success because a proportion of those who might have been trapped managed to squirm through the network of Allied contacts while the pocket was being sewn up tight. The true word to describe Chambois was 'débâcle'.

As the sound of gunfire died away around Chambois and as the Allied armies rushed to reach the Seine crossings, peace of a kind began to descend on the Normandy of Cobra, Goodwood and Totalize. But the killing continued. The brutal aftermath of battle, anti-personnel mines under the ground and booby traps above it, continued to maim the unwary who wore no uniform and whose only concern was to rebuild the ruins.

On 1 August near Lessay, 16-year-old Helene Boucard and 18-year-old Daniel Vengeons were blown up and killed by a mine when crossing the marshes near Renneville. 12 August: Pierre Lemoigne trod on a mine in his own garden and died in an American field hospital. 23 August: Jean Digne, agricultural labourer, dug into a mine and died. 26 August: Pierre Gourdan was killed by a mine when working in his field. 10 September: Pierre's brother, Henri, died in the same way. And so it went on. Exactly one year after D-Day two local men clearing ruins disturbed and were killed by a mine.

Then, in the perverse way war selects its victims: 22 October 1945, Hermann Daasch, German prisoner of war, also clearing ruins at La Montagne near Lessay, was killed by another German mine.[26]

CHAPTER TWELVE

VERY UNFRIENDLY FIRE

Andrew Dewar, Sherman driver, together with Terry Boyne, had seen his commander, Major Powell, killed by that vicious weapon, too familiarly known to many as Moaning Minnies or, to the Americans, Screaming Meemies. That had been on the 2 F&F charge up Bourguebus Ridge on 19 July. Now it was Andrew's turn for the 'bullet with my name on it'.

2 F&F were advancing along the Vire road on the Anglo-American boundary. Andrew's new commander, Sgt Mathers, had pushed so far forward that he had overtaken a German ambulance. Tigers halted their progress along a sunken road. Mathers called for rocket Typhoon support. USAAF Thunderbolts were overhead and took the call. It was a hot day. The turret flaps were wide open. There was a scream of aero engines. Bullets ricocheted off the turret and down inside the confined space, sounding like angry wasps. Once again the air pilots had been confused by friendly tanks being too far forward. Guns large and small were firing all over, along the land and out of the sky. Andrew's Sherman suffered repeated shocks. The crew bailed out.

From the ditch beside the road the crew could see that a large shell had entered one end of the tank, bored right through the entire tank and exited the other end. Andrew was aware of blood at shoulder and calf. A German ambulance man jumped into the ditch and began to attend to their wounds. He located shrapnel in the shoulder, upper arms and knee, and saw to Andrew and Mathers being evacuated safely. It was all a bit like the parable of the Good Samaritan: 'Who then is the neighbour . . .?'[1]

There had already been an outbreak of a very unfriendly fire of words which would last beyond the turn of the century. Patton and Montgomery had been like two tom-cats on a hot roof screeching at each other. As mentioned earlier, it was not just international unfriendliness: there were internecine quarrels as well. Tedder was seeking Montgomery's blood. Americans Hughes, Lee and Bedell Smith were hurling accusations at each other. Verbal thrust and counter-thrust became the subject of academic investigation leading to academic positioning on main issues. These included the jibes that the 'Brits and Canuks' had advanced too slowly, thus causing the Americans to lose an inordinately high number of casualties, or, on the other hand, that 'the Yanks had an easy ride' in Cobra because the other Allies were bearing the brunt of the major SS Panzer attacks.

It is therefore relevant to look at some of the criticism, especially in regard to the 'failure' of Goodwood and the 'success' of Cobra, from the point of view of experts and also from a worm's eye view. Recently an interesting debate had been instigated about the validity of the worm's eye reminiscences of participants, as in this book, when exposed to expert, that is to say professional or academic historians', scrutiny. This current debate was born out of a French Resistance issue which went to a court judgement (in favour of the reminiscing participants). It affected two French Resistance heroes, Raymond and Lucie Aubrac, whose memoirs had been challenged by historians. This led to various commentators raising questions such as, 'Who has the right to "make" history? Should their [witnesses'] words carry equal weight to those of a professional historian? Are we seeing the democratization of history with historical actors commanding the same respect and attention as established historians?' Comments during the debate have included that of a French historian, Henry Rousso, that 'Historians become prisoners of their mode of analysis.'[2]

Certainly a study of some thirty or more historians' views of Cobra and Goodwood will reflect diametrically opposed 'findings', ranging, for instance, from that of Belchem (Montgomery's head of operations), that the victory in Normandy conformed to Montgomery's pre-invasion master plan,[3] to Carafano's suggestion that Montgomery's 'pre-invasion master plan is a fiction'.[4] It is interesting, therefore, to look at some worm's eye comments as well as recent professional summing-up.

Sgt Sid Jones, right at the sharp end, said of Goodwood, 'We should have stopped at the finish of the area that had been bombed by the RAF and USAAF . . . and waited for infantry support. 2 NY went a railway too far.'[5] Maj Close, leading the first tank squadron of Goodwood, had already felt at the time that a traditional advance by a series of bounds would have been better than the suicidal second charge over that 'railway too far'.[6] A young tank gunner who survived remarked that, 'At reunions of veterans after fifty years it is not unusual to hear tank crew members wondering at the mentality which sent parades of tanks up those open slopes under the noses of the most fearsome guns ever used in a major war.'[7]

Continuing to look at Goodwood specifically, the then Capt Charlie Robertson was a little more fatalistic:

When we [7th Black Watch] moved forward to take over the village of Cagny from a unit of the Guards Division, we considered the ground gained to be a considerable achievement, and I doubt if any of us really thought a complete breakthrough had been a possibility. The strategy of tying down the German armour on the Caen sector of the bridgehead could only be made to work by our armour being a repeated active threat, and the consequence of this was, unfortunately but inevitably, a series of bloody noses.[8]

One official 11th AD review of Goodwood considered that, 'This air bombardment should have been split, and the second half of it launched against the Bourguebus Ridge; during this latter phase, also, guns could have been brought forward to support a further advance.'[9] The Guards commander during Goodwood, Adair, was suspicious of Montgomery's later assertion that the ground gained in Goodwood was, more or less, the extent of his intentions at the time. 'It had not attained all that was planned . . . I am sure [Monty] would have been ready to extend a limited break-out if all had gone to plan. Sadly, it didn't.'[10]

A modern historian and tank expert, reviewing all the evidence available after fifty years, considered that 'the planned campaign as outlined by Montgomery had no "Cannae" strategy', that is a close encirclement like the Roncey or Falaise pockets.[11] Another recent historian, himself a general, commenting on Montgomery's claim to have substantially 'written down' German armour, calculated the German losses as 'only 20 per cent of the total German armoured strength in the 1 SS Panzer Corps sector'.[12] It has been pointed out that, due to the thin German front line, much of the initial impetus of Goodwood was lost on virtually empty space.[13]

Colonel von Luck, the arch-villain (or hero, according to perspective) of Goodwood, had a clear idea as to why Goodwood failed to penetrate farther:

Our defence did hold a greatly superior British force – the reasons were – on the British side –

a) their tanks were outgunned by our anti-tank defence.

b) they did not make the best use of the air and artillery bombardment.

c) until the attacks on Bras and Hubert Folie they did not use all arms in a coordinated attack.[14]

A study for the US Army War College class of 2000 follows similar lines. It insists that not only did the authors of Goodwood hope to reach Falaise, 'Dempsey . . . was being conservative for he had in mind Argentan . . . 15 miles beyond Falaise.' Reasons why the advance broke down included:

First, the massive bombardment severely cratered the roads and obstructed the axis of advance.

Second, the Germans based their defense lines on defense in depth, so the carpet-bombing area did not cover the area where the German 88mm flak guns were located.

Third, the bombardment failed to take out the German anti-armour units and reserves located further back.

Additionally, the Allies were experiencing unexpected difficulty in coping with the fighting qualities of the individual German soldier.[15]

Montgomery has been widely criticized for his misleading statements. Dempsey was guilty of the unbelievable decision to forbid armoured personnel carriers. O'Connor was at fault, as corps commander, for not providing personnel carriers which Simonds did three weeks later. Others have pointed to the absence of adequate infantry close up to the lead tanks.

Dempsey himself, in his comment, stated that Goodwood 'was not a very good operation of war tactically, but strategically it was a great success, even though we did get a bloody nose. I didn't mind about that. I was prepared to lose a couple of hundred tanks. So long as I didn't lose men. . . . If we had tried to achieve the same result with a conventional infantry attack I hate to think what the casualties would have been.'[16] Dempsey seems to have been stuck at the 'either/or' stage of thinking, either a tank attack or an infantry attack, when the Germans had long moved on to an 'all arms' approach which did not send in tanks or infantry alone. And in Totalize armoured carriers put their infantry onto objectives with few casualties.

The commander of the leading division in Goodwood, Pip Roberts, has generally enjoyed 'a good press' regarding Goodwood. He was able to put his own quite convincing point of view early on after the war, his division later achieved considerable fame, and many of his men revered him in the way Patton's men revered their commander. However, his touch might appear to have been less certain in Goodwood.

He did not plan to use flails to clear mines, until persuaded otherwise by his one-time commander, Hobart. And mines there were. He considered afterwards that more infantry should have been provided with the spearhead instead of wasting time around Demouville.[17] Only four companies out of three battalions were actually involved in action in clearing the two villages, but he allowed the remainder of his infantry to stay there some four hours after many of them could have been on the move. And he did not insist strongly enough on using armoured personnel carriers. In fact, from the beginning he was not happy with some of the plan which he was going to implement.

It is true that even major-generals must obey orders, although Roberts himself took leave to stray from precise orders in Bluecoat. Most critics have accepted Roberts's statement that, when he objected strongly to the problems foreseen in the Goodwood plan, he was offered the alternative of 'letting another armoured division' lead the way.[18] Who then was fooling whom? The Guards were still landing some of their rear formations on the beaches and were unblooded. The 7th, at that stage, were not trusted by Montgomery. Their commander, Erskine 'thought the whole operation a waste of armour',[19] while both he and his armoured brigadier were listed to be sent home (which they soon were) in Montgomery's mind. Also the 7th were equipped with Cromwells, even less suitable for open tank country than Shermans. What other armoured division then was available in the British Army in Normandy? Even if major-generals, and lieutenant-generals, must obey orders, it might appear that O'Connor and Roberts were somewhat to quick to surrender on decisions which they could, to some extent, have influenced or varied within their own remits.

Goodwood has been described as one of the most researched of all battles. There has been less criticism of Cobra, perhaps because its success was so clear and far-reaching. Military defeats in the Second World War seem to attract more critical attention than victories. Of the many books in the bibliography taking an overall view of Normandy, all allocate considerable space to Goodwood, while only four give a detailed appraisal of the Totalize night march, one of the most brilliant feats of arms in the war. Even those texts spend more time on the eventual disruption of the second stage of Totalize than on the successful first phase.

Leaving aside the facile idea that 'Cobra was an easy ride', there have been historians who considered that it could have been planned and managed better. The appalling loss of American life through friendly fire in the air bombing of the first two days is an obvious target for criticism. Gen Bradley has usually been regarded as a good leader, but dissonant words have also been written about him. 'General Bradley's generalship, however, was not flawless. His most serious error was in the safety precautions put in place before the carpet bombing on 25 July . . . General Bradley assumed an excessive risk and his soldiers paid the price.'[20] Whether that is fair comment or not, the obdurate air commanders exacerbated the risk by refusing to fly a parallel route. Two weeks later Totalize demonstrated that it was preferable to fly parallel to the advance, and the safety zone then was far smaller (800 to 1,000 yards) than Bradley allowed.

More severe American censure has been aimed recently at some of 'Lightning Joe' Collins's decisions. His 'contributions to Cobra have been overrated . . . Collins's gravest error was insufficiently weighting the strength of the attacking forces on the first day of the attack. . . . As the battle unfolded and new operational opportunities opened up to widen and deepen the penetration, General Collins was slow to exploit them.'[21] Yet a writer who served at the sharp end in Normandy felt that Collins's decision to commit the armour before the infantry situation was clear was a major and brave stroke of generalship.[22]

If any ideas of an easy American ride still persist, Canadian Terry Copp points out that 'no breakthrough was possible until the GIs had won the battle of attrition in scores of small battles which cost the Americans more than 20,000 fatal casualties and 120,000 wounded – Western Front [1914–18] conditions and losses. . . . Operation "Cobra", the American breakthrough, was a result of attritional warfare, not an exception to it.'[23]

If some voices were raised accusing American infantry of advancing too slowly and being reluctant to press home attacks, peripatetic German medic and battle watcher, Walter Klein, had an answer to that:

I personally don't quite agree with that opinion. The American command wanted to sacrifice as little personnel as possible. And if the American infantry did not approach our lines, it was not from cowardice, but because they were ordered to withdraw, as soon as they met strong resistance, and to wait until the air force and the heavy weapons had exhausted the enemy. Our infantry men, who could not count upon any help, and who had seen the Russian infantry, could not have had a better opinion of the American infantry.[24]

The US Army War College study presented some main reasons for the success of Cobra, including:

1. The key Panzer Lehr Division was virtually destroyed in the carpet bombing.
2. Allied air attacks paralyzed German efforts to bring up reinforcements.
3. The bombardment destroyed much of the communications between front line units and HQs.
4. The Americans weighted their attack with mechanized forces striking at a small point on the thin German line.
5. The simultaneous British [and Canadian] attack at Caen kept German forces pinned down there.[25]

Gen Patton had been convinced that he could have closed the Falaise pocket much faster by continuing to drive north with three divisions. He was ordered to halt, and some writers have taken up his cry that he could have achieved it. Bradley doubted whether Patton's force could have withstood the inevitable counter-attacks. Some later opinions have supported Bradley's view. Terry Copp again comments:

If Patton had been permitted to continue north towards Falaise, his two armoured divisions would surely have been engaged in a pitched battle with most of the German armour and a number of infantry divisions. Could two US and one French division have closed the Falaise Gap and kept it closed when attacked from three directions . . . [by] the German army, still an organized force with an equivalent strength of eight to ten divisions?[26]

The Poles and Canadians, engulfed in the fury of fighting around Mount Ormel and St-Lambert, would probably have answered, 'No!'

One strange factor which has not been widely noticed refers to the return to *bocage* country around Falaise. Both the British in Goodwood and the Americans in Cobra struck out for open country through which their armour could race at high speed. The largely unplanned development of the final pocket around Chambois saw them back in difficult country of small fields, high hedgerows, tiny farms, thick woods, and deep streams, very similar to the *bocage* from which they had tried so strenuously, and for so long, to escape.

The problem of inferior guns and other equipment was a constant strain on the morale of Allied troops, especially in sending out Shermans to wrestle with Tigers. One incident in Villers-Bocage illustrates the extremes to which men had to go against the Tiger. On the occasion mentioned when Pat Dyas had seen his shots bounce off a Tiger at 20 yard range, a Lt Cotton was seen walking along the street carrying some blankets and gasoline cans, and holding an umbrella over the blankets in the rain. He entered a door and soon appeared at an upstairs window above the Tiger. He then soaked the blankets with gasoline and dropped them on to the exhaust pipe of the Tiger. The resultant blaze was enough to flush the crew out of the tank.[27]

A recent film on the Sherman (2002) stated that 'we' had no answer to the Tiger's 88mm gun. That is untrue. The 17pdr mounted on the Sherman Firefly was demonstrably a better gun, although the Firefly itself still suffered from inadequate armour. A technical study referred to the 'small but significant battle' of St-Aignan during Totalize, which 'was to show that if employed in a manner which protected its weak points the M4 Sherman in its Firefly guise could take on and defeat the much feared German armour.' The same study also pointed out that the Tiger itself had severe technical problems. 'The intricate semi-automatic Maybach Olvar gearbox was often unable to cope with the strains of the 56-ton machine and, as a result, was the most common cause for the demise of a Tiger . . . what might be referred to as "over-engineering".'[28]

There seems to have been somewhat less welcome in British and Canadian armies to lower-rank initiatives than was evident in the US forces. Canadian tank ace Maj Radley-Walters 'was distinctly unimpressed when an armoured corps staff officer, visiting the front, upbraided him for having his tanks piled with extra treads [as additional armour]. Added weight, the officer complained, would wear out tank engines prematurely.'[29] Compare this with American top brass interest in the brainwave of two humble sergeants with their Rhino adaptation.

Whatever disadvantages were suffered by the Allied infantry and tankers were more than compensated by mastery of the air and the volume of artillery fire always available. Added to that was the endless roller delivery of equipment replacement from vast factories. Adair of the

Guards summed it up neatly, 'Tank for tank none of ours could take on German tanks. But we had more fuel, more tanks and greater mobility.'[30]

Since the war a 'school of historians' has lauded the individual German soldier and deprecated the skills and dedication of the Allied soldier. Terry Copp, in an easily accessible final chapter of Whitaker's book, has followed this thread through from Liddell Hart via Van Crevald to the present day. Van Crevald spoke of the German soldiers' 'morale, elan, unit cohesion and resilience', but the GI, the British Tommy, and 'Johnny Canuk' were the 'tired, the poor, the huddled masses' commanded by officers who were 'less than mediocre'.[31] Copp refutes this. In fact almost anyone who was 'there', while confirming the quality of the best German soldiers, would see Van Crevald's view of the Allies as meriting the accusation made against St Paul: 'much learning hath made thee mad'.

No German gunner could have fired more accurately than Firefly Joe Ekins (of the huddled masses?) at St-Aignan, with three Tigers destroyed by three shots. No soldiers could have behaved more abjectly than the three thousand Germans who surrendered at Le Havre naval fortress, equipped with 14in guns turned inland, when fired at by two Shermans.[32]

Perhaps one of the most sustainable criticisms of the Allied armies relates to the failure to conceive of and plan for what would be the realities of fighting in Normandy. The success of certain tactics in the African desert cannot be used as an excuse for employing incorrect tactics in Normandy. The British and French had the experience of 1940 when, at Arras and on the Somme, inadequately supported tank attacks failed to have the desired impact. There was also later experience for the Americans in Sicily. But a Canadian was able to say of Normandy:

> Misunderstandings between tankers and infantry were evident [at first] because neither knew as much about the other's roles, strengths and weaknesses as they might have. Instead of being organized in integrated units, infantry battalions and tank squadrons lived apart in their own distinct military worlds, coming together only sporadically for training. The cooperation of infantry and armour envisaged as being a wall of steel followed by a wall of flesh, or vice versa, does not exist. . . . By

Verrières Ridge [25 July] experienced tank crews were understandably wary about charging alone up open hillsides in their outmatched Shermans.[33]

Perhaps generals had, at times, to forget their humanity and treat other humans as what used to be called 'canon fodder'. One remark of Dempsey's is revealing, though its implications may have been unintended. Referring to Goodwood, he admitted that he was prepared to lose 200 tanks, 'so long as I didn't lose <u>men</u>'.[34] Only the Germans were using 'crewless tanks' in Normandy. Were there not men in the 200 brewed-up British tanks? And was not death in a blazing tank one of the worst of fates?

The world in which Dempsey had to work was concerned with pieces on a chessboard, map references, availability of numbers, enemy dispositions and so on, with little room for human sentiment. For that it is necessary to return to the individual tanker, like Louis Gerrard, wounded in the Flowers' fight among the hedgerows:

I remember German kids in front of our tank with their hands above their heads, they were young kids, crying. And some of our guys would say, 'Sonofabitches. Shoot 'em!' They didn't do it, but they were thinking about it, because they figured they were young kids and all, but they would kill you.

I was never angry at the Germans. I figured they were put into it just like I was. I mean, I didn't want to go to war, and I guess a lot of them didn't. But that nut was over there sending them in. You've got to kill them or they kill you. You have to do it. You say 'If . . .?' But you can't keep on iffin!'[35]

The gods of war are malevolent jokers with long memories. Joe Solarz confessed to not knowing the names of villages they had passed through. But he remembered one name: Buchenwald. His unit drew the unwanted and ghastly duty of guarding the newly liberated concentration camp. He was bitten by fleas and rats. Bacteria remained in his blood. In 1992, 47 years later, the bacteria activated. He was diagnosed as suffering from the blinding eye disease, Brill-Zinsser, by an elderly doctor who had seen it prevalent in concentration camp survivors. For Joe it was a tangible tragedy.[36]

For many it was the unseen sleeping cobra of psychological hurt, hibernating for years in the murky depths of the mind, which now struck, awakened by the serene dawn of advancing age and the prospering long-term memory.

And, for some, it could only be ameliorated by quasi-religious confession in the form of reticent reminiscences, exchanged at reunions or exposed in books.

NOTES AND REFERENCES

Unit war diaries or histories are not noted below unless the quotation is of special significance. Because of the variety of contact methods used, from e-mail to personal interviews, information from an individual is noted only as 'inf.', followed by the date.

CHAPTER 1. FLOWERS IN THE HEDGEROWS

1. This chapter is based on Aaron Elson's books and inf. 2001; also Lefauvre inf. 2001 and author's battlefield survey.
2. K. Tout, *Tank!* (Robert Hale, 1985/1995).
3. Bob Levine who gallantly climbed Mont Castre years later with Lefauvre.
4. Typical British tank crew training included about five weeks' infantry training out of perhaps 100 to 150 weeks' tank training pre-D-Day.
5. A.C. Elson, *Tanks for the Memories* (Chi-Chi Press, 1994).
6. Caesar, *Gallic War*, Book III.
7. Titman's memory is a little fallible. Even with extra storage bins welded on, his Sherman would not carry 100 rounds of <u>both</u> AP and HE.
8. J. Cary published his explanation in *Tanks and Armor in Modern Warfare* (Franklin Watts Inc., 1966).
9. Father of Aaron in 1 above.
10. The present author's tank career ended when a Sherman did precisely that.

11. At this point the synoptic accounts vary widely due to the anguish and shock experienced by participants.
12. 'Forbidden Zone' was not a common 1944 term but is used in a descriptive sense.
13. A.C. Elson, *They were all young kids* (Chi-Chi Press, 1997).
14. *Ibid.*
15. The Hill 122 action was not an integral part of Operation Cobra but, like other such actions, was a prerequisite to the establishment of a stable start line.

CHAPTER 2. THE SADNESS OF SERGEANT SID

1. S.E.M. Jones in *Northamptonshire Yeomanry Magazine*; and inf. 2001/2.
2. Surprisingly, some eminent historians seem to be unaware of the existence of this 'third' railway (see later chapters), passing Soliers and La Hogue. It is not marked on the Normandy maps in, among others, Belchem, Bellfield and Essame, Ellis, Hastings, Keegan, McKee and Man's atlas.
3. W.J. Mosely, *From Arromanches to the Elbe: A Tankie's Story* (self-pub., 1992) and *Northamptonshire Yeomanry Magazine*.
4. 'Hull-down' – with only the turret showing and the gun able to fire. 'Turret-down' with only the commander's head above the skyline and guns unable to fire.
5. Tank commander who wished to remain anonymous, 2001.
6. R. Spittles, tape recordings (Imperial War and Bovington Tank Museums); and *Northamptonshire Yeomanry Magazine*.
7. As 5 above.
8. 2nd Northamptonshire Yeomanry, armoured recce regt of 11th AD.

CHAPTER 3. HALT! WHO GOES WHERE?

1. E. Bellfield and H. Essame, *The Battle for Normandy* (Severn House, 1965).
2. L.F. Ellis, *Victory in the West*, vol 1, 'Battle of Normandy' (HMSO, 1962).

3.   Lt A.W. Faulkner, inf. 2001.

4.   L.F. Ellis, *op. cit.*

5.   M. Shulman, *Defeat in the West* (Secker & Warburg, 1947).

6.   McKee, *Caen, Anvil of Victory* (Souvenir Press, 1964).

7.   M. Green and G. Green, *Patton: Operation Cobra and Beyond* (MRI Publishing, 1998).

8.   C. Wilmot, *The Struggle for Europe* (Collins, 1952).

9.   J.J. Carrafano, *After D-Day: Operation Cobra and Normandy Breakout* (Lynne Rienner, 2000).

10. Panzer Lehr = 'Training' Division.

11. C.A. Acker, *Normandy Breakout: Strategic Decisions and Leadership Action in Operations Goodwood and Cobra* (US Army War College, 2000).

12. Bellfield and Essame, *op. cit.*

13. D. Mason, *Breakout, Drive to the Seine* (Ballantine, 1968).

14. 3rd AD history.

15. B. McAndrew, D.E. Graves and M. Whitby, *Normandy 1944: The Canadian Summer* (Art Global, 1994).

16. *Ibid.*

17. *Ibid*; also T. Copp and B. McAndrew, *Battle Exhaustion – Soldiers and Psychiatrists in the Canadian Army, 1939–45* (McGill-Queens, 1990).

18. Wilmot, *op. cit.*

19. *Ibid.*

20. M. Wood and J. Dugdale, *Orders of Battle: Waffen SS Panzer Units in Normandy, 1944* (Book International, 2000).

21. *Ibid.*

22. M. and G. Green, *op. cit.*

23. L. F. Ellis, *op. cit.*

24. Wilmot, *op. cit.*

25. K. Tout, *Tanks Advance!* (Robert Hale, 1987).

26. M. and G. Green, *op. cit.*

27. *Ibid.*

28. Reid Mitchell in P. Addison and A. Calder, *A Time to Kill* (Pimlico, 1997).

29. Tout, *Tanks Advance!*

30. J. Lucas, *Das Reich* (Cassell, 1999).
31. M. Pinel, *Chronique des Années de Guerre – Lessay* (Pinel, 1994).
32. F.W. Winterbotham, *The Ultra Secret* (Weidenfeld & Nicolson, 1974).
33. D. Belchem, *Victory in Normandy* (Book Club Associates, 1981).
34. L.F. Ellis, *op. cit.*
35. Acker, *op. cit.*
36. *Daily Telegraph*, 10 July 1944.
37. S.W. Mitcham Jr, *Hitler's Field Marshals and their Battles* (Guild Publishing, 1988).
38. H. Speidel, *Invasion, 1944* (Regnery, 1950).
39. K. Meyer, *Grenadiers* (J.J. Fedorowicz, 1994).
40. D. and S. Whitaker, *Victory at Falaise* (HarperCollins, 2000).
41. McAndrew *et al.*, *op. cit.*
42. D. Irving, *The War between the Generals* (Allen Lane, 1981).
43. Lord Alanbrooke, *War Diaries 1939–45* (Weidenfeld & Nicolson, 2001).
44. A. Chalfont, *Montgomery of Alamein* (Weidenfeld & Nicolson, 1976).
45. L.F. Ellis, *op. cit.*
46. Irving, *The War between the Generals*.
47. Tout, *A Fine Night for Tanks* (Sutton Publishing, 1998), p. 153.
48. *Sunday Despatch*, 18 July 1944.

CHAPTER 4. WORLD'S WORST TRAFFIC JAM

1. Later Maj F.A.O. Clark, inf. 2001.
2. Boscawen, *Armoured Guardsmen* (Pen & Sword, 2001) and inf. 2000.
3. 3 RTR war diary appendix.
4. Tout, *The Bloody Battle for Tilly* (Sutton Publishing, 2000).
5. Boscawen, *op. cit.*
6. McKee, *op. cit.*
7. M. Reynolds, *Steel Inferno 1 SS Panzer Corps in Normandy* (Spellmount, 1997).
8. Irving, *The War between the Generals*.
9. Acker, *op. cit.*
10. J. Keegan, *Churchill's Generals* (Weidenfeld & Nicolson, 1991).

11. See also Tout, *A Fine Night for Tanks*.

12. Irving, *The War between the Generals*.

13. M. Hastings, *Overlord* (Michael Joseph, 1984).

14. D.D. Eisenhower, *Crusade in Europe* (Doubleday, 1998).

15. As in L.F. Ellis, *op. cit.*

16. Whitaker and Whitaker, *op. cit.*

17. R. Holmes, *War Walks (Goodwood)* (BBC, 1996).

18. Curtis tape, IWM.

19. Tout, *Tanks Advance!*

20. Boyne inf. 2001/2

21. 1 NY and 6th North Staffs.

22. Spittles, IWM tapes; and inf. 2001

23. O'Connor's after battle summing-up.

24. Capt H. Ripmen, RAMC, in *The Armoured Micks*.

25. P. Mace and T. Wright, *Forrard (East Riding Yeomanry)* (Leo Cooper, 2001).

26. Maj C. Robertson, inf. 2001

27. R. Gwyn Evans, *RAMC Journal*, Jan–June 1947.

28. A. Borthwick, *Battalion* (originally as *Sans Peur*, 1946) (Baton Wicks, 1994).

29. As 23 above.

30. George Fyfe, *Daily Telegraph*, 19 July 1944.

31. Borthwick, *op. cit.*

32. G. Blackburn, *The Guns of Normandy* (McClelland & Stewart, 1995).

33. Cockbaine, inf. 2001

34. Boyne, inf. 2001/2.

35. Brookshaw, IWM Tapes.

36. *Taurus Pursuant*, 1945.

37. Van Rosen, during War Office study of Goodwood at Tidworth, 1947.

38. 8 RB war diary appendix.

39. Robbins, inf. 2001.

40. Tidworth Goodwood study.

41. Bell, IWM tapes.

42. *Taurus Pursuant*.

43. C. D'Este, *Decision in Normandy* (William Collins, 1983).

44. Stormont, D. and G. History.

45. Mace and Wright, *op. cit.*

46. Borthwick, *op. cit.*

47. Ralph Hill, 1 NY, inf. 2001.

48. Gwyn Evans, *op. cit.*

CHAPTER 5. THE BULL MEETS THE MATADORS

1. W. Close, inf. 2001; and *The View from the Turret* (Dell & Bredon, 2001).

2. J. Brisset, *The Charge of the Bull*, trans. T. Bates (Bates Books, 1989).

3. Unit diaries and participants inf. 2001. Roberts disagreed and blamed 159 brigade delays for later woes, as not his fault (Tidworth, etc.).

4. Tout, *Tanks Advance!*

5. L.F. Ellis, *op. cit.*

6. Holmes, *op. cit.*

7. Fidler, IWM tapes.

8. Hayward, IWM tapes.

9. Holmes, *op. cit.*

10. Fidler, IWM tapes.

11. Clark inf. 2001; and von Luck, Tidworth study.

12. Tout, *A Fine Night for Tanks.*

13. Shulman, *op. cit.*

14. Von Rosen, Tidworth.

15. Von Rosen, Tidworth.

16. Becker, Tidworth.

17. *Ibid.*

18. K. Jones, *Sixty-four Days of a Normandy Summer* (Robert Hale, 1990).

19. Close, Tidworth.

20. Stileman, Tidworth.

21. *Taurus Pursuant.*

22. Close, Tidworth.

23. Ellis, *op. cit.*

24. D'Este, *op. cit.*

25. Mayors of Soliers, Cagny, Tilly, inf. 1999/2001.

26. Stiller, 1SS LAH, inf. 2000.

27. Blackburn, *op. cit.*, quoting *Taschenbuch der Panzer* (1954).

28. Wood and Dugdale, *op. cit.*

29. Spittles, 2001. NB. Challenger = a 1940s Cromwell variant, not the sophisticated late twentieth-century main battle tank.

30. Reynolds, *op. cit.* And see also ch. 2, n. 2; and Tout, 1998 and 2000.

31. Mosely, inf. 2002.

32. *Ibid.*

33. G.P. Mitchell, *A Regimental Medical Officer in Armour.*

34. *RAMC Journal*, July 1941.

35. Tout, 2000.

36. Meredith, IWM tapes.

37. Mace and Wright, *op. cit.*

38. Borthwick, *op. cit.*

39. R. Tiemann, *Chronicle of 7 Panzer Companie* (Schiffer Military History, 1998).

40. Byrne, inf. 2002.

41. 8 Rifle Brigade reports 1944 (war diary appendix).

42. 23rd Hussars' history.

43. Jones, *op. cit.*

44. Brisset, *op. cit.*

45. Reynolds, *op. cit.*

CHAPTER 6. GRIM GUARDS AND HAMSTRUNG RATS

1. Mitchell, in *Armoured Micks.*

2. *Medical Services in an Armoured Division*, *RAMC Journal*, Oct. 1943.

3. Tidworth, Goodwood study.

4. Lord Carrington, *Reflect on Things Past* (William Collins, 1988).

5. From various reports and articles in *Guards Magazine.*

6. H. Essame, *Normandy* Bridgend (Ballantine, 1970).

7. From film, *Operation Goodwood.*

8. Carrington, *op. cit.*

9. Lacey, inf. 2001; and E.A. Smith, *Recce Troop Memories* (self-pub., 1997).

10. *Ibid.*

11. Carrington, *op. cit.*

12. Lindsay, *Guards Magazine*, 1989.

13. Tout, *Tanks Advance!*

14. Heywood, Brig. A.G., CBE, LVO, MC, *A Duel with a Tiger*, in *Guards Magazine*, 1989.

15. Boscawen, *op. cit.*

16. Boscawen, inf. 2001.

17. From Gorman BBC interview in *Armoured Micks*.

18. Teale, IWM tape.

19. Holmes, *op. cit.*

20. McKee, *op. cit.*

21. Roberts, Tidworth Goodwood study.

22. Dyas, inf. 2000.

23. Tout, *Tanks Advance!*

24. Tidworth, Goodwood study.

25. *Armoured Micks.*

26. I.C. Hammerton, *Achtung! Minen!* (Book Guild, 1991).

27. Lechipey, inf. 2001.

28. Evans in *Canadian Military History*, 8.1, winter 1999.

29. Tout, *The Bloody Battle for Tilly.*

30. Fully quoted in L.F. Ellis, *op. cit.*

31. D'Este, *op. cit.*

32. *Daily Telegraph*, 19 July, 1944.

33. *Daily Telegraph*, 20 July, 1944.

CHAPTER 7. CRESTFALLEN AT THE CREST

1. Reynolds, *op. cit.*

2. Col Charles Pearce, inf. 2000.

3. Mosely, inf. 2001

4. Close, inf. 2001. Both he and Langdon won the MC.

5. Boyne, inf. 2001.

6. Jones, *op. cit.*

7. The author when commanding a 'rear link' was never required to use the 'B' set (in 1 NY).

8. Tout, *The Bloody Battle for Tilly*.

9. Willis, *None had Lances* (24th Lancers Old Comrades Association, 1986).

10. G.P. Mitchell, *A Regimental Medical Officer* (LRI/7325, 23rd Hussars, *c.* 1946).

11. Maj Gordon Brown, inf. 1999.

12. *Burns in Wartime, RAMC Journal*, LXXVII/1/2.

13. Hayward, IWM tapes.

14. Blackburn, *op. cit.*

15. Robbins, inf. 2001.

16. Tout, *The Bloody Battle for Tilly*.

17. Cloudsley-Thomson, various articles and inf. 2001.

18. Tout, *The Bloody Battle for Tilly*.

19. Pearce, inf. 2000.

20. *Daily Telegraph*, 19 July 1944.

21. Mayor of Bourguebus, inf. 1999.

22. Evans, *Canadian Military History*, VIII/1/21, 1999.

23. Tout, *The Bloody Battle for Tilly*.

24. Lechipey, inf. 2001. By the time of the 11 September 2001 events, Mado, now an American citizen, had become a special assistant to President Bush.

25. Horne, inf. 2001.

26. *Armoured Micks*.

27. R. Vogel, 'Tactical Air Power in Normandy. Some thoughts on the Interdiction Plan', in *Canadian Military History*, 3, 1, 1994.

28. Lechipey, inf. 2001.

29. Lehmann and Tiemann, *Leibstandarte IV*.

30. Stiller, inf. 2000.

31. Brookshaw, IWM tapes.

32. G.P. Mitchell, *op. cit.*

33. Meyer, *op. cit.*

34. Borthwick, *op. cit.*

35. Robertson, inf. 2001.

36. Blackburn, *op. cit.*

37. Tout, *The Bloody Battle for Tilly*.

38. C. Wilmot, *The Struggle for Europe* (Collins, 1952).

39. Belchem, *op. cit.*

40. Compare Holmes, *op. cit.*

41. Boscawen, *op. cit.*

42. Acker, *op. cit.*

43. *Northamptonshire Yeomanry Magazine*, 1999.

44. Wood and Dugdale, *op. cit.*

45. Richard Holmes, commander of TA armoured units (*War Walks*).

46. 2 NY oral traditions.

CHAPTER 8. COBRA UNDER THE CARPET

The three chapters dealing specifically with Cobra generally follow the outlines of Blumenson, Carafano and Cary, all of which contain much detail, as well as AD histories. These are cited below only if the point is of special signficance.

1. Irving, *The War between the Generals*.

2. Wilmot, *op. cit.*

3. Goldstein, inf. 2002.

4. Whitaker and Whitaker, *op. cit.*

5. *Ibid.*

6. Reid Mitchell, in Addison and Calder, *A Time to Kill*.

7. Y. Buffetaut, 'Normandy la Percée: Operation Cobra', in *Militaria* (Histoire et Collections, Paris, 1998).

8. Essame, *op. cit.*

9. Cary, inf. 2000.

10. Broadhurst, IWM tapes.

11. Buffetaut, *op. cit.*

12. B. Cooper, *Death Traps* (Presidio, 1998).

13. Whitaker and Whitaker, *op. cit.*

14. Eisenhower, *D-Day to VE Day*.

15. Alanbrook, *op. cit.*

16. 3rd AD history.

17. M. Blumenson, *Breakout and Pursuit* (US Gov. Printing Office, 1961).

18. Anonymous GI, Inf. 2001.

19. Wilmot, *op. cit.*

20. Acker, *op. cit.*

21. Buffetaut, *op. cit.*

22. A.D. Chandler (ed.), *The Papers of Dwight D. Eisenhower* (John Hopkins, 1970).

23. Essame, *op. cit.*

24. Shulman, *op. cit.*

25. Acker, *op. cit.*

26. 39th Executive Officer's report,1944.

27. Blumenson, *op. cit.*

28. Cary, *op. cit.*

29. *Ibid.*

30. Raney, inf. 2001.

31. W. Klein, *Bombing and Operation Cobra* (MS AGIO, US Dept of the Army, 1949).

32. Acker, *op. cit.*

33. Len Cottell, in Tout, *A Fine Night for Tanks.*

34. Bellfield and Essame, *op. cit.*

35. Cary, *op. cit.*

36. Carrafano, *op. cit.*

37. Cary, inf. 2001.

38. Whitby, *Burns in Wartime, RAMC Journal,* 1941.

39. Gwynne Evans, *Medical Services, RAMC Journal,* 1947.

40. Ellis transcript in *Victory in the West.*

41. Author's own paraphrase.

42. From Rommell Papers in Cary, *op. cit.*

43. Klein, *op. cit.*

44. Raney, inf. 2001.

45. *Ibid.*

46. S.J. Zaloga, *Operation Cobra 1944 – breakthrough in Normandy* (Osprey, 2001).

47. O.N. Bradley, *A Soldier's Story* (Henry Holt & Co., 1951).

48. Whitaker, *op. cit.*

49. Blumenson, *op. cit.*

50. 'Super Sixth' history.

51. Cary, *op. cit.*

52. Winterbotham, *op. cit.*

53. P. Carrell, *Invasion They're Coming* (E.P. Dutton, Inc., 1983).

54. W.L. Shirer, *The Rise and Fall of the Third Reich* (Secker & Warburg, 1959).

55. Pinel, *op. cit.*

CHAPTER 9. COBRA STRIKES AT LAST

1. Cary *op. cit.*

2. J. Collins, *'Lightning Joe'* (Baton Rouge, 1979).

3. Cooper, *op. cit.*

4. Sgt Hank Jefferson, inf. 2001.

5. Bechtold, in *Canadian Military History*, 7.4.1998.

6. Winterbotham, *op. cit.*

7. Eberbach report, June 1948.

8. Martin Goldstein, film *Sherman Assualt*.

9. John Seemes, film *Sherman Assault*.

10. For example, Cooper, *op. cit.*

11. McAndrew *et al.*, *op. cit.*

12. Gatzke in 2 AD *Rolling Again*.

13. Hammell, inf. 2001.

14. Arte Krenn, inf. 2000.

15. Klein, *op. cit.*

16. Willhersby, *Redressing the Balance – the Successful Employment of Sherman Tanks, Normandy 1944* (Thesis 3500, Univ. of Leeds, 1998).

17. Bradley, *op. cit.*

18. Raney, inf. 2001.

19. Elson, *op. cit.*

20. Cary, *op. cit.*

21. 2nd AD history.

22. *'Hell on Wheels'*.

23. Raney, inf. 2002.

24. Pinel, *op. cit.*

25. Solarz, inf. 2001/2.

26. Oral in Whitaker, *op. cit.*

27. 3rd AD history.

28. cf. Lucas, *Das Reich.*

29. Klein, *op. cit.*

30. Oral in Whitaker, *op. cit.*

31. Author's own experience.

32. Report 12 of 2 Operational Research Section.

33. In Elson, *op. cit.*

34. D. Holbrook, *Flesh Wounds* (Methuen, 1966).

35. *Burns in Wartime, RAMC Journal,* 1941.

36. Rawling, in *Canadian Military History,* 6.1.1997.

37. Gatzke as 12 above.

38. Willis, *op. cit.*

39. Carafano, *op. cit.*

40. Pinel, *op. cit.*, and Aubert's own statement.

41. Klein, *op. cit.*

42. Oral in Whitaker, *op. cit.*

43. Tout, *The Bloody Battle for Tilly.*

44. Essame, *op. cit.*

45. Winterbotham, *op. cit.*

CHAPTER 10. COBRA HYDRAHEADED

1. Belchem, *op. cit.*

2. This and subsequent – 2nd AD history.

3. *'Hell on Wheels',* p. 226.

4. Raney, inf. 2001.

5. Lucas, *op. cit.*

6. 'Super Sixth' and Solarz, inf. 2001.

7. Eisenhower, *D-Day to VE Day.*

8. Klein, *op. cit.*

9. *'Hell on Wheels'.*

10. 'Most Secret Report' in Ellis, *op. cit.*

11. Cary, *op. cit.*

12. Klein, *op. cit.*

13. Cary, *op. cit.*

14. *'Hell on Wheels'.*

15. 3rd AD history.

16. Arte Krenn, inf. 2001.

17. Col Tom Gillis, inf. 2000/2.

18. A.C. Elson, *They were all young kids* (Chi-Chi Press, 1997).

19. Solarz, inf. 2001.

20. Tout, *The Bloody Battle for Tilly.*

21. Elson, *They were all young kids.*

22. Maj Gen R.J. Blackburn, *RAMC Journal*, April 1946.

23. Bechthold, in *Canadian Military History*, 8.1.1999.

24. 3rd AD history.

25. Gillis, inf. 2000.

26. Feinberg, inf. 2000.

27. Solarz, inf. 2000.

28. Cary, *op. cit.*

CHAPTER 11. SHAMBLES AT CHAMBOIS

1. Combat interviews, 5 September 1944.

2. Col Pearce, inf. 2001

3. Irving, *Hitler's War.*

4. Whitaker, *op. cit.*

5. *'Hell on Wheels'.*

6. *Ibid.*

7. 3rd AD history.

8. *Ibid.*

9. *Ibid.*

10. *Ibid.*

11. Klein was debriefed at POW detention centre, Versailles, October 1945.

12. Lutcavish statement (D Coy 712 TB) per Elson.

13. cf. Tout, *A Fine Night for Tanks* and *The Bloody Battle for Tilly*.

14. Whitaker, *op. cit.*

15. *Ibid.*

16. 'Hell on Wheels'.

17. Irving, *op. cit.*

18. Mitcham, *op. cit.*

19. Patton's diary quoted in Blumenson, *The Patton Papers* (Houghton Miflin, 1974).

20. *Ibid.*

21. Stiller, inf. 2001 and in Tout . . . *Tilly*.

22. Whitaker, *op. cit.*

23. Tout, *A Fine Night*.

24. Cary, *op. cit.*

25. Cooper, *op. cit.*

26. Pinel, *op. cit.*

CHAPTER 12. VERY UNFRIENDLY FIRE

1. Dewar, inf. 2002, but still swinging a club at St Andrews where he lives.

2. H. Diamond and C. Gorrara, 'The Aubrac Controversy' in *History Today*, March 2001.

3. Belchem, *op. cit.*.

4. Carafano, *op. cit.*

5. Jones, inf. 2001/2.

6. Close, inf. 2001/2.

7. Tout, *A Fine Night for Tanks*.

8. Robertson, inf. 2001/2.

9. *Taurus Pursuant*.

10. Adair, *A Guards General* (Guards Armoured Division).

11. Jarymowycz, *Canadian Military History*, 7.2., 1998 (Note 108).

12. Reynolds, *op. cit.*

13. K. Macksey, *Panzer Division* (Ballantine, 1968).

14. Tidworth Goodwood study.

15. US Army War College, 2000/ Acker, *op. cit.*

16. Interview by Chester Wilmot, 1945.
17. Tidworth Goodwood study.
18. *Ibid.*
19. Reynolds, *op. cit.*
20. Carafano, *op. cit.*
21. *Ibid.*
22. Cary, *op. cit.*
23. *Canadian Military History*, 7.4., 1998.
24. Klein, *op. cit.*
25. Acker, *op. cit.*
26. Copp, as 23 above.
27. Dyas, inf. 2000.
28. Willersby, *op. cit.*
29. McAndrew *et al.*, *op. cit.*
30. Adair, *op. cit.*
31. An Israeli historian's study for the Pentagon, 1983.
32. Tout, *Tanks Advance*, the author commanding one of the tanks.
33. McAndrew *et al.*, *op. cit.*
34. Acker, *op. cit.*
35. Gerrard in Elson, *They were all young kids.*
36. Solarz, inf. 2001/2.

BIBLIOGRAPHY

SOURCES AND FURTHER READING

Does not include war diaries or official units histories unless published commercially.

Acker, C.A., *Normandy Breakout: Strategic decisions and leadership action in Operations Goodwood and Cobra* (US Army War College, 2000)

Addison, P. and Calder, A., *A Time to Kill* (Pimlico, 1997)

Alanbrooke, Lord, *War Diaries 1939–45* (Weidenfeld & Nicolson, 2001)

Ambrose, S.E., *Citizen Soldiers: US Army from the Normandy beaches* (Simon & Schuster, 1997)

Beal, P., *Tank Tracks* (Sutton, 1995)

Bechthold, B., 'The Development of an Unbeatable Combination (US Close Air Support)' in *Canadian Military History [CMH]* (8.1. winter 1999)

Belchem, D., *Victory in Normandy* (Book Club Associates, 1981)

Bellfield, E. and Essame, H., *The Battle for Normandy* (Severn House, 1965)

Bernage, G. and Cadel, G., *La Bataille Décisive* (Ed. Heimdal, 1984)

Blackburn, G., *The Guns of Normandy* (McClelland & Stewart, 1995)

Blackham, R.J., 'US Army Medical System', in *RAMC Journal*, April 1946

Blumenson, M., *Breakout and Pursuit* (US Gov. Printing Office, 1961)

——, *The Patton Papers* (Houghton Miflin, 1974)

——, *The Battle of the Generals; The Untold Story of the Falaise Pocket* (Morrow, 1993)

Bodelson, A., *Operation Cobra* (Elsevier/Nelson, 1979)

Borthwick, A., *Battalion* (originally as *Sans Peur*, 1946) (Baton Wicks, 1994)

Boscawen, R., *Armoured Guardsmen* (Pen & Sword, 2001)

Bradley, O.N., *A Soldier's Story* (Henry Holt & Co., 1951)

Breuk, W.B., *Death of a Nazi Army: The Falaise Pocket* (Scarborough House, 1985)

Brisset, J., (trans. Bates, T.) *The Charge of the Bull* (Bates Books, 1989)

Buffetaut, Y., 'Normandy La Percée: Operation Cobra', in *Miltaria* (Histoire et Collections, Paris, 1998)

Carafano, J.J., *After D-Day: Operation Cobra and Normandy Breakout* (Lynne Rienner, 2000)

Carrell, P., *Invasion. They're coming!* (German account) (E.P. Dutton Inc., 1983)

Carrington, Lord, *Reflect on Things Past* (William Collins, 1988)

Cary, J., *Tanks and Armour in Modern Warfare* (Franklin Watts Inc., 1966)

Chalfont, A., *Montgomery of Alamein* (Weidenfeld & Nicolson, 1976)

Chandler, A.D. (ed.), *The Papers of Dwight D. Eisenhower* (John Hopkins, 1970)

Close, W., *The View from the Turret* (Dell & Bredon, 2001) (from 27 The Dell, Bredon, GL20 7QP) and see also Roberts

Collins, J., *'Lightning Joe'* (Baton Rouge, 1979)

Cooper, B., *Death Traps* (Presidio, 1998)

Copp, T., re Attrition in Normandy, editorial comment, *CMH* (7.4., August 1998)

——, 'A Last Word' (versus revisionism) in Whitaker, *Victory at Falaise*

Copp., T. and McAndrew, B., *Battle Exhaustion – Soldiers and Psychiatrists in the Canadian Army, 1939–45* (McGill-Queens, 1990)

Copp., T. and Nielsen, R., *No Price too High* (McGraw-Hill Ryerson, 1996)

De Guingand, E., *Operation Victory* (Hodder & Stoughton, 1950)

D'Este, C., *Decision in Normandy* (William Collins, 1983)

Diamond, H. and Gorrara, C., 'The Aubriac Controversy' in *History Today* (March 2001)

Dugan, H.W. and Peterson, D., *'Third Armored Division'* (Turner Publishing, 1972)

Eccles, C.E. and Perkins, H.K., 'The Medical Services in an Armoured Division', in *RAMC Journal* (October 1943)

Eisenhower, D.D., *Crusade in Europe* (Doubleday, 1998)

Ellis, J., *The Sharp End, The Fighting Man in World War II* (Windrowe & Green, 1990)

Ellis, L.F., *Victory in the West*, vol. 1, 'Battle of Normandy' (HMSO, 1962)

Elson, A.C., *Tanks for the Memory* (Chi-Chi Press, 1994)

——, *They were all young kids* (Chi-Chi Press, 1997)

English, J.A., *The Canadian Army and the Normandy Campaign – A Study of Failure in High Command* (Praeger, 1991)

Essame, H., *Normandy Bridgehead* (Ballantine, 1970)

Evans, C., 'The Fighter Bomber in the Normandy Campaign', in *CMH* (8.1., winter 1999)

Evan, Gwyn, 'The Medical Services in North-West Europe', in *RAMC Journal* (Jan–June 1947)

Fiddes, F.S., 'Surgery in the Front Line' in *RAMC Journal* (November 1945)

Fletcher, D., *The Universal Tank: British Armour in the Second World War* (HMSO, 1993)

Florentin, Eddy, *Battle of the Falaise Gap* (Elek, 1965/Hawthorne, 1967)

Fraser, D., *And We Shall Shock Them* (Cassell, 1999)

Freeman, R., *The Mighty Eighth War Diary* (Arms & Armour, 1990)

Furbringer, H., *9 SS-Panzer Division* (Munin Verlag, 1987)

Gersdorff, R. von, *The Campaign in Northern France (25 July to 14 Sept.1944)* (Foreign Military Study B-725, USAEUR, 1946)

——, *Normandy, Cobra and Mortain* (FMS A-894, USAEUR, 1949)

Graham, D., *The Price of Command* (Stoddart, 1993)

Green, M. and Green G., *Patton, Operation Cobra and Beyond* (illustrated) (MRI publishing, 1998)

Hallinan, V., *From Cobra to the Liberation of Paris* (thesis) (Temple University, 1988)

Hammerton, I.C., *Achtung! Minen!* (Book Guild, 1991) (2nd ed. self-published 2000)

Hastings, M., *Overlord* (Michael Joseph, 1984)

Hofman, G.F., *The Super Sixth* (6 Armored Div. Association, 1975)

Holbrook, D., *Flesh Wounds* (Methuen, 1966)

Holmes, R., *War Walks (Goodwood)* (BBC, 1996)

Houston, D.E. *'Hell on Wheels': The 2nd Armored Division* (Presidio Press, 1977)

Hunnicut, R., *SHERMAN – A History of the American Medium Tank* (Taurus Enterprises, 1978)

Irving, D., *The War Between the Generals* (Allen Lane, 1981)

——, *Hitler's War* (Focal Point, 1991)

Jarymowycz, R.J., 'Canadian Armour in Normandy . . . the Quest for Maneuver' in *CMH* (7.2., spring 1998)

Jones, K., *Sixty-four Days of a Normandy Summer* (Robert Hale, 1990)

Keegan, J., *Six Armies in Normandy* (Penguin, 1982)

——, *Churchill's Generals* (Weidenfeld & Nicolson, 1991)

Klein, W., *Bombing and Operation Cobra* (MS A910, US Dept. of the Army, 1949)

Lehmann, R. and Tiemann, R., *Die Leibstandarte IV/I* (Munin Verlag, 1986)

Lucas, J., *Das Reich*, Cassell, 1999 (Arms & Armour, 1991)

Mace, P. and Wright, T., *Forrard (East Riding Yeomanry)* (Leo Cooper, 2001)

Macksey, K., *Panzer Division* (Balantine, 1968)

Man, J., *Atlas of D-Day and the Normandy Campaign* (Penguin, 1994)

Mason, D., *Breakout: Drive to the Seine* (Ballantine, 1968)

McAndrew, B., Graves, D.E. and Whitby, M., *Normandy 1944: The Canadian Summer* (Art Global, 1994)

McKee, *Caen, Anvil of Victory* (Souvenir Press, 1964)

Meyer, H., *History of the 12th SS Panzerdivision Hitlerjugend* (J.J. Fedorowicz, 1994)

Meyer, K., *Grenadiers* (J.J. Fedorowicz, 1994)

Milner, M., 'Reflections on Caen, Bocage and the Gap', in *CMH* (7.2., spring 1998)

Mitcham, S.W. Jr., *Rommel's Last Battle* (Stein & Day, 1983)

——, *Hitler's Field Marshals and their Battles* (Guild Publishing, 1988)

Mitchell, G.P., *A Regimental Medical Officer in Armour* (LR1/7325, 23rd Hussars, *c.* 1946)

Mitchell, Reid, *The GIs in Europe*, in Addison & Calder

Moseley, W.R., *From Arromanches to the Elbe: A Tankie's Story* (self-pub., 1992)

Murphy, 'What is "Tank Country"?', in *CMH* (7.4., autumn 1998)

Oldfield, M.C., 'Burns in Wartime', in *RAMC Journal* (July 1941)

Perkins, N.H. and Rogers, M.E., *Roll Again Second Armored* (Kristall Productions, 1988)

Pinel, M. *Chronique des Années de Guerre – Lessay* (Pinel, 1994)

Rawling, B., 'Canadians and Combat Surgery', in *CMH* (6.1., spring 1997)

Reynolds, M., *Steel Inferno 1SS Panzer Corps in Normandy* (Spellmount, 1997)

Rohmer, R., *Patton's Gap* (Beaufort Books, 1981)

Roberts, G.P.B., *From the Desert to the Baltic* (Kimber, 1987)

Roberts, G.P.B., Close, W., von Luck, H., *et al.*, Tidworth Goodwood Study, 1976 (Tank Museum, Bovington)

Shirer, W.L., *The Rise and Fall of the Third Reich* (Secker & Warburg, 1959)

Shulman, M., *Defeat in the West* (Secker & Warburg, 1947)

Sloan Brown, J., 'Colonel Trevor N. Dupuy and the Myth of Wehrmacht Superiority: A Reconsideration', in *Military Affairs* (January 1985)

Smith, E.A., *Recce Troop Memories* (self-published, 1997)

Speidel, H., *Invasion 1944* (Regnery, 1950)

Stacey, C.P., *The Victory Campaign (Official History of the Canadian Army in the Second World War, vol. 3)* (Queen's Printer at Ottawa, 1960)

Suchcitz, A. and Suchcitz, T., *1st Polish Armoured Division in Battle, (1st Dywyzja Pancerna w Walce, 1945)*, in preparation (Polish Institute, London)

Sullivan, J.J., 'The Botched Air Support of Operation Cobra', in *PARAMETERS* 18 (March 1988)

Taylor, L., 'Wittmann's Last Battle', in *After the Battle*, 48

Tiemann, R., *Chronicle of the 7 Panzer Companie* (Schiffer Military History, 1998)

Tout, K., *Tank!* (Robert Hale, 1985/1995)

——, *Tanks, Advance!* (Robert Hale, 1987)

——, *A Fine Night for Tanks* (Sutton, 1998)

——, *The Bloody Battle for Tilly* (Sutton, 2000)

Trahan, E.A. (ed.), *A History of the Second United States Armored Div.* (Albert Love Enterprises, 1975)

US Army, *The Armored Division in the Double Envelopment* (Research Report, Fort Knox, 1949)

——, *The Employment of Four Tank Destroyer Battalions in the ETO* (Research Report, 1950)

——, *World War II Combat Interviews* (University Publishers of America, 1989)

Van Crevald, M., *Fighting Power: German and US Army Performance 1939–1945* (Arms & Armour, 1983)

Verney, G.L., *Desert Rats* (Hutchinson, 1954)

Vogel, R., 'Tactical Air Power in Normandy. Some thoughts on the Interdiction Plan', in *CMH* (3.1., spring 1994)

Von Luck, von Rosen, see Roberts

Warlimont, W., *Inside Hitler's HQ* (Praeger, 1964)

Westphal, S., *The German Army in the West* (Cassell, 1951)

Whitaker, D. and Whitaker, S., *Victory at Falaise* (HarperCollins, 2000)

Willis, L., *None had Lances* (24th Lancers Old Comrades Association, 1986)

Wilmot, C., *The Struggle for Europe* (Collins, 1952)

Winterbotham, F.W., *The Ultra Secret* (Weidenfeld & Nicolson, 1974)

Willersby, E.D., *Redressing the Balance – The successful employment of Sherman tanks, Normandy 1944'* (thesis Hist. 3500) (University of Leeds, 1998)

Wood, M. and Dugdale, J., *Orders of Battle: Waffen SS Panzer Units in Normandy, 1944* (Book International, 2000)

Zaloga, S.J., *Operation Cobra 1944 – breakthrough in Normandy* (illustrated) (Osprey, 2001)

No. 2 Operational Research Section, 21st Army Group, 'Analysis of 75mm Sherman Tank Casualties suffered between 6th June and 10th July 1944', in *CMH* (7.1., winter 1998)

Guards Armoured Division, Adair, *'A Guards General'*

Irish Guards RHQ, *The Armoured Micks* (1941 to 1945, 1947)

11th Armoured Division, *Taurus Pursuant* (1945)

33rd Armored Regiment (US), *Men of War* (year not known)

GENERAL INDEX

References to plates are underlined.

Abrams, Col C.W. 179
Adair, Maj Gen A.H.S. 94, 195, 201
Air action, American *see* (Units)
    USAAF
  British *see* (Units) RAF
  German *see* (Units) Luftwaffe
Alanbrooke, F/M Lord 47, 55, 108,
    132
Allan, T4 F. 169
Allied air domination 43, 45, 82, 126,
    145, 162, 200
Animals in war 64, 89, 173, 174 ff.,
    191 ff., 25
Argentan 189, 196
Armour, Lt 191
Armoured cars 55, 56, 108
Arras 202
ARV, amoured recovery vehicle 28
Atlantic, Operation xvi, 86, 107
Aubert, Louis 160, 29
Aubrac controversy xvi, 194
Avranches 170, 172, 179, 180,
    184

Baggeley, Tpr 27, 17
Bailey, Lt A. 119
Bailey, Sgt J. 8, 18
Banneville 62
Barkmann, Lt E. 32, 156
Baron, Cpl J. 101

Baron, Pte W. 179
Bassett, Gdsm 99
'Battle Exhaustion' *see* Psychiatric
Baum , Col 170
Bayerlein, Maj Gen 135, 140 ff., 145,
    163, 28
Bayeux 32
Bealke, Col J., 9
Beauvoir Farm 120
Becker Maj 76 ff., 90, 103
Bell, Lt J.W. 67
Bell, Pte T. 177
Benmore, Tpr W 27
Belchem, Maj Gen 194
Bergeron, Lt P. 107
Bertenrath, Pz Cpl F. 157
BLA, British Liberation Army 32
Blackburn, Lt G. 63
Bletchley Park 44, 145, 163
Bluecoat, Operation 181, 189, 197
Boardman, Capt T. 187
bocage, 3 ff., 25, 40, 129, 161, 181,
    200, 2
Bois de Bavent 61, 88
Booth, Brig L. 188
Borgert, Lt W. 46
Boscawen, Lt R. 50, 100
Boucard, Helene 192
Bourguebus Ridge 25, 71, 81 ff., 111
    ff., 163, 193, 195

Bourguebus village 62, 81, 110, 118,121, 190

Boyne, Cpl T. 57, 64, 89, 92, 110, 112, 193

Bradley, Gen O. xv, 40, 42, 128, 132 ff., 145, 148, 184, 190, 198, 200, 30, 31

Bras 19 ff., 54, 79, 90, 107, 109, 111 ff., 196, 6

Bretteville-le-Rabit 54

Bretteville-sur-Laize 54

'Brewing up', tanks burning 12 ff., 21 ff., 74, 85, 90, 97, 110, 116, 158 ff. 183, 185, 192

Brittany 53, 180, 189

Broadhurst, Pte J. 130

Brooks, Maj Gen E.H. 148, 166, 173

Brookshaw, Lt P. 64

Brown, Maj G. 116

Buchenwald 203

Buckley, Christopher 109

Bulldozers/bulldozer tanks (Shermans) 130, 168, 176

Caen 5, 19, 35, 39, 53 ff., 86, 109, 170, 186, 195, 200, 7

Cagny 62, 73, 78, 87, 96 ff., 104, 108, 112, 118, 195

Canissy 161

Carothers, Capt T.H. 182

Carrington, Capt Lord 96

Cary, Capt J. 8, 136

Casualty statistics 36, 39, 109,127, 129, 135, 153, 188, 189, 199

Caswell, Sgt J. 71, 91

Challenger (1944) tank 83, 112

Chambois 190 ff., 200

Chapelle-en-Juger, la 141, 144, 145

Chatelain, Pierre 108

Cherbourg 36, 160

Churchill, Mr W.S. 36, 47, 117, 170

Clark, Gdsm (Maj) F.A.O. 49, 59, 75, 95

Close, Maj W. xvi, 68, 71, 78 ff., 99, 110 ff., 195

Cloudsley-Thompson, Lt J. 118 ff., 125, 175, 18

Cobra, Operation xv, 40, 53, 61, 128 ff., 147 ff., 165 ff., 181 ff., 192, 194, 198 ff.

Cockbaine, Maj D.E. 64

Code names 53, 55, 181, 182, 186, 187

Coleman, Lt Col W.D. 166

Collins, Lt Gen J. 133, 142, 144, 145, 147 ff., 161, 177, 199

Colombelles 52, 66, 68, 73, 86

Combat Commands, US (CCA,CCB) 148, 154

Cook, Tpr 20, 27

Cooper, Lt B. 131, 192

Cooper, Lt P. 178

Cooper, Sgt G 115

Copp, Terry xvi, 199, 200, 202

Corbin, Pte C.R. 177, 183

Corlett, Maj Gen 132

Cormelles 79, 111, 113, 117, 186

Cotton, Lt 201

Coutances 161

'Cowardice', see Psychiatric

Cowhey, Col 131

Cox, Cpl R. 74

Cramesnil 54, 186

Crerar, Gen 38

Cromwell tank 19 ff., 82,105, 118, 198

Cropanese, Pte S. 5

Crosthwaite, Maj I. 98

Culin, Sgt C 131

Currie, Maj D., VC 191

Curtis, Lt Col A.D.E 57

Cunningham, Tpr A. 23

Cuverville 25, 54, 68, 72, 83

Daasch, Hermann 192

D-Day 32, 35, 52

Deception tactics 57, 139
Decker, Cpl K-H 46
de Felice, Capt M. 161
Demouville. 25, 30, 25, 62, 68, 72,
    83, 105, 108, 125, 195
Dempsey, Lt Gen Sir M. xv, 53, 56,
    109, 126, 197, 203, 4
Dewar, Tpr A. 193
Diamond, Gdsmn A.98
Dietrich, Gen S. 38, 58, 76
Digne, Jean 192
Dives, River 108
Dixon, L/Cpl D. 23
'Dougie', (Sgt D.Bellamy) 22
Douglas, W/O 131
Dyas, Capt P. 105, 201

Eastern Front xvi, 48, 101, 199
Eberbach, Gen H. 82, 189
Eddinger, Lt 160
Eddy, Maj Gen 144
Ehrhardt, Cpl R. 89
Eisenhower, Gen D.D. 'Ike' 47, 53, 55,
    132, 134, 151, 170
Ekins, Tpr Joe xv, 187, 202
Elson, Aaron 7
Elson, Maurice 8
Emerson, Sgt 50
Emieville 62, 11
'Enigma' code-breaking, 44
Epsom, Operation 53
Erskine, Maj Gen G.W.E.J. 89, 198
Esquay 57
Evrecy 132

Falaise gap/pocket xvi, 189 ff., 196,
    200
Falaise town 54, 71, 108, 186, 189,
    196
Feinberg, Pte H. 179
Fetch, W/Op J. 152
Fidler, Tpr G. 74
Finnis, Capt J. 115

Firefly tank, see Sherman
Flail tanks 66 ff., 86
Flint, Col H. 135
Flowers, Lt. J xvi, 1 ff., 158,160, 174,
    203, 3
Fontenay-le-Pesnel 57
Four, 92 , 111, 112
Frank, Lt Sir H. 99
'Friendly fire' 1, 64, 105, 134, 137,
    139, 12/1, 12/8
French Resistance/Free French 44,
    107, 108, 146, 156, 160, 172 ff.,
    194
Frenouville 122
Fuller, Lt F. 158
'Funnies', specialist armoured vehicles
    42, 66

Galvin, Capt J 192
Gamache, Lt G. 120
Garcelles-Secqueville 64
Gary, Pte H 14
Gaskins, Capt 191
Gatzke, S/Sgt A. 151, 159
Geneva Convention 10
Gentle, Cadet H.A. 18
German soldiers' behaviour 44, 90,
    124, 171 ff.
German soldiers, non-nationals 89,
    155, 171
Gerrard, Cpl L. 9, 174, 203
Giberville 62, 86
Giblin, Cpl W. 161
Gillis, Col T.D. 178
Goebbels, J. 156
Goering, Reich/M H. 173
Goldstein, Pte M. 129, 151
Goodwood, Operation xvi, 19 ff., 39,
    49 ff., 71 ff., 94 ff.., 110 ff., 128,
    132, 143, 157, 186, 194 ff.
Gorman, Lt J. 101
Goubert, Jean 146, 9
Gourdan, Henri and Pierre 192

Grant, Maj Sir A. 96
Greene, Lt G. 182
Grentheville 68, 78, 84
Grimesnil 165
Gun, 17pdr 99, 102; 37mm 96, 185;
    75mm 4, 96; 76mm 134, 151;
    88mm 2, 75, 103, 158
Gun, self-propelled (SP) 77, 151
Gwatkin, Brig N.W. 95

Habetin, Rfn N. 90
Hammell, Lt J. 151, 158
Hammerton, Capt I. 106, 107
Hannah, Sgt 168
Harbinson, Sgt 102
Harding, Lt Col R.P. 59
Harris, Air/M Sir A. 61
Harvey, Brig R. 111
Hausser, Gen 163, 170, 171
Hawkins, Lt Col J. 155
Hayward, Tpr G. 74, 116
'Heavy armored divisions' 148, 153
Hebecrevon 21
Helms, Lt E.V. 147
Heywood, Capt A.G 99
High Commands,
    disagreements/antipathy 46, 76,
    108, 189, 194
Hill, Gdsm 106
Hill, Tpr R. 69
Hinde, Brig W.R.N. 'Looney' 60, 87,
    105
Hitler, Reich Chancellor A. 34, 44, 46,
    125, 126, 146, 170, 172, 180,
    182, 189
Hobart, Maj Gen P. 42, 66, 197
Holford, Sgt F. 107
Honey (Stuart) tank 79, 96, 150, 166,
    185
Hook, Lt F.A 107
Horne, Tpr A. 123
Hubert Folie 19, 78, 79 ff., 107, 111
    ff., 122, 196

Huebner, Maj Gen C.A. 148
Hughes, Gen E.S. 47, 194
Hunter, Lt Col J.A. 86
Hurtado, Pte 'T' 182

Ifs 79, 112, 117

Johnson, Capt W.C. 167
Jones, Lt K. 113 ff.
Jones, Sgt S. 19 ff., 85, 126, 195, 4, 5,
    6
Julius Caesar 6

Keating, Lt B. 107
Keller, K.T. (Chrysler) 154
Kent, Gdsmn K. 97
Kibala, Pte G 9
King, Lt Col 'R'. 155
Kirkman, Sgt T. 181
Kite, Sgt 114
Klein, Medic W. 137, 141, 160, 163,
    171, 172, 184, 199
Korean War 16
Kreipe, Gen W. 182
Krenn, S/Sgt A. 151, 157, 158,
    174

Lacey, Gdsmn L. xvi, 96, 104, 106,
    116
La Hogue 105, 108
Lammerding, Brig 170
Langangke, Lt F. 171
Langdon Lt 110 ff.
Langton, Lt S. 60
Lastelle 10
Lebissey 43, 50
Lee, Gen J.C.H. 47, 194
Leigh Mallory, Air/M Sir T. 134
Lemon, Capt 73
Lechipey , André 122
Le Havre 202
Le Mans 161
Lemoigne, Pierre 192

Lessay, 18. 128, 146, 153, 161, 192, 23

Levine, Cpl B. 3, 17, 1

Liège, Operation 182,184 ff.

Lotz, Sgt R. 161

Louvigny, 117

Lovett, Lt C. 16

Luftwaffe, bombing raids *see* (Units) Luftwaffe

Lutcavish, S/Sgt M

McCartney, Capt J.R. 168

McColl, Tpr W. 26

McConahey, Capt W.M. 175

McGillycuddy, Maj M. 113, 114, 127

McNair, Gen L.J. 35, 139

Malaria 70

Mann, Sgt J 26

maquis, *see* French Resistance

marais, swamps 10, 33, 41, 69, 161

Marigny, 144, 148, 21

Mark IV tank 82, 190

Marsden, Gdsmn G. 104

Marshall, Gen G 134

Mathers, Sgt 193

Matterne, Lt G. 155, 162

Medical treatment 1944 style 17, 26, 28, 85, 94, 115,139, 159, 184

Medics, treating enemy wounded 15, 115, 160, 184, 193

Meredith, Tpr B. 88

Merle, Guy 107

Mesnil-Frementil, Le 54, 72, 84, 95

Mézidon 108

Middleton, Maj Gen T. 145, 153, 178

Miller, Capt J.E.F 74, 111

Mines/Minefields, 56, 66, 98, 153, 169, 183, 192, 23

Miracle, Cpl 183

'Moaning minnies' *see* Nebelwerfers

Mock, Gdsmn J. 96

Model, F/M 189

Mont-Castre 6, 1

Montgomery, Gen Sir B.L. xv, 35, 47, 53, 55, 108, 126, 128, 164, 181, 189, 194 ff., 9

Moore Lt Col R. 96

Moore, Sgt R. 120

Moreton, Lt C. 88

Morse, Sgt F. 153

Mortain 170, 177, 182, 189

Mosely, Cpl W 22 ff., 84, 110

Mosquito (plane) 63, 69

Mosquitoes (insects) 69, 125

Mount Ormel 200

Moverley, Sgt 88

Mulberry artifical harbours 39

Nebelwerfers 11, 79, 96, 106, 112, 119, 128, 193

Nelson, Lt Col R. 161

Niblock, Tpr J. 30, 84, 6

Nicholls, Maj C. 73

Niewinowski, Lt 191

Norman, Brig 60

Noyers-Bocage 47, 81, 132

OBOE bomb aiming system 138

O'Connor, Lt Gen Sir R. 53, 56, 89, 126, 186, 197, 9

'O' (orders) groups 58

OPs (artillery observers 79

Oradour massacre 156

Orne, River/bridges 5, 33, 50, 52, 56, 87, 107, 10

Packard, Tpr J. 83

Padberg, Lt W. 129

Panther tank, xvi, 82, 105, 147, 156, 191

Panzerfaust 11, 23, 119

Panzermeyer (Maj Gen Meyer) 32, 46, 111, 186

Paris 35, 55, 75

Parker, Gdsmn C. 123

Pas-de-Calais 35

Patterson, Lt 177
Patton, Lt Gen G. xvi, 35, 47, 131,
    139, 145, 151, 175, 180, 189 ff.,
    194, 200, 30, 31
Pearce, Capt C. 110, 120, 181
Peck, Maj T. 113
Pedderson, Sgt A.O.
Peiper, Col J. 111
Periers 18, 128, 134, 153
Personnel Carriers, Armoured 54,
    186, 197
PIAT, anti-tank projector 118
Pickert, Gen 76
Picot, Lt G. 103
Poemelière, la 147

Point 122 6
Poirier, Le 100, 111
Porter, Cpl O. 69
Powell, Maj J.H.C. 111, 193
Prawdzik, Bn/Sgt Maj V. 155
Pretot 6
Prieure, Le 90, 95, 99
Psychiatric cases, 'bomb happy' state
    28, 37, 65, 75 , 140, 159
Psychiatric cases, refusal to fight 8, 18,
    119, 153, 155, 171
Pyle, Ernie 129

Quesada, Air Gen E.P. 139, 149 ff.,
    164, 176
Quillan, Lt Col A.R. 168

Radley-Walters, Maj. S.L. xvi, 201
Railway, embankment 19 ff., 78 ff., 88,
    100, 112
Raney, Lt T. 136, 142, 152, 153, 168
Rannville 50
Red Cross 172, 184
Religion/beliefs 9, 123, 174, 185
Reminiscence, xvii, 204
Resistance movement see French
    Resistance

Rettlinger, Maj 91
Reynolds, Maj Sir J. 123
Rhino bulldozer tank 131, 169, 176,
    178, 201, 24
Ripman. Capt H. 94
Robbins, Sgt R. 65, 117
Roberts, Col T. 159, 162
Roberts, Lt H.A. 183
Roberts, Maj Gen G.P.B. 'Pip' 54, 56,
    66, 71, 77, 89, 95, 104, 126,
    186, 197, 13
Roberts, Sgt (US eng.) 131
Robertson, Capt C. 61, 195
Rommel, F/M E. 34, 35, 45, 125
Roncey pocket 176, 177, 191
Roosevelt, President F.D. 36, 154
Rose, Brig/Maj Gen M. xvi, 42, 148,
    151, 152, 166, 169, 177, 27
Rothschadl, Cpl J. 1 ff.
Royal Tiger tank 101
Russia 44, 48, 58

St-André-sur-Orne 54
St-Aignan-de-Cramesnil 54,186, 201,
    202
St-Gilles 144, 148, 152
St-Lambert 191, 200
St-Lo 5, 18, 33, 128, 132, 135, 146
St-Sylvain 54
Salisbury Plain 19
Sannerville 62
Scholes, Gdsmn 101
Scott, Lt Col A.B.J. 58, 111
See, River 177
Seibold, Pz Sgt E. 156
Seine, River 48, 55, 190, 192
Semmes, Sgt J. 150, 155
Sheppard, Lt J. 8, 11
Sherman tank (75mm/general) 1, 6,
    9, 82, 150 ff., 157, 202, 12, 22,
    26, 35
Sherman Firefly tank 36, 82, 99, 102,
    120, 187, 201, 202, 14, 33

Sienne, River 171, 177
Silvertop, Lt Col D.A.H. 58, 79, 114
Simonds, Lt Gen G.G. 42, 186 ff., 197
Smith, Lt Gen Bedell 47, 194
Smith, Sgt E.A. 'Dusty'. 96
Soignolles 54
Solarz, Sgt J. xvi, 154, 174, 179, 182, 203
Soliers 19, 89, 105, 112, 118, 122, 6
Somme 202
Spandau, machine-gun 13, 88, 128
Spearman, 1st Sgt B. 2
Spitfire fighter plane 106, 121, 123
Spittles, Cpl R. 25 ff., 58, 17
Spring, Operation xvi, 163, 186
Stalingrad 171
Stancomb, Maj 28
Stallings, Capt G 183
Stiller, Gerhard, xvi, 124, 190
Stileman, Lt D.M. 79
Stimson, Mr 132
Stuart tank, see Honey

TDs (US tank destroyers) 151, 168, 182
Teal, Gdsmn G. 103
Tedder, Air/M Sir A. 47
Thunderbolt plane 121, 176, 193, 12/1
Thurdley-Wicks, Maj A.R. 104
Tiger tank, xvi, 32, 64, 82, 99, 105, 186, 191, 201
Tilly-la-Campagne 19, 108, 190
Tinchberry 181
Tite, Sgt 24
Titman, Sgt K. 6, 17
Titurius Sabinus 6
'Tommy Cooker' 1
Totalize, Operation, xvi, 61, 186 ff., 192, 197, 201
'Total Surrender' doctrine 46
Touffreville 62

Tractable, Operation 187 ff.
Training/ lack of 42, 181
Troarn 69
Troteval Farm 119
Tychsen, Col 170
Typhoon rocket plane 106, 121, 193

Uhlig, Fritz 3
'Ultra' code-breaking 44, 81, 145, 150, 163, 170, 184

Van Crevald 202
Venelli tribe 6
Vengeons, Daniel 192
Verrières 54, 120, 175, 203
Vickers-Smith, W/O J. 155
Villers-Bocage 32, 201
Vimont 54, 108, 118
Vincent, Pte H.W. 184
Vire 181, 193
Vona, Pte M 17
Von Bock, Gen F. 135
Von Choltitz, Gen 129
Von Kluge, F/M H. 38, 44, 126, 135, 145, 163, 170, 189, 32
Von Luck, Col H. 75 ff., 103, 111, 196, 8
Von Rosen, Capt 64, 76, 103, 105, 111
Von Rundstedt, F/M G. 34, 38, 46, 76
Waldmuller KG 111
Walker, Maj Gen 'B' 14
Watson, Maj Gen L.H. 131, 177
weather 39, 125, 132, 134 ff., 182, 22
Webster, Capt M.G.T. 96
White half-track 20
White, Brig Gen I.D. 166
White, Sgt 99
Whitewood, Tpr L 28
Whittington, Sgt H.B., CmoH 165

Wiley, Lt J. 7
Wisch, Maj Gen T. 111, 190
Wittmann, Maj M. 32, 111, 118, 156, 186
Wolfe, Lt H. 158
Wolff, Capt W. 111, 9
Women soldiers 167, 173
Wood, Maj Gen 'P.' 162 , 179

Workman, Sgt 102
Wunsch KG 111

Yeburgh, J. 60
Yockey, Cpl W.D. 169
Young, Sgt J. 147

Zemitus Pte L. 183

Index of Units Mentioned

AMERICAN
Army:
First Army 128, 134
Third Army 184
Corps:
VII Corps, 132, 144, 147 ff.
VIII Corps, 144, 153
XV Corps, 190
XIX Corps, 132 , Army Medical
Corps 175 ff., 185
Military Police 34
Divisions:
Armored:
2nd Armored 'Hell on Wheels' 18,
132, 143, 144, 147 ff., 154, 162,
166, 170, 189
3rd 'Spearhead' 18, 37, 132 , 143,
144, 148, 154, 173, 176 ff.
4th 145, 162, 164, 176, 179
6th 'Super Sixth' 145, 162, 164,
171, 179
Infantry:
1st 148, 177
4th 132, 144, 177
9th 35, 132, 144
30th 35, 129, 132, 135, 136, 142,
144, 171
79th & 81st 153
Combat Commands:
CCA, 2nd AD 148, 166, 169
CCB, 2nd AD 148, 176

CCA, 3rd AD 177
CCB, 3rd AD 177
Regiments (= Brit.Brigades)
Armored:
33rd 155 , 183
41st 171
62nd 167
66th 147, 154
67th 174
78th 167
Infantry:
22nd 154
36th armored infantry 184
39th 135
119th & 120th 142
310th 158
314th 129
Battalions:
4th /37th Arm 179
2nd /41st Arm 166
3rd /49th Inf 142
2nd /66th Arm 152, 183
3rd /66th Arm 147
1st /67th Arm 161
69th Tank bn 179
82nd Recce bn 173
702 TD bn 154, 168
712 Tank Bn 1 ff.
712 TD bn 192
14th Arm. Field Artillery 154
305th Eng. Combat Unit 174

US Army Air Force:
8th USAAF 149
9th USAAF 62, 149
IX TAC 176
Bombing raids 48, 62, 134 ff., 137 ff., 195
Air Support Parties/Visual Combat Posts 149, 176

BRITISH
Royal Navy:
HMS Roberts 72
Army:
Corps:
VIII 53, 54, 61 ff., 72 ff., 94 ff., 110 ff.
Divisions:
Armoured:
Guards 49 ff., 56, 59, 87, 94 ff., 108, 112, 118, 195, 198
7th (Desert Rats) 27, 56, 60, 69, 87, 89 ,104 ff., 108, 112, 118, 198
11th (Charging Bull) 49, 56, 60, 66, 71 ff., 94, 100, 110 ff.,195
79th ('Funnies') 4, 26, 66
Infantry:
3rd 88, 112
43rd Wessex 37
51st Highland 37, 68, 88, 186
Brigades:
Armoured:
5th Guards Armoured 59, 69, 94 ff., 112
22nd 69, 87
29th 22, 54, 91, 111
33rd 186
Infantry:
32nd Guards 95
159th 54, 72, 121
Regiments (armoured and infantry):
2nd (Armoured) Grenadier Guards 95 ff.

1st (Armoured) Coldstream Guards 50, 100, 103
2nd (Armoured) Irish Guards 59, 94, 100 ff., 105, 123
1st (Motorised) Grenadier Guards 95, 104
5th Coldstream Guards 95
3rd Irish Guards 95
1st Welsh Guards 95
2nd (armoured recce) Welsh Guards 100
7th Black Watch 61. 121, 126, 195
4th County of London Yeomanry 87, 105, 110, 118 ff., 181, XXII Dragoons 95, 106
East Riding Yeomanry 61, 69, 88, 106
2nd Fife & Forfar Yeomanry 58, 64, 68, 72 ff., 92 ff., 111, 114, 193
1st Herefordshires 65, 68, 72, 117
13th/18th Hussars 88
23rd Hussars 59, 68, 90 ff., 106, 115, 121
Inns of Court 54
24th Lancers 115
Lothian and Border Horse 67
2nd Monmouthshires 68, 72, 121
1st Northamptonshire Yeomanry 69, 186
2nd Northamptonshire Yeomanry 19 ff., 54, 68, 72, 83, 92, 112 ff., 195, 5
8th Rifle Brigade 65, 67, 79, 86, 92, 112, 114
144 RAC (Royal Armoured Corps) 186
4th Royal Northumberland Fusiliers 100
2nd Royal Ulster Rifles 88
1st RTR (Royal Tank Regiment) 69, 87, 105, 123
3rd RTR 58 ff., 64, 66 ff., 71 ff., 91, 93, 110 ff.
5th RTR 64, 87, 105, 118

2nd Seaforth Highlanders 69, 125
Royal Army Medical Corps 61, 94, 175
Royal Artillery 21 A/tk regt 107
Royal Engineers R Force (deception) 57
Royal Corps of Military Police 51, 87
RAF:
Bomber Command 61
Bombing raids, 43 , 61, 186, 188, 195 ff., 11
83 Group recce 106

CANADIAN
Regiments:
Black Watch 163
De la Chaudière 86
Essex Scottish 117
Fusiliers Mont-Royal 120
1st (Can.) Hussars 86
Maisonnueve 120
Queen's Own Cameron Highlanders of Can. 125
Queen's Own Rifles of Can. 86
Regina Rifles 48, 107, 116, 121
South Albertas 191
South Saskatchewans 117
Stormont, Dundas and Glengarry Highlanders (the Glens) 51, 86

GERMAN
Army:
Seventh Army 163
Corps:
1st SS Panzer Corps 196
84 Corps 129
Divisions:
Armoured:
1st SS Panzer LAH 38, 52, 81, 82, 114, 124, 127, 155, 190

2nd SS Panzer Das Reich 44, 133, 134, 155, 157, 163 ,166, 170, 171, 180
9th / 10th SS Panzer 81
12th SS Panzer Hitlerjugend 35, 103, 170, 189
17th SS Panzer Goetz von Berlichingen 3,11, 133, 170, 180
2nd Panzer 81,
21st Panzer 82, 163
Panzer Lehr 35, 38, 128, 133 ff., 140ff., 145, 157, 161, 166, 170, 171, 200
Infantry:
Fifth SS Parachute 9, 45, 141, 143, 171, 180, 3
77 / 91 / 243 Infantry 180
271 / 272 Infantry 45
275 Infantry 145, 180
276 / 277 / 326 Infantry 45
346 Infantry 52
352 Infantry 161
353 Infantry 145, 171
16 GAF (Luftwaffe) 45, 65, 163
Regiments:
Deutschland 184
15th SS Parachute 9
Hermann Goering (GAF) 111
858 88
Battalions:
503 heavy (Tiger) 82
Luftwaffe:
Bombing/strafing raids 31, 48, 57, 92, 106, 107, 121

POLISH
Division:
1st Armoured 186, 187, 193, 200, 33